PROBLEMS OF PEACE

FIFTH SERIES

PROBLEMS OF PEACE
FIFTH SERIES

LECTURES DELIVERED AT
THE GENEVA INSTITUTE OF
INTERNATIONAL RELATIONS
August 1930

Essay Index Reprint Series

 BOOKS FOR LIBRARIES PRESS
FREEPORT, NEW YORK

First Published 1930
Reprinted 1970

INTERNATIONAL STANDARD BOOK NUMBER:
0-8369-1808-8

LIBRARY OF CONGRESS CATALOG CARD NUMBER:
71-121470

PRINTED IN THE UNITED STATES OF AMERICA

INTRODUCTION

THIS volume is the fifth series of the Proceedings of the Geneva Institute of International Relations, and contains the lectures delivered last August by high officials of the Secretariat and International Labour Office, and by such authorities as Professors J. L. Brierly, André Siegfried(French), Salvador de Madariaga (Spanish), W. Rappard (Swiss), Manley O. Hudson (American), and Dr. Kastl (German), on the main lines of development of the League and the International Labour Organization and the chief problems arising out of the attempt to organize the peace of the world through the League.

The volumes of the Proceedings of the Geneva Institute by this time contain a unique symposium of views and information on the nature and growth of the League and the possibility it affords to governments and public opinion for securing the peace of the world. Not only have the lectures they contain been delivered for the most part by men and women who are authorities on their respective subjects and speak with inside knowledge as active participants in the work they are describing; the fact that they now go back over a period of five years and reflect the points of view of many nationalities and that the subjects selected, although varying from year to year, preserve a certain continuity by centring on the League and the problems arising out of its growth and purpose, make them a valuable running commentary on the history of the post-war efforts to secure peace by world organization.

An hour's lecture cannot of course be exhaustive, but may claim only to be suggestive. It has not always been possible to obtain the very best speakers on each subject and the lecturers chosen have not always given of their best. Imperfection and 'unevenness' are inherent in all symposia. But it may fairly be claimed already that the five numbers of *Problems of Peace* contain material not to be found elsewhere, and of the highest value for students and lecturers and all who are interested in the great purpose for which the League of Nations stands.

The lectures in the present volume are planned to constitute so far as possible an organic whole. The editor's task this year is therefore a little wider than usual, for it includes bringing out the unity underlying this series of lectures:

The first, which is entitled 'The Beginnings of World Government', examines to what extent the League of Nations may be regarded as a nascent world government, that is, how far it fulfils for the whole of mankind the functions that are performed by governments within the borders of each state. It should be remembered that not only is the League at the outset of its career, but that a world-wide association of States can never come very close to the organization of a single State or even of a Federation, for the simple reason that all existing States or Federations are organized on the assumption of the need for making war against other States; this need does not exist in the world community, since we have as yet no reliable communications with Mars, and the organization of such a community must therefore proceed on widely different lines.

The lectures on 'Parliaments, National and International'

and on the 'Past, Present, and Future of the International Labour Organization' are, as it were, an amplification of the theme of the first lecture, that is, portray certain aspects of the growing world organization, and discuss constitutional and 'procedural' problems arising out of the movement towards a world government. (Previous volumes contain lectures on the origin and structure of the League and the Labour Organization, on their working and relation to current problems, &c.)

The other lectures are designed to cast light upon various functions performed by the League regarded as a nascent world government. The lectures on 'International Banking and Finance' and on the 'Economic Causes of War' show the necessity for international organization in the field of financial and economic relations and the extent to which this need is being met. (Previous volumes contain lectures on the economic and financial work of the League.) World public health has long been a matter which nations have become accustomed to regard as of common concern, requiring international machinery working on the basis of joint obligations. Colonial administration as an international trust, the principle of national tolerance as an international obligation, and the administration of international justice are all descriptions of what is being done and an indication of what still remains to be done if a world loyalty and a world government are to become enough of a reality to make peace secure. Dr. Kastl's vigorously expressed views on the Mandates system are particularly interesting, as he was until recently the German member of the Mandates Commission.

Professor Brierly's discussion on the legislative function in international relations, Mr. W. A. Forster's brilliant lecture on what we have to give up if we really mean business with renouncing war, and Mr. Garvin's strongly urged plea for subordinating League coercion of a peace-breaker to agreement with the U.S.A., and hope that the latter may undertake to enter into conference for averting threats to peace, accept some definite procedure for settling disputes, and not insist upon trading with a violator of the Peace Pact, cover between them some of the vital problems that arise in organizing the world for peace. Professor Madariaga's lecture on the difficulty of disarming also proceeds from the view that peace and the view of sovereignty which contends for the national right of self-judgement and self-help are incompatible.

The final lecture touches on what is perhaps the most fundamental problem of all, namely, the training for world citizenship of the men and women whose opinion ultimately determines the fate of governments.

The editor wishes to express the thanks of the Committee to all those who contributed to making this session of the Institute a success. In the first place, the lecturers, but also those who consented to serve as chairmen and who did all the thousand and one things necessary to make this gathering of 400 people of many nationalities run smoothly and pleasantly. Special thanks are due to the Secretariat for their kindness in again allowing the lectures to be held in the famous Glass Room.

For those who are not familiar with the previous volumes it may be as well to recall that the Geneva Institute grew out of the holding of summer schools at Geneva first by the

British League of Nations Union and then jointly by the Union and the American League of Nations Association. The Proceedings are conducted in English, but the Institute is open to men and women of all nationalities. The sessions are generally held in August and last for a week. In 1931 the session will be held in the week beginning 16 August.

THE EDITOR.

Particulars of the Meeting of the Geneva Institute of International Relations for 1931 can be obtained from:

The Secretary, League of Nations Union, 15 Grosvenor Crescent, London, S.W. 1.

The Secretary, League of Nations Association, 6 East 39th Street, New York.

And during the summer months from:

The Secretary, Geneva Office, League of Nations Association, International Club, Geneva.

CONTENTS

Contents

Contents

CHAPTER I

THE BEGINNINGS OF WORLD GOVERNMENT

Professor W. E. RAPPARD:

i. *Introduction.*

THIS is the fourth occasion on which I have the honour
and the pleasure of addressing the Geneva Institute of
International Relations.

Heretofore I had been called upon to describe the origins
and the evolution of the League of Nations, to estimate its
significance as an historical fact, and to attempt to forecast
its probable future.[1]

To-day my task is different. I am to speak on the beginnings of 'international government', and, if I interpret correctly the intentions of my task-masters, thereby to initiate
an Anglo-American audience into the nature of the great
institution they have come to study at Geneva. When this
most flattering but equally arduous duty was imposed upon
me I felt somewhat appalled. The topic is not one which
I would have chosen had I been left to consult my individual
preference. On the other hand it did seem to offer a convenient vantage point from which to consider all the efforts
at international co-operation which centre around Geneva.
That is why, in spite of my misgivings, I accepted the task
set me.

The originality, if any, to which my three previous lectures
could pretend, was due to the novelty of at least some of the
facts presented therein. To-day, having no startling dis-

[1] Cf. *Problems of Peace*, 1st, 2nd, and 3rd series, London, 1926, 1927,
1928.

B

coveries to reveal and still wishing to be concise and not too unbearably trite, technical, or dull, I shall attempt to analyse a few fundamental concepts with the hope of shedding some new light on them. Should this analysis appear in any respect original, it may very likely, on critical examination, prove to be fallacious. And although, unlike many more brilliant scholars in the field of politics, I hold deliberately fallacy to be too high a price to pay for originality, even a fallacy, if it be both honest and novel, may more usefully challenge thought and thereby promote the discovery of truth than scores of humble platitudes pompously reiterated and dumbly accepted.

In no science is boldness of conception more necessary than in that of international politics to-day, and in none is it more difficult. It is urgently necessary, because if we continue to accept, in times of peace, the existing organization of human affairs, with all its anarchical and threatening national rivalries and antagonisms, as the only possible scheme of things, we and our children will be condemned for ever in the future to suffer the consequences of what has for ever in the past been its inevitable concomitant: recurrent and increasingly destructive war.

On the other hand, boldness of conception is exceptionally difficult in international politics. Especially is this so for those who like myself are of a positive and historical turn of mind. To conceive of a world in which peace, founded on a basis of recognized and guaranteed justice, would and should always prevail, to conceive of a world in which war would not only be outlawed in the abstract, but effectively banished and repressed as, say, the crime of piracy is to-day, such boldness would seem to defy the whole course of human events.

In the first sentence of his monumental *Grammar of Politics*—a work which deserves the epithet not only by reason of its titanic proportions, but also because it truly constitutes a monumental landmark in the otherwise rather dull scenery of current political thought—Professor Laski writes: 'A new political philosophy is necessary to a new world'.[1]

Without inquiring whether the old world ever possessed a political philosophy adequate to its needs, there is no doubt in my mind that to-day we have none. A 'new world' is in itself a bold phrase. The political, economic, and social foundations of our nationalistic and capitalistic world are assuredly over a century old. What seems new, however, and what is undoubtedly characteristic of our times, is the more vivid realization of the unfitness of our international organization. The growing interdependence of nations, combined with the increasingly devastating technique of war, have led at least some of us to appreciate more clearly than we did before 1914 the wicked folly of the doctrine of absolute national sovereignty.

That doctrine as an ideal is to-day condemned by most clear-sighted and independent students; but it is still proclaimed and indeed extolled by practically all politicians. The glorious and tragic exception of President Wilson but confirms the rule, as he was a student in politics rather than a politician. This opposition between those whose business it is to think and those whose practice it is to talk, is not solely due to the fact that thought invariably precedes talk, in the evolution of affairs at least, if not in the habits of all politicians. The reason for this opposition unfortunately lies much deeper. A student, if he be worthy of his calling, thinks with

[1] H. J. Laski, *A Grammar of Politics*, 3rd ed., London, 1928, p. 15.

a view to discovering the truth. A politician, if he be a practical democrat, talks with a view to being elected or re-elected. This implies no criticism. Such are the rules of the game to which he is obliged to conform. If he failed to do so and thus forfeited his usefulness, he might be a brilliant student, but he would be a poor politician.

Now, to exalt national sovereignty as the guiding principle of future evolution towards peace would be for the scholar the shortest road to disastrous error, but for the politician it is the safest road to success at the polls. In other words, as we shall see presently, the people, the true sovereign in all so-called enlightened countries, while they want peace and prosperity, are insistent on committing their chosen repre-sentatives to an international philosophy which cannot but breed war and misery.

It may or may not be regrettable, but it is certainly obvious that the task of directing from day to day the practical affairs of mankind devolves upon the politician and not upon the student. It is for the student, therefore—it is particularly for such a group of students as this—to seek to discover the truth, in order that, having discovered it, we may convert our respective peoples and through them our respective politicians to a saner view of international relations. May we succeed before it is too late!

As a would-be clear-sighted student and certainly as a pedantic professor, I shall now, addressing myself to my subject, attempt first of all to define international govern-ment and to determine its implications. I shall then inquire whether and in how far international government thus defined and understood exists to-day. Finally I shall seek to ascertain why mankind in its blind aspirations and awk-ward efforts towards a state of affairs which true international government—I shall then have been led to call it world government—can alone bring about, should still be so reluctant to accept what appears a necessary means to a salutary end.

ii. *Definition and Implications of International Government.*

In the preface to her *Study of International Government*, published about 1924, Dr. Jessie Wallace Hughan, an unmistakably American author, thus defines her topic:

> ' "International" carries two simple and related meanings: pertaining to two or more nations, and concerning different nations in common. "Government" signifies the exercise of authority in the administration of the affairs of a state, community, or society. "International Government", therefore, is the exercise of authority in the administration of the affairs of two or more nations.' [1]

This is simple, short, and snappy, as are many American phrases coined for a people who are daily taught to think in headlines, to read in subways, and to worship what a clever author has called 'the ideal of acceleration'. Now as a sincere admirer of American business methods, and, besides, as the grateful owner of an American motor-car, I should be the last to sneer at the process of thinking in headlines and reading in subways, or at the cult of acceleration. But if there is one thing which cannot be profitably done in a hurry, it is abstract intellectual analysis. Let us, therefore, with as much old world leisure as the distinctly new world aestival atmosphere of Geneva will permit, consider these concepts a little more closely. The definitions we will arrive at will doubtless be less simple, short, and snappy than the above.

[1] Jessie Wallace Hughan, *A Study of International Government*, London, undated, p. xv.

Possibly, however, by positing while not pretending to solve what is assuredly a complicated problem, they may no less usefully contribute to its elucidation.

If, discarding all dictionaries and disregarding all academic discussion, we analyse the notion of government in the light of historical experience, I believe we shall agree that it contains two essential elements, without either of which there can be no true government. The first of these is authority, that is the competence and ability to command and to be obeyed in the political sphere. The second is order, that is a certain scheme, or method, or plan to which the governed are made to conform.

There may be authority without government, as in the case of the purely arbitrary rule of a brigand chief or a political boss. And there may be order without government, as in the elaboration of a treatise on politics. But when there is both order and authority, political authority exercised to enforce some kind of political order, then there is bound to be government.

The authority may be dictatorial, as in fascist Italy, or liberal, as in classical Athens. The order may consist in a multitude of hard and fast rules, as in the Soviet Union of the five years plan; or it may consist in a few general principles, as in 'muddling through' Great Britain. Whenever and wherever is authority and order, then and there is government.

Now what about international government? By that term we may mean—and it is well not to confuse the different meanings—either government by two or more nations, or the government of two or more nations.

Examples of international government in the first sense are the rather unfortunate historical instances of so-called *condominia,* or the present administration of the Saar Basin. In the latter case, a territory has been governed for the last ten years by an international commission, appointed by the Council of the League of Nations, an international body. If the mandated areas were administered by the League of Nations, as was at first proposed, and not by mandatory powers on behalf of the League of Nations, as is actually the case, we should have there another example of international government in the first sense. As a matter of fact, the mandate system does not afford an example of international government. This is so, not because the League of Nations is not an international body, but because the powers it exercises over mandated territories are not those of government, but only of supervision.

Examples of international government in the second sense, that is to say the government of an international community, are, for very significant reasons, much more difficult to find. The monarchical ruler of two or more countries bound together in a personal union, such as the King of England and Hanover before 1837, or the King of Sweden and Norway before 1905, might have been said to exercise international government. As a matter of fact they were not. Likewise, during peace negotiations, the power or powers victorious over a coalition of allies, enforcing its or their will simultaneously on two or more defeated enemies, might be spoken of as temporary international rulers. I do not know whether the term has ever been used in that connexion.

The Peace Conference of Paris in 1919, to be sure, is sometimes given as an example of international government. That is so, however, rather because the victorious governments formed an international group, than because they laid down the law for the international community of the defeated. Nor is the government of a confederacy or of a federal State, such as the British Empire or the United States of America or the Swiss Republic, ever spoken of as an international government.

If we pass in review all historical examples of government in which several political units were subjected to a common rule, we shall never, I believe, be led to discover a single example of what any of us would be tempted to call international government. And still it was with a view to speaking of the States assembled in the League of Nations that I was asked to discuss the beginnings of international government. What then is the explanation of the riddle ? The explanation is very simple, or rather there is no riddle at all, but only the loose expression of a vague idea.

Some of us are apt to think of the League as an example of international government, less because the members of the League may seem to form a community of governed, than because they may seem to form a community of governors. They are thought of as governing, not as being governed. Of governing one another it is true, but not as being governed one by another.

If one were to suggest in public that a State Member of the League of Nations was being governed by any one but by its own exclusive self, he would be evicted from office if an official, defeated at elections if a candidate, and possibly censured even if only a mere professor. In my opinion, such treatment, although excessive, would, in the case of the professor at least, not be unreasonable. As we shall see presently, it is not true to say to-day, although I sincerely hope that it may become less untrue at a not too far distant date, that a State Member of the League of Nations is governed by the international body of which it is a part.

It of course follows that if the members of the League are not really governed from Geneva, they together, as a League of Nations, govern no one, except, as we have seen, the Saar Basin, and that only as a temporary expedient. If, therefore, the League is not engaged in international government in the second sense of the term, it cannot truly be said to be engaged in it in the first. If no State and no group of States consent to be the object of international government, the community of States forming the League can clearly not be an agency of international government.

Indeed, if we wished to sacrifice current linguistic usage to logically precise phraseology, we could show that there is a contradiction involved in the term 'international government'.

Government, as we have seen, is authority to enforce order. A nation or a State is, according to orthodox theory, a sovereign unit. Even if we discard the classical doctrine of absolute sovereignty as an ideal, we must admit that in ordinary parlance a nation or a State ceases to be a nation or a State when it submits to a superior authority. New York is not a state in the international sense, in spite of its size, wealth, and population, which in Europe would almost entitle it to rank as a great power. Nor do New Yorkers constitute a nation. Why not ? Simply because, submitting as they do, in theory at least, to the will of the federal government, they are not politically independent.

Now if a nation forfeits its status as a nation by bowing to the authority of a superior government, then clearly international government is a misnomer. Either there is government, and then it is not international, but supernational, or rather world government; or there are independent nations and then there is no international government although, of course, there may be international co-operation or organization.

The term international government is therefore ambiguous or over-ambitious. It is ambiguous if used to describe a hypothetical world government, as ambiguous as the term inter-state government would be to describe the constitutional system of the United States or the term inter-cantonal government to describe that of Switzerland. And it is over-ambitious if used to describe what goes on in Geneva, for, as we shall see, that is hardly government at all.

Now this is not a mere quibble, as it may seem to some at first glance. All those who expect the League of Nations effectively to prevent war, to promote disarmament, and to reorganize the world in accordance with the best economic interests of the inhabitants of the globe, more or less consciously think of it as a super-State or a world government. When they do so consciously and intelligently they may be bold enough to admit it, as did for instance Mr. Oscar Crosby in his book entitled *International War: its Causes and its Cure*,[1] or more recently Mr. H. G. Wells in several of his writings. But when they do so unconsciously, as vast numbers of people all over the world do to-day, they are apt to allude to the League as an institution of international government, in that case a convenient term for the muddle-headed and a phrase adequate only for the expression of a confused idea.

My insistence on this point is not due to any academic verbal frenzy, such as we professors sometimes seem to indulge in with the delight of perversity. My wish is only to call attention to the dangers of a term which, unless clearly understood, necessarily promotes loose thinking on what is to my

[1] Oscar T. Crosby, *International War: its Causes and its Cure*, London, 1919.

mind one of the fundamental questions in international relations.

In order to soothe those whom this pedantic discussion may have irritated and to show that my views, even if they be deemed startlingly heterodox, are not confined to academic circles, let me quote, in concluding this first chapter a passage from the illustrious author of the *Outline of History*. In this statement, drawn from an article entitled *Delusions about World Peace*,[1] the main point I have sought to make is particularly stressed. It is, indeed, stressed with an emphasis which would seem impertinent and which would be exaggerated on the part of any one not an intellectual genius who legitimately enjoys the novelist's privilege of over-statement.

'One real test of pacifist sincerity is to be found in the pose towards national independence. To any one who will sit down for five minutes and face the facts squarely it must be evident that the organization of world peace, so that war will be impossible and disarmament secure, involves some sort of federal authority in the world's affairs. At some point there must be the certainty of a decision upon all disputes of races and peoples and nations that would otherwise necessitate war. And this authority must clearly have the power to enforce its decisions. Whatever navies and armies survive, other than police forces for local and definite ends, must be under the control of this central authority. It may be a committee of national representatives or what you will, but a central authority there must be. Pax Mundi, like the Pax Romana or the Pax Britannica, must be the only sovereign power within its realm. If you are not prepared to see your own country and your own flag so far subordinated to collective control, whatever protestations of peaceful intentions you make are

[1] H. G. Wells, *The Way the World is Going*, London, 1928, pp. 149–50.

either made unintelligently or else in bad faith. Your country cannot be both independent and restricted. Either you are for Cosmopolis or you are for war.'

iii. *Does International Government thus Defined and Understood exist To-day?*

We have seen that, strictly speaking, international government is a misnomer. Taking it, however, in the sense of super-national or world government, let us see whether any beginnings of it may be said to be apparent on the international horizon to-day.

Let us examine, therefore, first whether there is any order in the relations between States and then whether there is any authority competent to enforce that order.

It has become the fashion amongst students of international affairs to speak of our contemporary world as offering the spectacle of international anarchy. This significant phrase should not blind us to the fact that there is to-day much more order in international relations than there ever has been in the past, that order, in fact, has come to be looked upon as the rule and disorder as the exception. Likewise, Socialist critics are apt to insist on the anarchy of the capitalistic régime. While also partly justified, the implied criticism would be unfair if it were construed to mean that anarchy was the essence of capitalism. In the field of international politics, as in that of social and economic politics, order has come to be looked upon not only as a theoretical ideal, but also as the normal state of existing affairs. So true is this that the admittedly surviving elements of disorder have come to be resented as the avoidable symptoms of an abnormal and abhorred anarchy.

That is why it is characteristic of the present age—an age

in which war has for the first time in history been authoritatively branded as a crime—that the cry of international anarchy should be raised to-day. There have been long periods during which war was the rule and the brief interludes of peace the exception. No one then spoke of international anarchy. To quote Professor Rostovtseff, one of the greatest historians of antiquity: [1]

'The fundamental conceptions of international relations in the ancient and in the modern world are utterly different. The modern world considers the natural condition of life in our society to be the state of peace. War is nothing but a temporary suspending of this natural condition and is regarded as an abnormal state. Free intercourse between different nations is normal; restrictions and limitations of the rights of foreigners are abnormal and require serious reasons. Such, briefly, are our ideas as they developed during centuries of existence of the family of European nations. But in the ancient world, generally, the natural attitude of one state towards another was that of potential and actual enmity. Hence, war, not peace, was the foundation of international relations.'

Not only has peace to-day come to be regarded as the normal condition of international relations, but by far the largest number of political, economic, and intellectual dealings between different States and their nationals take place without injustice or friction. In case of difficulty, national laws or international treaties, recognized as valid by both parties and administered by unchallenged national or international tribunals, provide a peaceful and orderly means of settlement.

Unfortunately there still remain, however, several possi-

[1] M. I. Rostovtseff, 'International Relations in the Ancient World', in *The History and Nature of International Relations*, New York, 1922, p. 35.

bilities of disagreement and among them some of the gravest sources of conflict.

I shall not attempt to enumerate all the classes of cases in private international law where no one guiding principle of solution is adopted by all States and which are, therefore, not susceptible of a settlement legally satisfactory to all parties. Such cases, numerous and troublesome though they be as occasions of disputes between individuals and as symptoms of international disorder, are not the most serious. They are seldom more than pretexts for inter-state conflicts. Moreover, their number tends to diminish with the not too difficult progress of private international law.

The real subsisting international anarchy lies elsewhere. It is to be found in the fundamentally unsatisfactory and unsettled relations between the States themselves, much more than in those between the respective citizens.

Briefly to define this anarchy, we may say that it springs from three distinct sources.

One of these is the still persistent reluctance of most States to agree once and for all to accept the jurisdiction of an independent tribunal and to abide by its decision whenever there is a generally recognized law or legal principle applicable to the case in dispute. The recent very noticeable progress of so-called compulsory arbitration tends to narrow this source of disorder. But it will subsist until all States have, without any reservation and without any time limit, accepted the compulsory jurisdiction of some international court of justice. Up to date[1] twenty-eight signatories out of some seventy so-called sovereign States have finally accepted the jurisdiction of the Permanent Court of International Justice, under paragraph 2 of Article XXXVI of

[1] 28 July 1930 ; thirty-four by October 1930.

its Statute. But among them there are as yet but two great Powers, Germany and Great Britain, and in no case has this step been taken without some often important reservations or conditions.

We are here, however, in the presence of a rapidly spreading system of legal international order. It is to be hoped and, I think one may add without undue optimism, expected, that our generation or the next may see the completion of this very happy evolution. It is coming to be more and more generally recognized that, as M. Briand had the courage to say on the platform of the ninth Assembly, 'There is no dishonour even for a Great Power to go to The Hague and to return disappointed.' As Professor Laski has rightly stated:[1]

'To suggest that a nation is humiliated by being proved in error is as wise as to suggest that trial by battle is likely to result in justice. A power, indeed, which urges its prestige as a means of evading international jurisdiction is fairly certain to be wrong.'

The progress of compulsory arbitration, important as it is, is, however, far from tending to the establishment of a complete international order. The second element of anarchy in the present situation is the absence of any pacific means of modifying international law without the consent of all States concerned. Now existing international order may be fundamentally unfair on certain important points and it is bound, unless altered, to become more and more so in course of time.

Certain frontiers may be indefensible on grounds of justice. The very unequal distribution of colonial possessions and natural resources may be rightly resented, not only by those who have been despoiled, but even by the large majority of mankind. Certain limitations of independence may seem

[1] H. J. Laski, op. cit., p. 167..

unjustified, not only by people struggling for emancipation, but even by the disinterested onlooker.

No matter how revolting to the general sense of justice and no matter how threatening to peace, international law, even if administered by a court of justice whose jurisdiction would be universally recognized, affords no redress in such cases. Diplomatic negotiations, mediation by the Council of the League, consultation by *ad hoc* commissions, international conferences, or discussions before the Assembly under Article XIX of the Covenant, may achieve something, but only if the beneficiary of an unfair advantage consents to relinquish it. If not, the international community is helpless. It is in the position of a State whose constitution would refuse to allow for legislation by majority and which contained no provisions permitting its own amendment. As Professor Brierly said in the course of his remarkable lecture on *The Function of Law in International Relations* here two years ago:[1]

'The problem of the peaceful incorporation of changes into an existing order is the supreme problem of statesmanship, national or international. Whenever it is not frankly faced and solved, revolution in the national, and war in the international, field will always in the long run burst the fragile dams of legal formulas by which we vainly try to stabilize a changing world. The paradox of all law is that it cannot keep its vitality unless there exist legal means of overriding legal rights in a proper case, but, if we believe that the law exists for men and not men for the law, it is right that this should be so. Within a well-ordered State the pressure for change is more or less successfully canalized by a legislature, which can weigh demands and judge what changes are just, and when. In the international sphere the problem has not yet found its solution.'

[1] In *Problems of Peace*, Third Series, London 1929, p. 297.

Finally the third source of international anarchy lies in the fact that many phenomena of international importance are at present still beyond the orbit of international law. Whereas in the preceding case, an international tribunal, if consulted, is bound to render a decision contrary to the dictates of justice, because the law itself is unjust, here it cannot even be consulted, or is bound, if consulted, to remain mute, because there is no law for it to apply.

A State may strangle its neighbours by means of its tariff policy. It may oppress its own nationals or exclude all foreigners from the enjoyment of all its natural resources. It may make the most elaborate and threatening preparations for a war of aggression and thereby oblige its neighbours either to enter into a ruinous race of competitive armaments or to submit to any one of those forms of pressure and bullying to which disproportionate force has so often given rise in the past. The world of sovereign States, as it is at present organized, is equally helpless in presence of such policies, which, while not illegal, are as disruptive of international order as they are threatening to peace. To quote Professor Laski once more: [1]

' . . . the notion of an independent sovereign State is, on the international side, fatal to the well-being of humanity. The way in which a State should live its life in relation to other States is clearly not a matter in which that State is entitled to be sole judge. That way lies the long avenue of disastrous warfare of which the rape of Belgium is the supreme moral result in modern times. The common life of States is a matter for common agreement between States. International government is, therefore, axiomatic in any plan for international well-being. But international government implies the organized subordination of States to an authority in which each may have a voice, but in

[1] H. J. Laski, op. cit., p. 65.

c

which, also, that voice is never the self-determined source of decision. England ought not to settle what armaments she needs, the tariffs she will erect, the immigrants she will permit to enter. These matters affect the common life of peoples; and they imply a unified world organized to administer them.'

So much for international order, which, as we have seen, is the rule, and international disorder, which, while exceptional, is still and, I may add, increasingly dangerous in a constantly shrinking world.

Now how about authority, that authority without which even complete and perfect order is not government?

Without the authority to impose and to enforce order, there is not only no government, but there can likewise be no security. That is, in fact, the only justification for government on the international, as on the national plan. If nations or individuals could be relied upon willingly to accept and faithfully to observe, as self-imposed law, all the suggestions of a duly qualified advisory agency, then government, national or international, would be superfluous, as it is necessarily always more or less oppressive. No government! Such is, therefore, the plea of the thorough-going anarchist. He is an anarchist not because he favours disorder, but because he believes in the possibility of spontaneous order. In the national field, however, the anarchist is looked upon as a dangerous Utopian, and by no one with as much suspicion and intolerance as by those conservatively-minded members of the community for whom the dangerous Utopian on the international plan is he who most insistently clamours for some form of supernational government.

Now supernational government and absolute national sovereignty are, as we have seen, logically and historically incompatible.

The authors of the Covenant of the League of Nations, wisely recognizing that any frontal attack on the sacrosanct citadel of national sovereignty was doomed to failure and would only, if attempted, spell disastrous defeat for their whole undertaking, deliberately refrained from it.

Who could blame them when, timid and cautious as they made the document, it still proved too revolutionary for the people of the United States and too threatening for their senators' sense of national independence? Who would blame them when the first Assemblies, interpreting Articles X and XVI, went still further in their desire to limit the authority of the League and to reduce the obligations of its members? Who could blame them when, later on, the draft treaty of Mutual Guaranty in 1923 and the Protocol of Geneva in 1924, which were conscious reactions against this tendency, proved unacceptable to all non-European States? And who could blame them to-day in Europe when, more than ten years later, even M. Briand, perhaps the boldest internationalist on the front of the political scene, has felt bound, in his famous Memorandum, to insist on his fervent respect for the absolute sovereignty of the States between whom he proposes to establish a federal bond?

The League, therefore, having no authority over its members, because its members will accept no binding obligations towards it, is not an institution of government. It is, if you please, a government by persuasion. But that is a literary phrase without any scientific meaning. Government by persuasion is persuasion and not government.

But, it may be asked, are there at least some beginnings of government in the League? Are there no moral forces at work in Geneva which, even without governmental authority, tend to guide the wills of the sovereign States towards some common goal? Taken in this sense, I think we may reply in the affirmative. Although much has been said about the famous 'spirit of Geneva' which may sound well in a political speech or in a post-prandial address, but which would be out of place in a scientific lecture, there is no doubt in my mind that there is here an environmental influence which does contribute to promote international co-operation. It is not, as some of my fellow-citizens like to believe, the influence of the historical city-republic of Geneva. It is rather the result and the expression of an international *esprit de corps* which may well prove to be the embryo of a future world patriotism.

When leading statesmen of fourteen countries meet three or four times a year as members of the Council in Geneva, or when leading statesmen of some fifty nations spend a month together as members of the Assembly, discussing and trying to solve problems of common concern in a spirit of conciliation and friendliness, they do become thus something more than mere plenipotentiaries of their respective sovereign States. A new loyalty towards the League, or even towards mankind, as a whole, is sometimes discernible, which does make for mutual concessions and thereby for something in the nature of a common policy. The best proof of the reality of this intangible and imponderable spirit is to be found in the fact that, when these statesmen return to face their respective national parliaments, they are invariably accused by their respective nationalists of having succumbed to the diplomacy of their sly and wicked foreign antagonists.

Neither the Assembly nor the Council govern the world, or the League of Nations, or any of its members. But they do undoubtedly exercise a certain influence on the shaping of national policies. In this sense, beginnings of international government may be detected in Geneva.

What there is, really and obviously, on the other hand, is international co-operation and international organization.

In the evolution which seems to carry the nations of the world from absolute isolation to real federation, three successive phases may be distinguished.

The first is that of free and spontaneous co-operation. This stage began with the beginnings of intercourse and diplomacy and progressed very rapidly with the progress of population, wealth, industrial science, and trade. Already before the World War it had reached such a stage of development and intensity that, in various technical fields, it had given rise to international unions, as in the political field it had since the most ancient times led to defensive and offensive alliances of different types.

The second phase in this evolution may be described as that of voluntary and self-imposed organization, of which such unions and alliances were the prototypes and of which the League of Nations is the most recent expression and the most perfect instrument.

In this phase, the source of all power and of all decision still remains with the individual nations, but they agree, under certain conditions, for a certain time, in certain contingencies, and for certain well-defined purposes, to conform their respective policies to certain generally accepted principles. They even go so far, in a few exceptional circumstances, as under the Optional Clause of Article XXXVI of the Statute of the Court, or under the General Act of 1929, or under various bi-lateral treaties, as to bind themselves to submit to the verdict of a foreign authority. In so far, but in so far only, international organization may be said clearly to foreshadow the third phase of this evolution, the final phase of world government.

In this progressive development, the State Members of the League are unequally prepared to participate, or rather, are not all prepared to go equally far.

France and her continental allies, who have everything to gain and nothing to risk by the establishment of an order of things in which present frontiers will be guaranteed by the combined forces of the League, seem in some respects ready to go farthest in the direction of world government. But when it is suggested that there, of course, can be no such government without the power to revise existing treaties, if the interests of the greater part of the community should demand such revision, then France and especially her eastern allies become most insistent on the sacred character of their sovereign rights.

The discontented States of the world, that is those against whom the peace treaties were framed—the defeated Central Powers—Italy, a disappointed victor, and China, the victim of her allies' triumph, assume the opposite attitude. They are for League government in so far as League government means the possibility of redrafting the map of the world, but vigorously opposed to it when it implies the collective stabilization of the present conditions.

The European ex-neutrals, who are all small States, wish to strengthen the League in its judicial functions, but they are very reluctant to endow it with more political power. They are content with international organization which, in their view, implies the general application of the principle of compulsory arbitration. But League government, which, they fear, would mean government by the great Powers, has no attractions and is, indeed, not without its terrors for them. The weakness of their position resides in the fact that, while they impatiently demand disarmament, they are unwilling to make the sacrifices of national independence which international guarantees—without which there can be no general disarmament—inevitably demand. The attitude of Great Britain in its present temper is not very different, although it is, of course, based on other political and geographical considerations.

The non-European States are, on the whole, still in the phase of international co-operation. They are sometimes ready to consider some measure of international organization, but they are always resolutely averse from any form of world government. Whether they belong to the League, as Japan, the British Dominions, and the smaller Latin-American republics; or whether they participate only in its technical activities, as the United States, Brazil, Mexico, and Argentine, their policy is fundamentally the same. They are for co-operation, because co-operation means enhanced prosperity. They are suspicious of organization, because organization may imply troublesome obligations. And, with the possible exception of Japan, they are violently opposed to world government, because world government would seem to threaten their privileged economic position, endanger their newly-won independence, and too closely associate them with all that is objectionable in this intolerable continent of Europe. For States so disposed, the platonic vows of the Kellogg Pact and the pious aspirations of disarmament discussions are the last word in the art of preventing war.

As for Soviet Russia it, of course, occupies a place by itself. In the eyes of Moscow, co-operation with capitalistic nations would be a futile farce were it not an adventure offering some opportunities for revolutionary propaganda and some possibilities of obtaining foreign credits. International

organization is meaningless and world government the sole
desirable goal, world government implying, of course, the
incorporation of the rest of the universe in the Union of
Socialist Soviet Republics.

Such, in very rough outline, is the map of the globe, as
I see it, when considered from the point of view of international relations. Even the most enthusiastic friend of
world government must admit that, from such beginnings
to that goal, 'it's a long, long way to Tipperary'!

iv. *Why World Government is Desirable, and Why it is
still almost Universally Opposed.*

Let us, in conclusion, ask ourselves why mankind should
appear to be blindly groping for some form of world government, and why it should still be so reluctant to advance
deliberately in that direction?

In our sceptical age almost all moral axioms may be and
are in fact questioned. Were one to ask, however, whether
peace was preferable to war, harmonious co-operation to
hostile rivalry, and prosperity to poverty—in a word, life to
death—even our agnostic humanity would almost unani-
mously answer in the affirmative.

Now without some form of supernational authority entrusted with the duty of maintaining peace, securing disarmament, and promoting prosperity, that is to say of
governing mankind in the exclusive interests of mankind,
the coveted goal would appear even theoretically inacces-
sible. 'Either you are for Cosmopolis or you are for war', as
H. G. Wells declared in the above-quoted lapidary formula.

The story of all recent and successful federations would
seem to confirm that view. 'Either you are for a United
States of America, for a unified Germany, for a Swiss Con-

federacy, for a kingdom of Italy, or you are for war, stagnation, and poverty.' Thus spoke the American federalists of 1787, the promoters of the German Zollverein in the first half of the nineteenth century, the Swiss progressives in 1848, and the Italian patriots of the *Risorgimento*.

But why does not all civilized, pacific, and forward-looking humanity speak like Wells to-day ? The reasons are obvious.

In the first place, there is as yet in the twentieth century no world patriotism comparable in vital intensity to the American, German, Swiss, or Italian patriotism of the eighteenth and nineteenth. The millenaries of common aspirations, strife, and suffering, which mankind has lived through since the beginnings of time, have not yet given rise to a true, strong feeling of world solidarity. The disruptive forces of different origin, race, tradition, language, culture, and religion are still far more potent than the uniting forces of common experience and common interest.

In the second place, the love of freedom and independence, perhaps the most powerful impulse of individuals and nations, still blocks the road to federation. Freedom and independence, the necessary conditions of self-assertion, are not only highly prized advantages, but they have come to be sublimated into sacred ideals. Generations in all countries have striven, bled, and died for the cause of freedom and independence. Is it surprising that men to-day should resent the very thought of a super State conceived as depriving them of these sovereign blessings ?

To be sure, any well-considered plan of world government should tend to enlarge and not to limit individual freedom, and indeed also national independence in the best sense of the term. By doing away with war, crushing armaments, suicidal rivalry, and all the hindrances and restrictions of national sovereignty, it should appear as an instrument of human emancipation and not of oppression. It would, of course, be not a foreign government, but a co-operative institution designed to protect individual and collective rights of self-determination, and not to impose any uniform system of local and national administration. Differences of culture, language, and religion would be treasured as intangible human values and as necessary conditions of life and progress.

All that may be true and, indeed, obvious; but it is not yet understood by the man in the street, be it Main Street, Wall Street, the Strand, Unter den Linden, la Rue de la Paix, or even the Quai Wilson. In that connexion I venture to suggest that the term Cosmopolis is exceptionally unfortunate as the name of a world State, since it would seem to evoke an imposed uniformity of type much more than a peacefully organized and harmoniously federated diversity of local and national units.

The third main obstacle on the road to a world government results from the very unequal stages of national development we have noted above. If set up to-morrow, a world State would almost necessarily imply a very unequal and therefore unfair distribution of benefits and sacrifices. Some countries, and above all the United States of America, are large, thinly settled in comparison to their natural resources, and relatively secure from any foreign aggression. Others, on the contrary, especially in Europe, are small, over-populated, and hedged in on all sides by threatening neighbours.

While the two previously mentioned obstacles, and especially the second, should be overcome with comparative ease by education and enlightenment, this one strikes me as insuperable for the present and the near future. Time alone, the progressive equalization of economic and social conditions which it seems likely to bring about, the cumulative experience of the dangers for all and even for the most protected of absolute national sovereignty, and the constantly growing realization of the real solidarity of the most fortunate and the least fortunate members of the human family may gradually lead us all on, with a more assured gait, towards some form of that supernational government of which we are to-day witnessing the timid and halting beginnings.

Let me close these all too lengthy and still all too hasty remarks with a last quotation from Professor Laski, which may serve, with some qualification, both as a summary and a conclusion: [1]

'The implication of modern conditions is world-government. The process, naturally enough, is immensely more complicated than the government of a single State. The spiritual tradition of co-operation has still to be created; the difficulty of language has to be overcome; the application of decisions has to be agreed upon in terms of a technique that is still largely unexplored. The only source of comfort we possess is the increasing recognition that modern warfare is literally a form of suicide, and that, as a consequence, the choice before us is between co-operation and disaster. That was the sense which, in 1919, led the makers of the Peace of Versailles to strive for the mitigation of its inequities by the acceptance of the League of Nations. The latter, indeed, is the façade of a structure which has not yet been called into being. But it has at least this great importance, that it constitutes an organ of reference which goes beyond the fiat of a given State. It is, in fact, either nothing, or else a denial of national sovereignty in world-affairs. It is upon the basis of that denial that we have to build.'

With the end of this statement, spirited and stimulating

[1] H. J. Laski, op. cit., p. 227.

as everything that flows from its brilliant author's pen, I find myself unable fully to agree. The League of Nations is a 'denial of national sovereignty' neither in the intentions of its founders, nor in actual practice. Still less is it 'nothing'. It is, as I see it, an attempt to build up international co-operation on the foundations of national sovereignty. As such it is not and cannot be an inviolable temple of peace. But it is more than a mere façade. It is, in my view, an invaluable structure, both in its present admittedly limited potency and especially—if I may be allowed a final architectural simile—as a most necessary bridge leading from the international anarchy of the past over into the well-ordered world government of the future.

CHAPTER II

PAST, PRESENT, AND FUTURE OF THE
INTERNATIONAL LABOUR ORGANIZATION

Mr. H. B. Butler:

i. *The Importance of Public Opinion.*

LADIES and Gentlemen, it is a great privilege and
pleasure to address you during this year's session of the
Geneva Institute of International Relations at Geneva. I
say that it is a pleasure because to find so large and representative a gathering is a proof of the great, and perhaps of
the growing, interest that is being taken both in the United
States and in Great Britain in the work of the League; and
perhaps, as a Britisher, I may add that it is particularly
gratifying to me to be able to say that the largest gathering
of this kind that we welcome in the course of the year comes
from the two English-speaking countries. It is a privilege,
because we realize more and more as we go on that the whole
success of our work depends in the last resort on public
opinion, on what the man in the street thinks, and on what
the statesman thinks after the man in the street; because I
think that is usually how it works. Therefore, to have an
opportunity of saying a few words about what we are doing,
about what we have done during the ten years that we have
been in existence, is an opportunity which I would have
been sorry to miss.

Perhaps some of you may have questioned a little the
statement I made a moment ago as to the power of the man
in the street, but I think if one reads history aright one
comes to the conclusion that even in matters of constitutional
change, constitutional law, and so on, it is ultimately public

opinion that brings changes about rather than the statesmen and the politicians themselves. I know I am taking a risk in making that statement, as we have some eminent statesmen and politicians in this room, but I think they would ultimately agree with me that they cannot put over things which public opinion in general in not prepared to accept, and if one looks at the development of constitutional history, either in Great Britain or in the United States, one finds that it has been profoundly influenced by thinkers, by outsiders so to speak, who have written and who have thought about politics, but who have had nothing to do with them directly. One only has to recall names like de Tocqueville, Bagehot, and Lord Bryce, to realize the truth of that statement, and I am hoping that among you there may be some who will pay attention to the constitutional development of the League as those three that I have mentioned did to constitutional developments in Europe and America.

ii. *The Machinery of the International Labour Organization.*

We have now been in existence for ten years, and the Constitution which was laid down for us by Part XIII of the Treaty of Versailles may be said to have worked; and that, I think, is the greatest merit that you can claim for any Constitution when addressing an Anglo-Saxon audience. It works. When it was drawn up ten years ago, there were a great many people who thought it would not. It was an entirely new experiment. There had been international conferences in the past at which Governments had met each other through their officially appointed representatives, but there had never been in history an official conference at which the representatives not only of Governments, but also of organized employers and organized workers, met on

an equal footing, each one having an equal vote, in order
to deliberate and to reach international agreements. That
departure was regarded by many as so audacious as almost
to be condemned to failure in advance. But, as the result
of ten years' experience, I think one may say not only that
it has worked, but that it could not have worked in any other
way to produce really satisfactory results. What I mean by
that is this. If you just bring Governments together to
discuss problems of industry, they are unable to reach really
far-reaching conclusions unless they have taken into consultation the employers and the wage-earners. By bringing
the employers and the wage-earners into direct consultation,
therefore, we took, so to speak, a short cut. They were there
to speak for themselves and to say exactly what they liked.
Of course, it not unusually occurs that their opinions do not
coincide with those of their Governments, and do not
coincide with those of each other. But by sitting together,
by talking together, and perhaps most of all by getting to
know each other as human beings, they have gradually built
up a technique of agreement.

Perhaps I must go a little more into detail in order that
you may understand how the machine works. There are
three parts. There is first of all the annual Conference, which
you may call the Parliament. That consists of four delegates
from every country—two Government delegates, one employers' delegate, and one workers' delegate; and the employers' and workers' delegates are official in every sense of
the word, that is to say, their credentials are sent in by their
governments, but they have to be chosen in consultation
with the most representative organizations of employers and
workers in each country.

The Conference assembles and by now it has acquired

a sort of Parliamentary tradition, with carefully drafted
Standing Orders, which are frequently amended and which
are, on the whole, surprisingly well observed. There is very
little disorder in the International Labour Conference; in
fact, a great deal less than in some other Parliamentary
assemblies with which you are probably familiar. Each of
the four delegates has a vote of his own. Naturally enough,
the two Government delegates nearly always vote together.
Of course, the employers and the workers vote entirely
separately from their Governments and, to a large extent,
they vote as a body. The employers' and the workers' groups
are officially recognized entities; they have their own meetings
every morning, sometimes more than once a day, at which
they discuss the group policy on each question as it comes
up, and very often they even go so far as to appoint a spokes-
man who will put forward the group point of view. The
practical result of that is that the Government Delegations,
which, of course, are the largest (that was done on purpose,
because it was felt that, if these were going to be effective
international agreements, the Governments must have the
major voice in drawing them up), really more or less hold
the balance between the employers and the workers. Further,
no agreement can become effective unless it carries a two-
thirds vote in the Conference. The Treaty and the Standing
Orders lay down what kinds of questions require a two-thirds
majority, but it may be said broadly that every first-class
decision has to be carried by a two-thirds vote. From that it
follows, of course, that a very large preponderance of opinion
is necessary, at least the employers' or the workers' group
voting with almost the whole Government group, in order
to get anything through.

When the Constitution was drawn up, two criticisms

were made. One was that you would never get a two-thirds majority, because there would be too much division amongst the governments, while the employers and the workers would cancel each other out. The other criticism was that the workers' group would always be in the minority and that therefore the scales were loaded against them. Neither of those criticisms has in practice been justified. No less than thirty-one Conventions have been adopted by the Conference by a two-thirds majority or over, and if you analyse the actual voting you will find that, so far from the workers' group being usually in the minority, they have been usually in the majority. There have been thirty-one Conventions adopted out of thirty-five presented to the Conference, so that four Conventions have been lost. Of course, one could argue about each of those four Conventions, and one can regret that they were not carried, but, expressing a personal opinion, I am inclined to think that the fact that none of them commanded a two-thirds majority showed that the time was not really ripe for those particular measures. When one considers that the proportion of failures is 4 out of 35, I think one may draw from that the assurance that the Constitution has worked quite as well as, if not better than, its framers could have anticipated.

I am not going into the details of the various Conventions; they cover a very wide range of subjects, such as hours of work, social insurance, prohibition of night work of women, limitation of child labour, and so on. But, of course, the adoption of a Convention by the Conference does not make it effective. All those thirty-one Conventions might have been adopted and the world might not have been a penny the better for it, because, after they have been adopted, they have to be put into operation by the Government in each

country. At the time when the Treaty was drawn up—and
it is equally true to-day—it would have been impossible to
make the ruling of a two-thirds majority in an international
conference of that kind binding on the States. Consequently
it was provided that there should only be this measure of
obligation: that each Government should present to what
is called its 'competent authority' the Convention once it is
adopted in the Conference. Its competent authority,
whether it be Parliament (as it nearly always is) or any other
kind of authority, is not bound to accept the Convention.
It can turn it down—it frequently does. But that provision
of the Treaty at least ensures that a Convention shall not
just be put away in a pigeon-hole and conveniently forgotten.
It has got to be brought out into the light of day and it has
got to be publicly discussed, and that, after all, is as far as
you can go. You have got to give public opinion the opportunity of expressing itself, of examining a Convention, of
saying what it amounts to, and of making up its mind whether
it will accept it. But further than that, at this stage, you
certainly cannot expect to proceed.

Once a Government or a Parliament has adopted a Convention, it treats it just as it would treat any other international treaty, that is to say, it sends a formal ratification
of it to the Secretary-General of the League of Nations, and
from that moment it becomes bound to ensure its observance.
At the present time there are, I think, 402 ratifications of
Conventions actually registered by the Secretary-General at
the Secretariat of the League. But you may say, 'Well, that
sounds all right; 402 is quite an imposing number, but what
guarantee have you that those ratifications are really made
good in practice? What guarantee have you that a Government, once it has ratified one of these labour treaties, carries

it out?' That is a pertinent question, and there again, at the beginning of our career, we were told that it was impossible to have any satisfactory mutual check between nations: that you have got to take a nation on its word and leave it at that. In practice it has not worked out quite that way, and the pressure on the whole is becoming appreciably stronger year by year in the direction of establishing some sort of mutual supervision—control is perhaps too strong a word. It has come to take two forms. In the first place, the mere existence of the Conference with representatives from the three groups, two of which are not bound by any traditions of official reticence, makes it always possible for delegates to get up and say that a Convention is not being properly observed, and a number of complaints of that kind have been made from time to time. As you will easily realize, when such a complaint is made the Government in question does not treat it lightly. No Government likes being held up to international opinion as not having fulfilled its engagements. As a matter of fact, when complaints have been made, there has been in practically every case a full answer forthcoming. But, in addition to that, some years ago the Conference decided to take another step and to set up a Committee of independent persons drawn from different countries. There are ten of them now and they meet together every year to examine the reports which every Government that has ratified a Convention sends in to the Office explaining in detail the steps which have been taken by legislation or by administrative action to carry it out. We receive those Reports every year and we publish them in a pretty thick volume. Of course, they are dry in detail and to the outsider very uninteresting, but the duty of this Committee of experts is to read that volume carefully and to prepare a

Report, bringing out any points of doubt that have been raised in their minds by its perusal. That Report goes to the Conference itself, which in turn appoints a Committee to take the experts' Report and examine it. In that way the practice is growing of putting questions in a perfectly friendly way to Governments as to the precise methods which are being adopted to carry out Conventions, and there is no doubt that that is affording a growing measure of guarantee as to the strict observance and the uniform interpretation of Conventions. After all, there is nothing unique about it. You can find parallels in League procedure. Take the Mandates Commission; there the Mandatory Powers have to give an account every year of their administration of the mandated territories, and there is less and less resentment towards the questions which are put. We are gradually finding the same thing. It is in that way that a spirit of mutual confidence is being gradually developed which is adding considerable strength to the whole system of international agreement on labour questions.

That in a very few words is the Conference and how it works. The second part of the Organization is what is called the Governing Body. That body consists of 24 persons, 12 Government representatives, 6 employers' representatives, and 6 workers' representatives. They correspond roughly to the Council of the League; that is to say, they are responsible for all the day-to-day questions of administration and policy which arise. In addition they have one very important function to perform, namely, to settle the agenda of the Conference itself. On the whole it is a very representative body because, by the Treaty itself, it is required to contain delegates of the eight chief industrial States, so that you are bound to get the big countries represented as of right. This body has done its work well, and the only complaint that has been made against it is that it is not large enough: that it does not contain a sufficiently large overseas representation. That complaint was made at the first Conference at Washington, and as a result an amendment to the Treaty was adopted extending the size of the Governing Body from 24 to 32. But here we come across one of the difficulties of having a Constitution laid down by Treaty. In order that that amendment shall become effective, it has to be ratified by three-quarters of the States Members of the League and by all the States Members of the Council. That is a severe requirement and, as a matter of fact, at the present time we are two short of the necessary number of ratifications. We are hoping, however, that by next year, when new elections of the Governing Body take place, we may have secured those two ratifications also and enlarge the Governing Body in such a way as to ensure more representation for the extra-European countries. At present there are already three such countries represented on the Governing Body, i.e. Japan, Canada, and India.

The third limb of the tree is, of course, the Office itself. The Office has grown from very small beginnings to a body of about 400 people. Our principal duties are twofold. In the first place we have to make all the secretarial arrangements for the Conference, its organization, and so on. We have to provide secretaries, interpreters, &c., and to see that the records are properly kept. But, long before the Conference meets, we have to prepare its actual work. The nearest analogy that one can take is the work of a Government Department preparing a Bill for consideration in Parliament. Supposing, for instance, that you put a question on the agenda such as health insurance. In order that the

Conference may know what it is talking about, it is necessary
that it should know exactly what has been done in each of
the countries represented, and to find that out and to put
it clearly and concisely and intelligibly is no easy thing. As
a matter of fact, on that particular question we presented
the Conference with a volume of 1,264 pages. You may think
that they probably did not read it; I won't say that all of
them did, but a good many of them read enough to find out
exactly where they were. The report was, of course, provided with tables, to make it fairly easy to find out by a
quick glance exactly what was done in each country on each
branch of the question. It is perfectly certain that without
that nothing could have been done effectively, because there
would have been endless confusion and misunderstanding
as to the systems in operation in different countries, and a
month at least would have been spent in people trying to
find out what was each other's practice. But all that
preliminary work had been done, and when the Conference
met it had a solid basis from which to proceed to work out
the greatest common measure of international agreement.

That, we find, takes two years. Originally we tried to get
a Convention through in one session, but experience showed
that you could not move as fast as that if you were going
to move surely. What we do now is this. The first year the
Office presents the facts and the Conference has a preliminary
discussion, a first reading, to see what are the main questions
which have to be dealt with internationally, and it draws
up a series of principles. The Office then elaborates a questionnaire based on those principles and sends it to each of
the Governments. The Governments send very full answers.
We print those answers in full and from them we try to decide
the draft of an international agreement. That draft is usually

taken as the basis of discussion at the Conference, and what comes out in the end is something which usually resembles it fairly closely, although there are changes and amendments. The general lines, however, are nearly always set by the Office, because, after a little experience, when you put the answers together you can foretell pretty accurately on what points you can expect to get agreement and on what you will not get agreement. What we do then is to prepare a draft corresponding to the probabilities of agreement, and our forecast is usually justified in the main.

That, then, is the procedure as laid down by the Treaty, which, on the whole, has worked fairly well. But, if I have a few more minutes, I should like to go a little deeper into the subject and deal with one or two new problems which are now beginning to emerge.

iii. *The Difficulty of Questions not Universal in Character.*

There are some questions which are not universal in character, that is to say, they concern either one industry alone or certain countries alone. Of the first class, the most obvious instance is the shipping industry. All countries are not maritime; in fact,. of the 55 States Members of the League, I suppose you would say that 18–20 at the outside are maritime countries. Objection was taken at a fairly early stage in our proceedings to questions relating to conditions of work on board ship being dealt with by all the countries Members of the Organization, because some of the maritime countries said, 'That is all very well, but we may get our conditions being determined by countries which do not know one end of the ship from the other'. The second class of question limited in scope is the class relating to a certain number of countries only, to the exclusion of others.

The most striking instances of that kind with which we have had to deal are two. The first is the question of native labour, which, of course, primarily concerns only the nine countries possessing colonial territories. There, again, you have the same kind of objection—that countries knowing nothing about colonial administration, who have never seen the entirely different conditions which exist in Africa or Asia, are not competent to pass any kind of judgement on matters affecting native labour. The other question is the regulation of hours of work and conditions in coal mines in Europe. That is a particular question which concerns only nine countries in Europe—it does not even concern the whole of Europe, except in so far as all Europe burns coal. There, again, you have the same kind of difficulty.

I would like to run very rapidly through the stages by which the Constitution is being modified in order to meet cases of that kind, because I think it may have much greater developments in the future. As regards maritime questions, we tried to get over the difficulty in the first instance by having a special session of the general Conference dealing only with maritime questions. It was thought that a good many of the countries that had no interest in the sea would not attend, and that, therefore, you would get a discussion practically confined to the maritime countries. Up to a point, that expectation was realized. A good many countries that had no seaboard did not attend, but, even so, there is no doubt that some of the delegates could hardly be described as experts in maritime questions, and consequently it was felt that some other procedure should be adopted to secure a more technical discussion on these particular subjects, at any rate before they came to the general Conference.

In the case of native labour, we adopted a rather different

procedure. We appointed a Committee of Experts drawn from the Colonial countries, consisting of men who had spent all their lives in the Colonies, and who knew exactly what they were talking about; men, I might add, who on the whole were exceedingly sympathetic with the aspirations of the native. Those men did not represent their Governments; they were just there to express a personal opinion as to what could and could not practically be done to improve the conditions of native labour, particularly as regards forced labour, which was the first aspect of it which we tackled. That body of experts drew up a Report upon which we founded our Convention, and I am glad to say that that Convention went through this year at the Conference by a very large majority, in spite of a good deal of opposition. And there is one further point to be borne in mind—that, although it is claimed that Colonial questions only concern Colonial Powers, that is a claim which cannot really be altogether substantiated. In the development of a whole continent such as Africa, for instance, the opinion of the world at large has an immense importance, and I believe that the fact that these questions of native labour have been brought before the International Labour Conference, on which the opinion of the world at large is brought to bear, is a very important departure. I am quite sure, from the little that I myself know of conditions in Africa, that the mere fact of such a discussion is going to have a very great influence.

But still, there again you will notice there was really only the General Conference which dealt with the question, and it was when the problem of coal arose that an entirely new experiment was made. As you know, coal is a highly technical question; if you talk to a coal-miner about mines, he despises your ignorance as much as a sailor does if you talk to him about ships. It was only by getting the coal-owners, the coal-miners, and the Government Departments who were interested in coal into consultation that you could get a discussion that was really worth anything. We did that by means of a special technical Conference at which only the nine countries were represented. They sat for a fortnight in January, and they took the whole of that fortnight to try to argue out how they worked in the various countries. For instance, the British system of calculating time spent underground was entirely different from all the continental systems, and the continental systems varied a good deal between each other. Also, the technical terms were very difficult to translate absolutely correctly, and it took a fortnight, as I say, before the ground was sufficiently clear for everybody to be certain what the others meant when they talked. That preliminary Conference was, to my mind, absolutely indispensable. It was criticized at the time on the ground that it had not reached any agreement. But it did two things: it created a common language, so to speak; it created confidence among the delegates that they really understood each other's meaning (and that is essential before you can hope to get any agreement); and, on the other hand, it narrowed down the points of difference to three. When the coal question came before the General Conference in June, the discussion was continued from the point where it left off in January, and finally it was lost by a very narrow majority only, on account of disagreement on a single point. On the whole, I think that that new method, the method of having a technical Conference, purely advisory in character, without any power to take binding decisions, simply reporting back to the General Conference, has been successful. That that is more or less the general opinion is shown by the fact that the same procedure is to be applied in the case of maritime questions. Next year we are going to have a technical maritime conference of an advisory character confined only to the maritime countries, before the question of hours at sea comes to the General Conference.

iv. *Conclusion.*

We shall have to see how it works out. It may not work out well, but what I would try to impress upon you is that we are still in a very early stage; we are still in the stage of experiment. We are feeling our way, and as time goes on we find new requirements here, defects there, which have to be met somehow or other. But what I think is also true is that, in these ten years that we have just been through, we have shown that the Constitution as it was originally drawn up was a sound Constitution, sound not only in its theoretical structure but also as a piece of working machinery. We are also in process of demonstrating that it is a living institution, in the sense that it is capable of adaptation; that it is not just a static charter, put there in the Treaty and incapable of adaptation, but that it is a living organism which works and which is capable of expansion and modification in order to meet the needs of practical life. That, to my mind, is the essential feature. Of course, there have been mistakes, there have been failures, there may be others in the future, but I think the real point I would like you to carry away is this: that we are not just 'staying put'. We are not going to stick in the mud; there is sufficient sap running in the tree to make it capable of further growth and to make it capable of meeting the new demands of the new ages that are in front of us.

CHAPTER III

PARLIAMENTS, NATIONAL AND INTERNATIONAL

Mr. G. A. JOHNSTON:

THE reaction against parliamentary government in Europe, coinciding with the rapid development of parliamentary institutions in Asia, has stimulated research in many countries into the technique of parliamentary procedure, the mechanics of conference method, the psychology of 'thinking together'.

It is not without interest, as a contribution to the study of parliamentary procedure, to survey the development of the mechanism of an international institution to which the term parliamentary has sometimes been applied, which has now celebrated the tenth anniversary of its existence. The first International Labour Conference of the League of Nations was held in Washington in November 1919, and since that time conferences under the auspices of the permanent International Labour Organization have continued to meet at least once a year.

The purpose of this paper is not to assess the economic and social results obtained by the International Labour Organization, but solely to examine, as a contribution to the science of parliamentary institutions, the system of procedure of this international house of representatives.

i. *Parliamentary Representation*

What are the main characteristics of a parliamentary institution? In the first place it aims at being a representative body. A national parliament is the nation in little. In this microcosm the main tendencies of the public opinion of the country as a whole are represented *in petto*. Parliamentary representatives are supposed to represent the common interests of their constituents. 'This is the first principle of democracy', writes Mr. Chesterton in his *Orthodoxy*, 'that the essential things in men are the things they hold in common, not the things they hold separately.' A national parliament is essentially representative of the things that men hold in common. The International Labour Conference is also, in spite of appearances which sometimes suggest the contrary, a representative body in this sense. For the general philosophical conception on which the system of representation in this industrial parliament has been based is that there is an essential community of interest in the whole industrial field, and that the best way to make people realize this fundamental community of interest is to get representatives of the various groups together to discuss freely and frankly the questions of primary concern to them. It is representative not only of the various nations which compose the League of Nations and the International Labour Organization, but also of the main interests concerned with industry.

At the International Labour Conference, which meets at least once a year, each Member State has the right to be represented by four delegates. Two of the delegates are Government delegates, acting on Government instructions; but the other two have to be nominated by the Government in agreement with the most representative organizations of employers and workers in the country concerned. The obligation of the Government to consult the employers' and workers' organizations is no mere formality. The object is to secure the genuine expression of opinion of the organized employers and workers of the world; and the Conference has always shown itself very scrupulous in scrutinizing the credentials of the delegates. The basis of the composition of the Conference, therefore, is to secure the direct representation of the Governments, the employers, and the workers of all the various States Members of the League of Nations.

The system of representation in the Conference has been exposed to two main criticisms. In the first place it has been maintained that the constitution of the Conference consecrates a form of industrial organization which is, after all, transitional. There is no certainty that the tripartite division into Governments, employers, and workers possesses any finality. All sorts of suggestions are being made in the world with a view to revolutions in this system of division. The Soviet system in Russia at one time attempted to suppress everybody but the workers. There have also been endeavours, of a less revolutionary kind, through the co-operative movement, democratization of industry, guild-socialist organizations, and in other ways, for the worker to become also an employer. But the experience which we have of such experiments shows that, even when the workers unite to employ themselves, there is apt to emerge a difference of interest between the worker *qau* worker and the worker *qua* employer.

From a very different angle, a striking suggestion has been made by Mr. Owen D. Young. Speaking of industrial relations, Mr. Young said:

'Perhaps some day we may be able to organize the human beings engaged in a particular undertaking so that they will truly be the employer buying capital as a commodity in the market at the lowest price. I hope the day may come when these great business organizations will truly belong to the men who are giving their lives and their efforts to them, I care not in what capacity. Then they will use capital truly as a tool, and they will all be interested in working it to the highest economic advantage.'[1]

However the structure of industrial society may change, it seems probable that there will always be at least two main groups in addition to Governments, a group of 'workers' whose main function is to devote their manual strength and intellectual ability to the routine work of industrial production, and a group of 'employers' whose main function is to organize and manage the labour of the first class with the assistance of their own and other people's capital. I have said at least two groups, because, as industrial society gradually changes, and the distinction between the functions of management and capital-supply becomes more marked, it is possible that the employers' group may split into two: (*a*) the management group, (*b*) the capital-supplying group. We may, in the future, find it necessary to modify the constitution of the Conference, to provide for representation of three non-Governmental groups instead of two. But that is not a development of to-morrow or yet of the day after to-morrow. What appears certain is that, however the non-Governmental groups may be constituted, the Government group will remain substantially a single group. The Government must always represent an attitude and an interest different from that of a non-Governmental group. In the first place, the interests of the workers and employers are primarily the interests of producers, but both groups are composed of individuals who have interests as consumers. These interests are represented by the Government. Further, the Government also represents the manifold interests of a non-industrial sort, not directly involved, perhaps, in labour legislation, but

[1] *New York Times*, 5 June 1927.

indirectly liable to be affected. All the interests and institutions which are the soul of the community must continue to be represented by the Government.

The second criticism to which attention must be devoted relates to the right of workers and employers to sit on an equality with Government delegates in the Conference. The importance of this innovation is not always recognized. For the first time in the history of international law it was provided, in the constitution of the International Labour Conference, that individual citizens representing group interests within a particular country should sit side by side with Government delegates, possessing the same rights as they and not bound in any way by the instructions or even by the influence of their Government. Is it not a very dangerous principle, it may be asked, to give such power to group interests? Does such an arrangement not suggest to these interests that, in their own countries also, they may arrogate to themselves a place on an equality with the Government in all matters relating to labour and industry? Does it not encourage the emergence of group interests possibly at variance with those of the State as a whole, as represented by the Government? Is it just that Governments should be bound by decisions for the taking of which they are only partially responsible?

The reply to this question is, in a word, that the powers of the Conference are, in the last resort, not immediately legislative. The decisions of the Conference embodied in draft Conventions and Recommendations cannot be immediately enforced anywhere by the Organization. They must first be submitted to the Parliament or other competent authority in each country concerned before they can be put into application. The decisions of the Conference, however great may be their moral importance as the solemn agreements of the nations of the world in meeting assembled, are not in themselves laws. The decisions of the Conference do not automatically bind the States. In view of this, no real objection can be felt, from the standpoint of political philosophy, to the presence at the Conference, with full rights, of workers' and employers' delegates.

It is, indeed, of positive value to have the direct representation in the Conference of the two groups directly concerned in industry. This direct representation constitutes a safeguard against the danger that the work of the Organization should become theoretical, academic, or bureaucratic. The discussions of the Conference, in virtue of the presence of those directly interested in the questions at issue, preserve that vitality and reality which is encouraged when the principle of personal contact is respected.

The Conference is thus in one aspect an interesting example of an experiment in functional representation. Its constitution involves, in fact, a compromise between the traditional principle of the representation on territorial lines of the community as a whole, and the insistent demands which have been made for the direct representation of occupational interests.

One of the interesting conclusions which emerges from Bryce's detailed examination, in his *Modern Democracies,* of the working of the system of representative government in the most important democratic States is that this system of general and non-technical representation has been found to complete itself, officially and unofficially, by the adjunction of permanent or temporary institutions of a technical or occupational kind.

In some countries the consultation of technical experts

E

usually takes place through Commissions or Committees. When a question requiring special technical knowledge comes before Parliament, Parliament recognizes itself incompetent in the details of the question, and a special Commission, composed of experts of recognized standing, is appointed to examine the question in all its aspects and to present a report to Parliament. On the basis of this report and of the evidence on which it is founded, Parliament then, in the light of general principles, takes a decision on the legislation that it considers necessary. This procedure seems perfectly consistent with the principles of representative government, nay, seems even to be a necessary corollary to it. For if the sovereign Parliament of representatives possesses *ex hypothesi* no special technical knowledge, it is necessary that it should have recourse to the advice of publicly-constituted bodies of experts.

Less legitimate, however, is the development within Parliament, or in close contact with it, of groups representing not the general interests of the citizens as a whole, but the special or exclusive interests of a particular section of the community. These groups are organized not to represent the citizens as a whole in certain circumscriptions, but to watch the interests of a particular section of the community and to influence the decisions of Parliament in favour of their interests. If the activities of these groups were public, little harm might result. It is when subterranean means are used that the system of the representation of interests becomes demoralizing to the whole structure of representative government.

These considerations, among others, have given rise to the increasing demand in various countries for the frank and open establishment, alongside the ordinary political Parliament, of a permanent body on which would be directly represented, not the general interests of territorial circumscriptions, but the special functional interests of groups of producers and consumers. In accordance with this demand, bodies such as the Reichswirtschaftsrat and the Conseil National Économique have been set up in various countries. In so far as these bodies repose on a system of functional representation, they present certain analogies, which, however, must not be pressed too far, with the constitution of the International Labour Conference.

ii. *Parliamentary Procedure*

The second main characteristic of parliamentary institutions is that every Parliament develops its own system of procedure. Sometimes this system of procedure has come to be established by a slow growth from precedent to precedent; in other cases it is regulated by a written constitution. Procedure is important; for it is as true of Parliament as it is of law that, as Sir Henry Maine said, progress is secreted in the interstices of procedure. The International Labour Conference has its written constitution, but provision is made in it for amendment. Like every living and growing institution, its system of procedure is in process of development.

The main object of the procedure that is being developed by the Conference is to give every guarantee against the possibility of hasty and ill-considered decisions. Some of the earlier decisions of the Conference were attacked on the ground that they were insufficiently prepared and examined before being reached. It would be difficult to bring such a criticism against the present procedure of the Conference. Its procedure is now so complicated that it is, perhaps, exposed to the criticism that it unduly compresses the springs of action.

The main lines of the procedure of the Conference may be rapidly indicated. The Governing Body of the Office decides to place on the agenda of the Conference a certain question. The various States Members of the Organization are notified officially of this decision and the Office prepares a report on the law and practice in various countries in regard to the question. This report is communicated to all the delegates to the Conference some time before the opening of the session. When the Conference meets, it examines the report by the International Labour Office, both in committee and in plenary session, and decides upon the main points on which it is desirable to consult Governments of States Members of the Organization, with a view to the adoption, at the next session, of a Draft Convention or Recommendation. A questionnaire is prepared by the Office and communicated to the States Members; their replies are received by the Office in due course, and, four months before the following session of the Conference, the Office communicates a report to all Governments, containing the text of the replies of the Governments to the questionnaire, together with drafts, based on the replies of these Governments, for Conventions or Recommendations. The Conference discusses, on the basis of the drafts prepared by the Office, in the light of the replies received from Governments, both in committee and in plenary session, the decisions which it finally adopts.

It will be seen from this brief account of the procedure of the Conference that, from the time when the Governing Body decides to place a question on the agenda until a Draft Convention or Recommendation is adopted by the Conference on that question, a period of over two years elapses. During all this period the various Governments are examining the question, the Office is collecting information upon it and is placing that information at the disposal not only of the Governments but of the general public.

Nor is this all. It generally happens that, before the Governing Body decides definitely to place a question on the agenda, the question has already formed the subject of preliminary exchanges of views, either in the Conference or in the Governing Body, or of inquiries by the Office, during a period of years.

It may be mentioned, in parentheses, that this so-called 'double discussion' procedure has taken the place of earlier forms of procedure which were found to work unsatisfactorily. One of these earlier forms of procedure was called 'second-reading procedure'. According to it the Conference, at the first of two successive sessions, discussed and decided by a first vote on the text of a Draft Convention or Recommendation. At the succeeding session of the Conference the text of the Draft Convention or Recommendation again came before the Conference with a view to adoption on final reading. It was originally intended that the second reading should be used merely to enable any alterations of detail to be made which were found to be necessary. As a matter of fact, experience showed that there was a tendency for the opposition shown to the Convention or Recommendation at the first reading to crystallize in the intervening year and for questions of principle which had been decided upon in the first reading to be raised again at the second reading. The second discussion, therefore, at the second Conference, went over the same old ground as was covered at the first Conference, and no useful purpose was served. This system was, therefore, abandoned in favour of the double-discussion procedure.

Three further points with regard to procedure may be

mentioned. In the first place, great use is made by the Conference of the system of committees. In most parliamentary systems, the committee plays a useful part. In the International Labour Conference, where questions of a highly technical character are often discussed, careful and detailed discussion in committee is absolutely essential. The members of these committees are appointed from among the delegates to the Conference, on the basis of their recognized competence in the subject under discussion, as is the practice in the case of committees of most national Parliaments.

Special attention may be drawn to the fact that the first draft of the text of the Convention or Recommendation is submitted to the consideration of the Conference and its committees by the International Labour Office. On the basis of replies to its questionnaires, on the basis of its study of public opinion in the various countries of the world on the particular question at issue, it draws up a draft for a Convention. In preparing this draft the Office does not, of course, seek in any way to override the authority of the Conference. The Conference may make any alterations it likes in the draft prepared by the Office; it may even reject it altogether. The primary object of the drafts prepared by the Office is to give the various committees appointed by the Conference something to work on, some *point d'appui* among the welter of possible conclusions.

There is, however, a more fundamental reason, deeply rooted in the principles of political philosophy, for this procedure. If the Office prepared no draft for submission to the Conference, individual States would certainly do so. The result would be the probable emergence of one or two conflicting drafts, prepared by powerful States, each of which would secure adherents among the smaller and less powerful

States, or among the workers' and employers' delegates. The Conference would be torn between two conflicting views, each supported *à outrance* by the prestige of a group of States, and no agreed conclusion would be possible. In the history of the Conference, the most striking example of the evil results of such a situation was afforded by the discussion at the Genoa Conference on the eight-hour day at sea. It is true that the Office did prepare and submit to the Conference a draft for discussion. But the authority of the Office was not at that time great, and the Conference rapidly found itself enmeshed in a discussion of two different solutions of the problem, one British, the other French. The point of view of the British Government, which proposed a fifty-six-hour week at sea and a forty-eight-hour week in port, with strict limitation of overtime, was supported in general by the Northern countries, Japan, and Spain. On the other hand, the French Government, followed by most of the other countries, provided for a forty-eight-hour week with unlimited overtime, compensated by additional wages or by off-time if in port. From the start it was almost a foregone conclusion, in view of the sharp national cleavage thus manifested, that no agreement would be reached by the Conference.

An individual Government could, in isolated cases, perhaps, supply as good a draft as the International Labour Office; but such a draft would suffer from a double political defect. It would definitely engage the prestige of the Government which sponsored it, and would almost inevitably involve opposition, probably quite unnecessary, on the part of other States. Under the present system, the draft prepared by the International Labour Office, with its international staff, comprising its estimate on the basis of all the data, of the probable line of agreement between the parties concerned, bears every guarantee as an objective and international document. It is thrown to the Conference as a new football is thrown to the teams in a cup-tie. The football may be kicked, and kicked hard, but the International Labour Office has no susceptibilities, and at the end of the match the same football usually emerges, with a dent here and there, perhaps, but essentially the same football as that with which the game commenced. This draft prepared by the Office engages no nation's prestige and, even more important, alienates no nation's sympathies. It can be, and is, discussed patiently and dispassionately on a basis rather of industrial than of national divergences of opinion.

In this respect the procedure of the International Labour Conference differs entirely from that of most national Parliaments. In most national Parliaments, bills are submitted by the Government, and the Government does its utmost to secure the passage of the bill against all the obstacles placed in its way by the Opposition. The proposed Draft Convention submitted by the International Labour Office to the Conference differs entirely in this respect from the bill submitted by the Government. The proposed Draft Convention is a neutral document established on the basis of the replies of the various Governments. The aim of the International Labour Office in preparing the draft is not to maintain any particular point of view, but to prepare a draft which, in the light of the replies of the Governments, seems most likely to be adopted by the Conference. The prestige of the Office is not engaged by the proposed Draft Convention in the same way as the prestige of a Government is engaged by a Bill. The attitude of the Office to its proposed Draft Convention is not analogous to that of a Government towards its Bill in a national Parliament, but rather to the attitude of a particular Government department which has been responsible, under the orders of the Government, for the drafting of the Bill. The attitude of the Office, in a word, is not a political attitude, but a scientific one.

Perhaps at this point the criticism may be made: 'This system of procedure seems indeed to be carefully constructed; it seems indeed to be of a nature to prevent hasty decisions, but, after all, the Conference constitutes a single Chamber. It does not have any second Chamber, constituted otherwise than the first Chamber, to provide a necessary guarantee against imprudent legislation.' The reply to that imaginary criticism is that, from the point of view of practical results, there is a second Chamber. The second Chamber is the national Parliament of each of the States Members of the Organization. No second Chamber could be more remote from the influences which have free play in its first Chamber than this. Sometimes Geneva is accused of having an atmosphere which in some mysterious way leads cautious and practical statesmen and industrialists into idealistic imprudences to which they would never have committed themselves at home. If there is any truth in that, it is clear that such an atmosphere can have no influence on the second Chamber, namely the national Parliament. The decisions of the International Labour Conference come before the national Parliaments and are submitted to their cold analysis in complete remoteness from the generous enthusiasm which is supposed to reign at Geneva.

iii. *Organized Discussion.*

Every national Parliament aims at reaching its decisions by a process of organized discussions. Students of political psychology have pointed out that the specific character of the decision adopted by a representative body is undoubtedly dependent on the process of reaching the decision. Of least value is a decision adopted simply as a result of the passive acquiescence of one side in the views of the other. Such a decision means that the discussion has consisted simply in the exposition of one view and the submission of the other members of the conference to this view. From the point of view of conference method, a better result than that of acquiescence is that of compromise, where each side, as a result of discussion, is prepared to modify its original standpoint with a view to reaching agreement. It is possible, however, to obtain even better results than compromise from conference procedure. Such results are obtained from the method of integration. This means that the whole conference is inventing or discovering new ways of reaching its ends better than any of the original views of any of the individual groups. The conference as a whole, through the method of integration, is getting plus value as a result of the emergence of the collective thinking of the group as a whole.

It is probable that in no Parliament is discussion always so well organized as to produce the maximum value of collective thinking. Mr. Graham Wallas, in his *Great Society*, draws an unflattering picture of the process of discussion as illustrated in Congress and in the House of Commons. It would be idle to assert that at the International Labour Conference the level of organized discussion uniformly reaches the stage of genuine integration of various opposing points of view. It is probable, however, that the level of organized discussion in the International Labour Conference is higher than it is in many national Parliaments. In so far as the standard of discussion at the Conference does not remain uniformly at a high level, the reasons are to be found in two main circumstances. In the first place, much of the real discussion at the Conference, as in national Parliaments, takes place in committee. There is a tendency for the plenary session simply to register the decisions of the committees. In certain cases, however, where the plenary session of the Conference has seen fit to discuss in detail the conclusions to which committees have come, examples of organized discussion of a high order have been exhibited. The standard of discussion at the Conference is adversely affected, in the second place, by the fact that a large proportion of delegates speak in languages not their own. It is only a very exceptional man who can be eloquent or convincing in a foreign language. His auditors may, indeed, understand what he is saying, but their understanding is not accompanied by the element of pleasure produced in his hearers by an eloquent orator. Account must also be taken of the occasional misunderstandings due to translation. A speaker, speaking in his own language, if the question with which he is dealing is a particularly difficult and delicate one, may spend hours in devising a formula and achieving the precise turn of phrase which he wishes to give to his thought. The interpreter is obliged to improvise his translation on the spur of the moment, and it is not surprising if he sometimes fails to convey precisely the nuance which the original speaker is particularly anxious to express. The fact that translation is necessary, however, is not an unmixed evil. In committee work, all the proceedings of the committee are conducted both in French and in English, and, where the members have some knowledge of both languages, it is a positive advantage to have translation. Such translation gives the members of the committee a little time to reflect on the precise bearing of the speech which has just been delivered, and enables the next speaker to marshal and arrange his thoughts more logically than he might have been able to do if he had been obliged to follow on immediately, without any interval, after the previous speaker. Translation has a further advantage. By making it impossible for one speaker to follow on immediately after another without an interval for interpretation, it allows a moment or two for passions which may have been aroused to subside, with the result that the 'retort discourteous' usually does not take place. It is perhaps in part for this reason that the International Labour Conference has known few, if any, really stormy sessions.

Closely connected with the question of organized discussion in parliamentary institutions is the question whether members of Parliament are to be regarded as representatives or as delegates. What precisely is meant by this distinction ? A representative is a man who is appointed with general indications as to the policy which he is to pursue, but with great liberty as to the precise formulation of this policy. A delegate, on the other hand, is a man who is bound down by precise instructions, even on points of detail. Members of national Parliaments are in almost all cases representatives. They are elected for a period of years on a general programme or platform which they have submitted to their constituents. They receive a general mandate to represent their constituents but, unless in exceptional cases, are not bound down on points of detail. The representative is obliged to use his judgement in the interpretation of his mandate, giving due weight to the consideration that, if he does not interpret aright the views of his constituents, he runs the risk of not being re-elected or even, as in some American States where the system of 'Recall' is in practice, of finding himself recalled and losing the confidence of his constituents before the normal period for which he has been elected has elapsed.

In the case of the International Labour Conference, most of the members may be regarded as representatives. They receive general instructions from their Governments, from their trade unions, or from their employers' organizations, but they are allowed considerable liberty in the precise application of these instructions. If, in certain cases, members of the Conference, particularly those representing Governments, receive precise and detailed instructions even on the smallest points, and thus are to be regarded as delegates and not as representatives, it should be remembered that even in these cases it may be possible for them, through the telegraph or the telephone, to secure alterations in their instructions. It is, in fact, indispensable in any representative assembly that the members of the assembly should essentially be representatives and not delegates. An assembly composed exclusively of delegates, in the strict sense—persons tied down in all details by precise instructions—would be an entirely paradoxical and useless institution; for *ex hypothesi*, inasmuch as all its members were entirely determined in their attitude by previous instructions, no amount of discussion would make it possible to secure a change in any of the points of view represented. If organized discussion is to have any meaning, there must be the possibility of influencing and of being influenced. This is possible only on the conception that the members of the representative assembly are representatives, and not delegates.

In connexion with organized discussion, the size of the body in which discussion takes place is of importance. Aristotle restricted the size of the City State because, in his view, if the State passed certain limits of size, it became too big to enable the citizens to participate adequately in its activities. Similarly, in the case of a representative body, the number of members may become too large to make it possible for all to participate usefully in the discussion. The question may be raised whether the limit of size has not been exceeded in certain national Parliaments, many of which contain several times the number of titular delegates to the International Labour Conference. The constitution of the International Labour Conference has ensured that the limits of size beyond which a deliberative assembly cannot satisfactorily work have not been exceeded.

iv. *Parliamentary Functions.*

Our examination of the organized discussion of the Conference brings us naturally to consider the two main functions of a parliament. These are, first, to pass legislation, and second, to focus the expression of public opinion. Parliaments aim not only at passing legislation, but at passing progressive legislation. If a Parliament did not lead to the adoption of legislation, it would very soon cease to exist. Further, while opinions may and do differ as to what constitutes progress, improvement, and reform, no Parliament wishes to be regarded as reactionary or even as wishing merely to maintain the *status quo*. Every Parliament desires that its legislation shall be progressive legislation—legislation which will secure a genuine improvement in the conditions of life of the people of its country.

The success of the work of a Parliament cannot be measured statistically, simply by the number of bills submitted to it or even by the number of Acts passed by it. If, then, the mere number of the legislative decisions of the International Labour Conference is not very great, that does not call for any apology or excuse. Thirty-one Draft Conventions and thirty-eight Recommendations have been adopted by the International Labour Conference. If we attempt to classify these decisions by subject, we shall find that they fall into ten categories: (1) hours of work (including rest periods and spare time), (2) wages, (3) unemployment, (4) migration, (5) industrial health, (6) industrial accidents, (7) social insurance, (8) the special protection of women and children, (9) technical education, (10) systems of inspection.

In speaking of the decisions of the Conference, the word 'legislative' has been used, and the decisions have been called 'legislative decisions', but the decisions of the Conference are not strictly in themselves legislation. They have no legislative effect until they become embodied in national legislation.

In order to secure as far as possible that the provisions of the decisions of the Conference shall be embodied as soon as, and as completely as, possible in the systems of national legislation of the various countries, all States Members of the Organization are obliged to submit all Draft Conventions to their Parliaments or other competent authorities within twelve months, or, in exceptional circumstances, eighteen months, with a view to their ratification. Up to the end of July 1930, 388 ratifications of Draft Conventions had been registered.

I do not propose to discuss the question of ratifications. An admirable examination of the situation has recently been made by the Chairman of the Governing Body, Mr. Arthur Fontaine, and published in the illustrated album issued by the Office to commemorate its tenth anniversary.

The second main function of Parliaments is to focus the expression of public opinion and to provide a forum for free and open discussion. There is a great deal of truth in the

French saying, that the worst chamber in the world is better than the best ante-chamber. In the worst chamber in the world there is an attempt at open discussion. Criticism is not only permitted, but welcomed. This parliamentary duty of criticism and discussion is more and more faithfully discharged by the International Labour Conference.

Attention was drawn to this function of Parliaments and of the International Labour Conference by the Deputy Director of the International Labour Office in the closing session of the 1927 Conference. Mr. Butler said:

> 'It is only in so far as it develops parliamentary qualities that the Conference, and the Organization which depends upon it, can really flourish and develop an organic spirit of its own. Parliaments do not devote the whole, or perhaps even the greater part, of their time to drawing up laws. Laws, like books, are excellent things, but it is possible to have too many of them, and if parliaments produced nothing but laws, I feel quite sure that they would go out of existence in a comparatively short space of time. Their other, and perhaps their principal duty, is to act as a reflection of public opinion, and to shape a policy on the great questions of the day. If I may say so, it seems to me that this Conference is doing that more and more each year.'

This parliamentary aspect of the Conference is becoming increasingly marked. In the general discussion of the Director's report it is now customary for some fifty delegates, representatives of Governments, employers, and workers, to take part. The speeches range over a wide field of questions touching the work of the International Labour Organization —national social policy in relation to international labour legislation; internal organization and practice; interpretation; relations between the Office and the States Members and non-Members; subjects for future examination; and many others.

The question which claims most attention is, however, the progress of the ratification and application of International Labour Conventions. Workers' delegates are apt to complain that progress is unduly slow; Governments contend that it is as fast as national economic conditions and other circumstances will permit; employers' delegates suggest that more speed might be imprudent.

The conference is, in fact, becoming an international tribune for the serious discussion of labour difficulties throughout the world. Declarations of government policy in labour matters, made by Ministers of State to the world public represented at Geneva, are more and more frequent and more and more expected. The Conference wants to know what Governments are doing or not doing, and wants to know why. It shows itself exceedingly respectful and sympathetic towards real national difficulties, more and more critical and impatient of mere hair-splitting and obstruction.

v. *Parliament and Civil Service.*

Finally, no analysis of the characteristics of a Parliament would be adequate which left out of account the Civil Service, which functions alongside of and ancillary to the parliamentary institution. Every Parliament has its officials and every Parliament depends, in part at least, for its smooth working, on a Civil Service. The International Labour Conference also has its Civil Service. This is the International Labour Office. This International Civil Service at Geneva has two main functions: in the first place to undertake all preparatory and secretarial work with the International Labour Conference, the Governing Body, and the various commissions and committees set up; in the second place to act as an information and research office on industrial and

F

labour questions. The work of the Office in this field has led to its being called 'an international clearing-house of information'. In this development the International Labour Conference has realized in the international sphere the desire expressed by Professor H. J. Laski that every national Parliament should provide for itself a small but competent Research Bureau.

It has not proved an easy thing to evolve a genuine International Civil Service. Each State has peculiarities of administrative organization, though all such systems may be regarded ultimately as variations of two or three main types. And the great problem of the Office has been to evolve a scheme of organization which would not merely be a compromise between these types, but would be an internally self-consistent system resulting from the adaptation to the needs of an international institution of the best elements in the various national schemes.

The information work of the Office is undoubtedly more difficult than that of the normal national Government Department. One important element is the language difficulty. The information collected by the Office naturally comes in various languages, not only those which are generally known to an international staff, but also such 'exotic' languages as Japanese, Czech, Polish, Hungarian, and Finnish, an acquaintance with which is a rare accomplishment. It is essential that the Office should be able to utilize this information in the interests of the completeness of its scientific research. The various departments of the Office contain representatives of over thirty different nationalities, and very few written languages are unknown to some or other of the members of the staff.

In spite of every endeavour, the language difficulty remains a real one for the Office. It suggested, in fact, to the first Chief of the Research Division the following law: 'The difficulty of gathering, compiling and publishing information increases with the number of languages involved, not in simple direct ratio, but in the cube of the number of languages involved.' In spite of this difficulty, the Office has been able to carry out its task of scientific research in the documentary preparation of questions for the Conference. The research worker must always be 'objective': he must study his subject with the same mental detachment as he would examine a bloodless specimen under the microscope. But the atmosphere of the Office is not academic. Its activities are not devoted to a theoretic end. All its work is 'directed to practice'. This apparent antagonism between the necessary disinterestedness of spirit of the research worker and the practical purposes of the Organization has suggested to some that there is a fundamental antinomy within the life of the Organization. But this is not so. The doctor who sets out to cure his patient must not only diagnose the disease from which his patient is suffering but must also know the specific remedies to apply. In the interests of practical action, research is necessary to discover the remedies.

Scientific research such as is carried on in the Office is an 'industry of transformation', which takes the crude ore of unverified statements, allegations, controversies, protests, claims, and counter-claims, and by a process of mental metallurgy converts it into the true steel that will serve the ends of human welfare.

vi. *Nationalism and Internationalism*

We have now passed in review the main characteristics of Parliaments, and have considered how far each of these characteristics can be predicated of the International Labour Conference.

But there is one essential feature of the International Labour Conference which is *ex hypothesi* to be found in no national Parliament. This is its internationalism. The first aspect of this internationalism that strikes the casual observer at the Conference is that more than one language is used. English and French are the official languages, and some other languages, notably German and Spanish, are frequently used. But a little reflection will show that the mere fact that more than one language is used does not differentiate the International Labour Conference from national Parliaments. In many national Parliaments more than one language is officially used. I need only mention Canada, South Africa, Switzerland, Belgium, and Finland. In all these countries, and there are others, more than one language is used in Parliament.

We must therefore look farther to find the essence of the international character of the Conference. Its internationalism is to be found primarily in the fact that all the States Members of the Organization have the right to participate on an equal basis in its work. The system of careful preparation for the Conference helps to ensure the genuinely international character of the Conference. When the delegates meet at the Conference they know the probable attitude that the other delegates will adopt, because this has been indicated in the replies of the Governments to the questionnaires sent out by the Office. But this attitude is rarely defined before the Conference in such a rigid form that the national pride of the particular country is engaged to support it. This is a great advantage from the point of view of genuine internationalism. Policies are brought into contact with one another when they are still in the making, before they have set in a mould, while modifications in the interests of international agreement are still possible.

Further, the Conference is the meeting-place not only of national interests but also of industrial interests. This naturally produces extremely interesting cross-currents. These cross-currents, paradoxical as it may seem, actually help to bring the ship safely into port. On the one hand, national differences tend to blunt the acuteness of industrial conflict, and, on the other hand, industrial differences take the edge off national claims. On the whole, while national points of view have sometimes been emphasized at the Conference, the battle is usually fought on industrial lines. On the one hand there is the workers' group, on the other hand the employers' group, with the Government delegates in the middle performing a mediating and conciliating function. Sometimes the employers' and the workers' groups vote as a solid block, but it frequently happens that a 'free vote' takes place and some of the workers or some of the employers may vote against the majority. In most cases the Conference has succeeded in finding a text for its Conventions and Recommendations for which the great majority of the delegates, Government, employers', and workers' alike, have been able to vote.

The decisions of the Conference are, in fact, genuinely international industrial decisions. They have been evolved by the free and frank discussion of national and industrial difficulties. They constitute the elements of a gradually growing international code of labour law, a gradually developing international standard. But they can result in a real improvement of conditions of life and work only when they have been submitted in each country to the free and unfettered decision of the national Parliament. The international parliament at Geneva is dependent upon national Parliaments, and the national Parliaments in their turn are dependent on the public opinion of the citizens of each country.

CHAPTER IV

INTERNATIONAL BANKING AND FINANCE

Sir ANDREW McFADYEAN.

PUBLIC interest in international finance is a fairly new thing; when war broke out in 1914 there were few people who understood in anything but the vaguest way the machinery of international trade and its financial basis. Finance and 'the City' were regarded as mysterious things in which ordinary men had a very indirect interest. In the last ten years painful experience has taught the humblest inhabitant of several countries that international finance has a very direct bearing on his daily life, and he has had to enlarge his horizon to take in not only 'the City' with which he was relatively familiar but all the larger capital centres, mutually dependent on each other's actions and reactions.

If this public interest in finance is a new thing the existence of official international finance is still newer; it has taken its rise from post-war conditions, and above all from the creation of public foreign debts on a large scale.

i. *International Indebtedness : a New Problem.*

We have been well enough accustomed at all times to see Governments floating loans abroad, and as investors we have had a certain interest, sometimes a sad one, in the solvency or insolvency of these foreign borrowers. It is easy to forget, however, just how new a thing it is for a Government to owe large sums, not to private bondholders, but to another Government repayable over two generations of men. Not only is large-scale indebtedness between Governments a new thing, but *pace* those students of the subject who see no difference between reparation, for instance, and ordinary foreign commercial indebtedness, it raises entirely new problems.

Consider, for instance, that the money which is borrowed abroad in the ordinary course of business is normally invested for productive purposes; it may prove that calculations have been faulty and that the investment is not so profitable as was expected, or it may prove that too great a burden of indebtedness has been contracted. The play of economic forces then adjusts the matter, for the debtor either goes bankrupt or writes down his capital, and little more is heard of or even felt about the matter. The private investor who has entrusted his savings to a foreign concern which fails feels little more soreness than if the concern was a domestic one; at any rate he can scarcely hope, even if he desires, to make a political question out of it.

Reparation and inter-allied debts—the two great categories of public international indebtedness—are different in every respect. They were contracted for unproductive purposes; the expenditure of the money lent did not make the world richer; it did not even leave the world where it was, which is normally the worst to be feared from unproductive commercial expenditure, but made it definitely poorer.

The amount of debt contracted (or imposed) had again no known relation to immediate or future capacity to pay. There was, and in some cases at least, is, no guarantee that the amounts owing between governments can be borne without undue strain, that is, without a lowering of the standard of living which might become socially dangerous in the paying country, and even repugnant to the conscience of the receiving country.

What is even more important, if a public foreign debt is in fact too heavy, it is not automatically adjusted by the bankruptcy of the debtor or a more or less automatic scaling down of his debts. A civilized country cannot afford the damage to its credit involved by bankruptcy; if it repudiates or appears to repudiate it will wait perhaps for generations before it can obtain fresh credit, and must be content in foreign trade to lead the kind of hand-to-mouth existence of Russia, which is almost a return to barter.

Finally, a public international debt is shot through at all its stages with political colour. Whatever the purpose for which the debt was contracted, the interest is taken from the taxpayer of one country, and it is paid over in relief of the taxpayer of another. All sorts of irrelevant considerations which never enter into the minds of commercial debtors and creditors arise to complicate the transaction and poison the political atmosphere. Private monetary transactions between nations are soon forgotten, or continue to affect nothing but commercial and financial relations. How long memories are for public debts may be exemplified by the constant resuscitation in my own country of claims against certain constituent states of the U.S.A.

A Government in its relation with other Governments should neither a lender nor a borrower be, and if it cannot avoid becoming one or other, should escape from the relationship with all convenient speed. For this reason the ideal method would have been to commercialize all these international public debts, by which means while some Governments would perforce have remained debtors, they would have been indebted not to other Governments but to private bondholders. This has not been possible, though it was long regarded as the goal of reparation, and is not now likely to be possible on any large scale.

It has not been possible because in the first place years

were wasted, thanks in a great degree to the way in which politics distorted a financial question, before there was any final or quasi-final determination, not of what the reparation debtor owed, an academic question comparatively easy of settlement, but of what he could pay. In the second place the reparation debt could not be treated in isolation from inter-allied debts. It was, and presumably is, the official view of the Government chiefly concerned as creditor, that that was no connexion between the two problems; I can myself see a limited sense in which there was no connexion, but they were in fact connected by the principal debtors, and to deny the connexion in these circumstances is about as helpful as to deny the objective existence of a so-called imaginary pain. Holding that the connexion existed, no inter-allied debtor would have been willing or could have been expected to commercialize his debt to the Governments of the U.S.A. or Great Britain unless and until reparation debts had been commercialized at the same time; as it was, circumstances compelled a settlement of war debts in advance of a final reparation settlement.

We have now reached the stage when that part of Germany's payments which is in excess of the sums required for inter-allied debt purposes will or can be commercialized, while as regards the balance a *de facto*, if one-sided, connexion is established between it and American claims on Germany's creditors; while therefore the problem of international public indebtedness unfortunately remains in being, reparation or its day-to-day administration has, by the mercy of Providence, ceased to be the concern of officials responsible to the recipients of reparation, and has thereby become of more general international, as opposed to inter-allied, concern, than it has hitherto been.

I think, as I have said, that public interest in international finance is in large measure due to the emergence of these public international debts. I may mention two other stimulants: the urgent need for reconstruction in the world at large, and the growth of an international consciousness. Some day, even if we have to wait until 1988, the complex of Governmental inter-indebtedness will be resolved—long before then we may be assured that reconstruction difficulties will have disappeared as the world has adjusted itself to new conditions.

ii. *International Finance as a Peace Factor.*

The internationalization of finance, and the growth of an international consciousness, which, like the prosperity of the United States of America, may have been hastened and stimulated by the war and its legacy, were phenomena which were bound, sooner rather than later, to affect the form of our civilization.

Your Institute has and should have a particular interest in international finance, which in my opinion is deeply concerned that peace should be maintained, has done much for the restoration of peace, and can and must in the future do still more to organize peace.

The financier is not a fisher in troubled waters; like any other business man, if the storm rises he will take into his net what he can catch, but perhaps more than others he is interested in the continuance of calm for his traffic. Stability of prices is of importance to all business; stability of credit and security prices, the commodities in which the international financier deals, is of paramount importance to him. The point needs no labouring; international business requires international security, and complete freedom to trade. In troublous times great astuteness may make great profits, but the backbone of any trade or industry is conservative, and desirous of increasing its profits by extending its activities and cheapening what it has to offer. The shock which the events of August 1914 caused to finance, the difficulties in which all the great centres of capital were immediately involved, can hardly have passed from your memories. The profound disturbance of the post-war period, with its un-settled financial problems, as evidenced by fluctuating currencies and high rates, has been a nightmare to all of us, but to none more inimical than the international financier.

He has at any rate acted as if he believed that resettlement was his special interest. I have mentioned two major problems—reconstruction and public international indebtedness—the latter covering both reparation and inter-allied debts. About inter-allied debts which have by the force of events been treated as a political problem, or at any rate handled exclusively by politicians and their executives, I propose to say no more. In the reconstruction of Europe, official international finance has, as most of my audience knows at least as well as I, done yeoman service of incalculable value. If in the long run the League of Nations was a political necessity, it has proved that in the last ten years it was absolutely indispensable to preserve that minimum of economic stability without which the material on which statesmen must work would have gone to pieces in their hands. It is easy to forget how near the greater part of Europe was to Bolshevism in the years immediately following the cessation of hostilities. Organized philanthropy was able to deal with the symptoms of disease, but with the drying up of that source and the disappearance of such international bodies as the Supreme Economic Council, the

League provided the framework within which the causes of disease could be treated radically. The disease was a derangement of credit, with State finances in disorder and national currencies chasing each other down a primrose path to a bonfire of useless paper. The League was a rallying-point and a framework, and it provided a brain; its Financial and Economic section and its Financial Committee were a public acknowledgement that healthy finances were the *sine qua non* of healthy public and social life, and that the world was interested in, and to some degree responsible for, the prosperity of all its parts. But the League could have done little without the unceasing collaboration of international finance, and particularly of the large central banks. I think I am doing nobody else an injustice if I venture the assertion that the governors of the big central banks have done as much, and as unselfishly, for the re-establishment of peace as either statesmen or officials.

ii. *The Reconstruction Work of the League.*

I do not propose to enter into details, which are possibly more familiar to you than to me. A start was made with Austria at a time when most people despaired of Austria's capacity to continue a hydro-cephalic existence. You perhaps remember the criticism which the Chinese philosopher offered some years ago to a defender of the view that the French Revolution had been a good thing for mankind; he mildly suggested that it was perhaps premature to come to any conclusion on the question. It might be still rasher to assert that the foundations of a reasonable separate life have been laid for Austria, and much must still depend not only on Austria herself, but on the trade policies of her neighbours; I imagine, however, that no one will deny that Austria was saved by action taken on the initiative of the League, and that the most dangerous centre of infection in Europe was thereby immunized for the time being, and has been maintained since in a condition of comparative health.

And after Austria came Hungary, Bulgaria, Greece, and other salvage work which has slowly but systematically endeavoured to restore the conditions of civilized life to the distracted and bewildered post-war world of Europe. If I pass over these activities of international finance somewhat cursorily I hope I have said enough to show that it is due to no want of a sense of their importance, but because I am more at home, and my audience perhaps less so, with the part which international finance has played in the peaceful treatment of the reparation problem.

iv. *Reparations.*

Reparation was from the outset primarily a financial and economic problem, with a political aspect and unavoidable political reactions. It was for more than four years treated as a political problem with a financial aspect of secondary importance. No progress was made towards its solution while this attitude of mind persisted in high places. An attempt was made in the spring of 1922 to take reparation out of politics when the Reparation Commission summoned a Committee of Bankers to study and report on the possibility of German loans abroad for the complete or partial liquidation of the reparation debt. The German debt then stood nominally at a figure (132 milliard gold marks) which has since been divided by something between three and four, and in the view of the French delegate to the Reparation Commission the Committee was not entitled to make any recommendations which involved a reduction of the capital debt. This being the attitude of Germany's principal creditor international finance could only throw in its hand, and content itself with saying that with things as they were there was no possibility of any foreign loans to Germany.

Towards the end of the year the German Government itself took the initiative in calling in the doctors to its own sick-bed and asked Messrs. Brand, Cassel, Dubois, Jenks, Karmenka, Keynes, and Vissering to advise them on the financial situation. This formidable array of talent made substantially the same diagnosis as the panel of doctors called in earlier by the Reparation Commission; Germany needed foreign assistance and could not obtain it until her capital debt had been reconstructed.

Thereafter we had the melancholy adventure of the Ruhr— let bygones by bygones; for eighteen months reparation was again treated as a purely political problem until at the beginning of 1924, when matters had reached a well-nigh desperate pass, international finance was called again into consultation and, with the institution of the Committee which has come to be known as the Dawes Committee, was given a free hand to make what recommendations it liked, with the moral certainty that any measures which it suggested would be enforced by all parties.

This is not the time or the place to discuss the technical merits of the Dawes Plan. It was framed by rigidly divorcing politics from finance, and by an insistence that in the future administration of reparation the divorce should be maintained. I suspect that the members of the Dawes Committee, who were unanimous in their recommendations, entertained widely divergent views as to the way in which the plan would work in practice, and I am sure that even at this date, when the Plan has been superseded, there is no general consensus of opinion as to the interpretation which should be placed on the financial experience gained during the currency of the Plan. The main purpose of the Plan was to ensure the 'Entpolitisierung' of reparation, to restore Germany's credit by setting her a task to accomplish, which, given the necessary political conditions, the experts were satisfied to be within her capacity, and so to gain a much-needed breathing-space during which passions could subside and an atmosphere be created in which a final solution of reparation could be approached.

Without offering any opinion on the question whether the reparation problem has now been disposed of, we can definitely assert that the main purpose of the Dawes Expert was achieved. Reparation, which had been the subject of weekly alarums and excursions in the Press, and had embittered the international atmosphere, ceased to be good copy except about once in six months when the Agent General's reports were published; whereas for five years it had been an insurmountable impediment to the re-establishment of good relations between victors and vanquished, it was for the next five years administered with a conspicuous absence of friction between creditor and debtor.

For five years the question of security, which is purely political, had made no progress and had needlessly complicated the question of reparation. A settlement, at least provisional, of reparation was not only desirable for financial reasons; it was essential to facilitate political progress. When once international finance had been allowed to do its own work and had done it successfully, quick progress was made in other directions; Locarno and the entry of Germany into the League of Nations only became possible by the adoption of the Dawes Plan.

After some four and a half years' experience of the Dawes Plan, international finance was again called in to prescribe a final solution of reparation. Half of the members of the Young Committee had already served on the Dawes Committee, and they have given up to the public duty of advising on the reparation problem more than six months of their valuable time; from personal experience of the earlier Committee and from what is common knowledge as to the proceedings of the later one, I may hazard a guess that the nervous strain and the responsibility involved were so great that the six months could be counted as twelve in any actuarial calculation of their expectation of life.

The Young Plan may or may not be the last word in the reparation problem, but if it is not this cannot be due to want either of knowledge or effort on the part of its framers; personally, I should describe it as a potentially final plan, and the best one possible in the circumstances; if it should break down, even temporarily, it is provided with its own safety-valve. For so soon as Germany, the sole judge in the matter, is convinced that she cannot continue to make the prescribed payments without endangering her own economic structure, she can declare a moratorium. She has no longer to submit to a body with a political complexion a request that her capacity to pay should be examined before she obtains relief, and incurs no risk of seeing matters go from bad to worse while the preliminary request is being considered and, if granted, acted upon. Automatically a Committee comes into being, composed of independent experts and with the power and duty of reporting on the whole situation. The Committee is purely consultative; its findings bind nobody; the same was true of the Dawes Committee and the same was true of the Young Committee; can any one doubt that the Committee automatically convoked in certain circumstances under the new plan is the lineal descendant of those earlier committees and will be invested with at least as much moral authority?

Whether difficulties arise in the future or not, the Young Plan has at any rate achieved two notable things. In the first place it has definitely and finally, as thoroughly as human foresight can provide, taken reparation out of the political sphere for the future and enabled the creditor Governments to liquidate the Reparation Commission and eliminate all forms of political or quasi-political control. In the second place the general adoption of the Plan has led to the complete evacuation of the Rhineland, the importance of which for international goodwill needs no emphasizing; this is, if you will, a very indirect result of the Young Committee's deliberations, and hardly to be credited to their account, but I have always had a sneaking suspicion that it was the desire to bring the occupation to an end, and the need for some pretext, rather than any urgency in the reparation problem itself, which was responsible for the institution of the Young Committee.

v. *The Bank for International Settlements.*

We have hitherto been talking mainly of what we may already think of as 'old unhappy far-off things and battles long ago'. But the main importance of the Young Plan lies not in its reparation provisions, which may or may not stand the test of time, but in the machinery which the Committee set up, ostensibly in the first instance for the administration of reparation, and only secondarily for wider ends. For the student of international finance the Bank for International Settlements has an importance far transcending reparation, and it is perhaps significant that in the outline for the organization of the Bank which the experts attached to their report, pride of place is given to the general international function of the Bank and reparation appears as a subordinate consideration—natural enough if, as we all hope, the Bank will remain in being long after reparation is a story remembered only in text-books. In the Committee's own words:

'In the natural course of development it is to be expected that the Bank will in time become an organization, not simply, or even predominantly, concerned with the handling of reparations, but also with furnishing to the world of international commerce and finance important facilities hitherto lacking. Especially it is to be hoped that it will become an increasingly close and valuable link in the co-operation of central banking institutions generally—a co-operation essential to the continuing stability of the world's credit structure.'

Please note the careful use of the words 'become' in these two sentences; what the Bank *is* is an embryo organism, and a human institution is very like a living organism in its capacity of adapting itself to its environment and becoming something very different from what it appears to promise when in embryo. The B.I.S. will almost certainly develop in ways which we do not at present foresee; in the meantime it is the first overt official acknowledgement of the necessity for daily international co-ordination in finance. I say official acknowledgement because it is plain that the Bank would never have been created without Government approval and support; but the Bank is, of course, not a governmental institution but a corporation controlled by the various central banks.

On that account fears were entertained in certain quarters that the new institution might prove to be an *imperium in imperio,* or financial super-State. My personal opinion is that these fears, at this stage at any rate, were in some respects exaggerated. The Bank's powers are closely restricted, and the criticism most commonly directed against it in Germany, at any rate when the Young Report was issued, was that it could do little with these restricted powers to confer the various benefits on mankind which are hinted at by the Committee. The Bank will be in the last resort as much subject to national controls as any other international cartel; more so, indeed, for some central banks are either Government institutions in name or in effect, and the Bank's powers are specially restricted when action in particular countries is involved. Each Central Bank, in fact, maintains its own sovereignty with the same jealousy as members of the League of Nations in the political sphere.

Modern opinion is that there is a balance of advantage in making a central bank independent of official control, with its possibilities of political manipulation, and I am not convinced that the attempt, rather half-hearted in nature, to create at the outset some official connexion between Basel and Geneva deserved to succeed. A Central Bank in a particular country is not a power above the State because it is not directly submitted to control by the Government of the day; the fact that the State cannot impose its will on the Central Bank does not mean that the Central Bank can impose its will on the State. In the last resort the State can always intervene, but its power should be invoked only on grounds of *salus reipublicae.* In the same way if and when we attain a larger measure of world government, I do not believe that there will be any difficulty in subjecting a central credit authority to the necessary control, though by that time it will probably be found that the Bank for

International Settlements will present, from this point of view, rather less urgent a problem than some other, if looser, forms of private international association in industry and commerce. In the meantime, steps have been taken in the Bank's Charter and Statutes to safeguard the future and prevent the Bank from enlarging its own domain, whether by annexation or furtive enclosure, and we may feel certain that the question of a liaison between the Bank and the financial organization of the League will be solved '*ambulando* as and when necessity arises.

The immediate utility of the new Bank is that it furnishes a centre at which those responsible for the credit policy of the world can meet periodically and can, when the need arises, quietly co-ordinate their policies without headlines in the newspapers or sensation in the money markets. A visit by Mr. Norman to New York, or by the Governor of the New York Federal Reserve Board to London and other European centres, gives rise to surmises and perhaps later to suspicions that one country's interests are being sacrificed to another's. A routine meeting entails no such disadvantages; perhaps it even has the opposite advantage that the Central Banks can hardly escape contact with each other even if they desire so to do.

There are very few national questions of any real importance at this stage of our civilization. There is little that any Government can do which has not international implications and reactions. Professor Jeans lately used a graphic illustration to convey an idea of the life of the world and mankind: if I correctly remember, we are to take the height of Cleopatra's Needle as representing the age of our planet before the appearance of human life upon it, and to balance a penny on the top of it to represent the time during which it has been inhabited by man; we must, then, if we want to forecast the probable future length of this world's life, stick stamps on the penny until our column is as high as the Matterhorn. We shall not reach far up the slopes before a great many of the problems and policies which seem to us exclusively and jealously national will be found to require international treatment. There is already nothing of greater international import than credit and price policies, and such questions as the use of gold. The real interdependence of the finance markets of the world has been only too painfully evident in the last twelve months. Sooner or later, it may be one or several hundred years away, the world will have to submit to common regulation in these as in other matters. In the meantime the Young Committee has planted a seed which may prove to be a mustard seed; the growth of the plant will doubtless raise new problems of control, but they will be problems, as I have hinted, which will demand treatment not only in the internationalization of finance, but in the growing internationalization of trade and industry. Much depends on the conduct of the Bank in its earlier years and in the degree of determination exhibited by those responsible for its administration that it really shall be as international in its spirit as the League of Nations. Those who stand aside from it will have to resist any temptation to pluck the plant up by the roots to see how it is growing. And before we leave the subject of the new Bank it is perhaps just worth observing in passing that every new institution for the co-ordination of national policies or activities is an additional safeguard of peace. It is commonly said, and I believe with truth, that if the League of Nations had been in existence in 1914 the Great War could not have broken out. If there is loyal and whole-hearted collaboration in the B.I.S., will it not become in ten years, with the development which we may legitimately expect, a powerful institution in the maintenance of peace ?

vi. *The International Character of Finance.*

I have tried to show, briefly and very imperfectly, something of what international finance has done in the last five years to restore and maintain peace, and to point out one recent development which contains promise for the future. Let me emphasize the fact that in its nature finance is more international than any other form of business activity. The change of bank rate in, let us say, New York has much more immediate effects in other financial centres, and these effects in their turn may have much more immediate consequential reactions on New York itself, than a new tariff, the rise of a new industry, the outbreak of a strike. We are in our commercial and industrial life so interdependent that any major event in any large country is a stone thrown into the pool, which sets up ripples which reach its total circumference. But the effects in finance are so much more immediate, and the consequence of failure to collaborate in a sense so much more potent, that collaboration in this field will probably be attained without the costly strife which accompanies commercial competition. And it is perhaps worth noting that in a world which appears to devote much of its energy to a restriction of international exchange, finance has been and remains a free trade undertaking. The commodity in which finance deals is far too fluid—and its fluidity increases with every day which passes—to be controllable by State-made barriers. In normal circumstances the import and export of capital are not susceptible of interference, except to a very limited extent and for a short period. Save in time of war, when all channels of communication can be strictly supervised, any attempts to prevent the export of capital are foredoomed to failure; witness the enormous sums sent abroad from France, in defiance or evasion of all restrictions, during the period of the franc's depreciation. Equally, attempts to check the normal inflow of foreign money into a country where economic conditions would produce an import of capital only tend to make credit dearer, cheapen security prices, and encourage the foreigner to purchase rather than to lend; the stream of capital is diverted slightly from its normal channel, but carves itself out another and less desirable one. And a consequence of this fluidity of money, which takes it where it will give the best return, and where inferentially it is most needed, is that capital-exporting countries are becoming more and more interested in the prosperity of other countries in which they have invested. I am aware that this interest has its dangerous side, but the best safeguard is that foreign investment should remain a perfectly free trade pursuit, that a borrower should be able to borrow in the foreign market which offers him the best financial terms, and that a lender should invest abroad where he thinks he can get the best return on his money, and be uninfluenced by political considerations of the baser sort. We may hope that the days are gone when a country can obtain a foreign loan for an unproductive purpose; in any case, collaboration between financial centres should make them more difficult of access to such a borrower. This indicates, perhaps, the only direction in which, in the sphere of finance, the natural spirit of competition will require curbing.

v. *To prevent War and punish the Aggressor.*

Finally, may I briefly allude to one other financial project which may be hailed as promising by those interested in the

maintenance of peace through international action ? I refer
to the proposals which are being canvassed for financial
assistance to a country threatened with aggression. They
raise, in rather stark a form, the hoary questions of deciding
in a threatening conflict which is the aggrieved party, which
lies in the political sphere where, without being an angel,
I fear to tread. I imagine, however, that when a general
formula or device has been invented and generally accepted,
whereby we can decide the question of aggression between
two conflicting parties, some of the worst of the difficulties
involved in organizing peace will *ipso facto* have disappeared.
I am apprehensive, too, that until we have reached this stage
we may find serious difficulty in applying the kind of convention which has been drafted if ever a case prima facie
demanding its operation arises. It is, however, an assumption
of the draft convention that the determination of the
aggrieved party presents no insurmountable difficulty, and
for our purposes we can accept the assumption.

The financial assistance proposed is on a modest scale; the
total amount which it is suggested should be made available
would not cover for long the capital needs abroad of any
country involved in modern warfare, and the amount which
it would fall to individual countries to guarantee would be
a bagatelle. When, however, a conflict threatens, any financial
assistance, however small, would be of a moral value quite
incommensurate with the monetary figure; and it would
work twice over by heartening the ever-aggrieved party and
cooling the aggressor. From the point of view of the guaranteeing parties, almost any financial assistance, however big,
would be money well invested if it were instrumental in
preventing a major conflict.

It inevitably occurs to wonder whether the proposals go

far enough. It has already been recognized as desirable to provide that the assisting Powers shall give no help, direct or indirect, to any Powers involved in hostilities with the assisted, that is aggrieved, party. The grant of assistance to the one party necessarily implies the refusal of assistance to the other, and the question arises whether it does not call for something more than negative action, whether the grant of supplies to one party should not sooner or later imply not merely a refusal to assist an aggressor, but a positive effort to hinder him from obtaining by any means financial supplies in the markets of those countries that are officially assisting the other party. It has been said that no country ever refrained from going to war, or broke off a war already entered into, for want of money, but under modern conditions no country of any size can conduct a single campaign without drawing upon other countries for food or raw material, and probably no belligerent country could continue for long to secure these supplies without financial assistance. I am aware that the question of sanctions is an exceedingly vexed political one, and I hesitate even to come within speaking distance of it. But it appears to me, as a mere uninformed spectator of such a political question, that when you have decided that one party to a dispute is the attacked party, and the other, therefore, an aggressor, and when you have reached such a stage of concerted action as to give active assistance to the aggrieved party, you can hardly avoid a consideration of sanctions. And I believe that when we have advanced farther on the path of international collaboration, international finance can provide, perhaps, the most effective and bloodless of sanctions for the punishment of aggression and the maintenance of peace.

CHAPTER V

THE ECONOMIC CAUSES OF WAR [1]

Professor ANDRÉ SIEGFRIED:

I DO not think I need examine at the moment whether economic interests are the principal or, in reality, the sole cause of war; neither do I consider it necessary to investigate to what extent, as compared with strictly political causes, economic tendencies may lead to war (in many—perhaps in the majority of cases—political and economic factors are so closely bound up together that it is impossible to analyse them separately). It will probably be more helpful to acknowledge at the start that the defence of economic interests may, and frequently does, lead either to the employment of force or to recourse to war—two forms of violence which it is often difficult to distinguish—and thence to proceed to ascertain in what form and circumstances and under what conditions economic interests are the cause of misunderstanding, friction, and war.

Private economic interests are naturally tempted to appeal to their Governments for support when those interests conflict with foreign interests: an attempt is thus made to replace pacific, reciprocal, and equitable agreements by arbitrary pressure—pressure which is virtually confirmed by force. Moreover, Governments often anticipate this desire on the part of private interests for political support, which gives

[1] The manuscript of his lecture submitted by Professor Siegfried for publication was taken from a memorandum which he had prepared for a League of Nations inquiry into the question of 'Economic Tendencies affecting the Peace of the World'.

them a pretext to intervene, apparently on economic, but in reality on political, grounds.

A risk of conflict may thus arise, and this is increased, or may even be created, if public opinion in any country regards, or is induced to regard, the dispute from a psychological standpoint, thus introducing an emotional element into the matter. Then the real cause of the trouble is no longer the economic dispute with which it began, but over-excitation of a strictly political sentiment.

With these qualifications, the principal causes of misunderstanding, friction, or war due to economic factors might be classified as follows:

1. First, we have causes relating to *conditions of production*, of which the chief cause in every country at the present time is undoubtedly the question of obtaining supplies of raw materials.

2. Then there are causes connected with factors relating to *international communications*: for instance, the international movement of ships, aircraft, railways, commodities, and even men; or, again, with the conditions under which a country communicates either with its colonies or with other countries by post, submarine cable, &c.

3. Lastly, there are causes connected with the *expansion of certain countries*; this expansion may take the following forms: the *expansion of trade* (exports and markets); the *expansion of capital* (foreign investments, exploitation of foreign countries or territories by means of capital investment, exploitation of colonies); the *expansion of population* (emigration and settlement colonies).

Once the principal causes likely to lead to friction, misunderstanding, or war have been recognized, we shall be able to draw up more accurately, by contrast, the principles of a policy capable of reducing or eliminating friction, mis-understanding, or war. If they were put into practice by Governments, these principles would help to create an atmosphere and economic conditions conducive to peace.

i. *Causes relating to Production.*

A country is hardly likely to attempt to procure capital by force; it will more probably have to defend itself at times against over-zealous investors who may nevertheless assert that they have the country's true interests at heart. Labour can be obtained by pressure or violence: by means of raids, for instance, or by methods of collective recruiting in which the contract is merely a matter of form. The main reason why such action does not lead to war is because it is generally taken against peoples who are too weak politically to resist.

It is the necessity of obtaining raw materials—the desire to procure or to monopolize the gifts of nature, freely bestowed in one case and denied in another—which is most likely to endanger peace and to cause force to be employed. The struggle is similar to that which ensues in connexion with the division of territory in all parts of the world. Industrial development has made this the primary cause of misunderstanding, friction, or war, because at the present time all great industrial countries have urgent need of raw materials which are unobtainable in their territory or are only procurable in quantities inadequate to meet their in-creasing requirements.

In the case of agricultural produce the need is less acute, because it is always possible to grow other crops in a similar climate; in short, there can here be no question of a mono-poly, at all events in the long run.

With minerals, however, it is a very different matter,

because it may only be possible to find them in a certain country; they can be sought for, discovered, and exploited, but they cannot be planted or produced elsewhere. The gravity of this position is increased because it applies, not only to raw materials proper, but to fuel and to the sources of power which have become absolutely essential to modern large-scale industry: while coal may be found to some extent everywhere, this is not the case with oil; water power may be obtainable in the vicinity, but on the other side of a frontier, and its use by a neighbouring country will depend on the policy adopted by the possessor.

Large industrial countries are becoming by an irresistible movement more and more dependent on others for their supplies of raw materials: at first they simply converted their own raw products, and this was the start of their development as manufacturing countries; later on, however, the course of their industrial development, which it is beyond their power to control, forces them to import an increasing proportion of the raw materials which they require. In the case of the most highly developed countries, the need to import certain raw materials becomes a necessity of their existence, which is no less urgent than that of obtaining food. The proportion of imports of raw materials to the total imports of those countries clearly shows the extent of their economic dependence on others.

We must here distinguish between the point of view of the buying country and that of the selling country. The buying country, rightly or wrongly, may fear that certain raw materials may become unprocurable by it, either because they may be kept by the producer or because others may monopolize them. In certain cases, this fear may become a veritable obsession. Naturally, the country will then endeavour to make sure of certain, lasting, and, if possible, permanent supplies of the products which it fears may become unprocurable; for instance, it may attempt to *control* (in the American sense of the word, i.e. to dominate) the undertakings which, in the selling country, produce the raw material required; or else it may urge the Government of that country not to reduce unduly, by means of export prohibitions, excessive export duties or export quotas, the quantity of products which it requires and which it may not be able to obtain elsewhere. Various methods may be employed in connexion with a safeguarding policy of this kind, ranging from an absolutely normal and pacific form of contract to war and conquest; effect may be given to this policy simply by the conclusion of a long-term contract or by contractual negotiations with the sovereign State in question; requests may, however, be accompanied by pressure, threats, or even by resort to force; the buying country may even attempt to obtain sovereign possession of the territory producing the coveted material, or, what practically comes to the same thing, to establish a protectorate *de iure* or *de facto* there. All these arguments are, of course, based on the assumption that the buying country is the stronger—otherwise pressure would be impossible; this shows the importance of force in connexion with the problem of raw materials.

The selling country by its attitude may create an atmosphere favourable to peace or to war. If it refuses to sell, conflict ensues; the supposition is, of course, absurd, but there is a wide range open between full consent and complete refusal. We should inquire to what extent the refusal, whether total or partial, may cause annoyance; it will be so if discrimination is exercised in the treatment of any particular country, or if (even without discrimination) the refusal is actually intended to apply to a single or what is practically a single buyer, or if a certain price has been intentionally fixed by agreement for the home market and another and widely different price for the export market, and, in general, if the consumer in question is led to think that he is being imposed upon. The irritating nature of such an attitude is, however, only apparent when the producing country is not in a position to transform its own raw materials. A country which keeps its raw materials and only exports them in the form of manufactured or semi-manufactured goods cannot be accused of acting in an aggressive manner. We must not, however, be too ready to assert that in such a case all possibilities of conflict are precluded.

What actually happens when one country possesses the raw material needed by another country? As a rule, the stronger (perhaps we should say the larger or the richer) gets its own way: if it is a producing country, it will dispose of its products as it wishes; if it is a consuming country, it will be tempted to requisition in one form or another the materials which it requires. In that case it will, perhaps, be wiser for the weaker country to give way to a sufficient extent to prevent the stronger from attempting to resort to force; it will often be difficult for it to ensure full respect for its sovereignty. It will usually be wiser for the stronger country not to go too far, because it can generally get what it wants without going to war, if not in every case without resort to force. If it desired to go farther, this would lead to the assumption that the economic argument was merely a thin disguise for an underlying political motive.

In these circumstances, a reasonable attitude on both sides is more likely to ensure peace. The sovereignty of the producing country doubtless gives it—in theory, at all events—

all rights, but it may be wiser for it not to make full use of them. If it does not take advantage of the position in order to obtain undue privileges, if it does not attempt to bully the consuming country, the latter—feeling confident that it will not be imposed upon and will be able to obtain regular supplies of the materials which it needs—will not be tempted to resort to pressure or violence.

What causes are likely to lead countries to adopt an attitude of moderation ? As a rule, their own interests will, or should, guide them to do so, because the seller obtains no advantage from bullying his customers or the buyer from threatening his supplier. If they are blinded or carried away by passion, it is still possible for third parties, who are always affected by a conflict, to intervene.

This intervention may be beneficially exercised by international opinion and abuses may thereby be prevented; if an enlightened opinion, conscious of its own powers, were created and developed, it could affirm the recognized principles of what we may call a code of international economic morality, in accordance with which certain practices would be condemned. The practical expression of an international opinion of this kind would take the form of the acceptance of common legislation based on general conventions, in accordance with the work already begun by the League of Nations.

Such legislation will not, perhaps, prevent the inevitable: certain tendencies, apart from their morality, are too strong to be resisted. Nevertheless, by regulating trade and organizing it on normal lines, we should relieve the buyer of the fear of being unable to obtain his raw materials, to which we have already referred; we should remove the temptation to which he is exposed—or, at all events, any justification for this temptation—to resort to force. The producer would be

H

protected from the excessive ambitions of the consumer, which might do him harm, and at the same time he would be discouraged from arbitrarily taking advantage of a situation the very privileges of which are likely to lead to threats and danger. Finally, the risk of a direct altercation fraught with the gravest dangers would be lessened or prevented.

ii. *Causes connected with Factors relating to International Communications.*

A self-supporting country will be little affected by factors relating to international communications. These are, however, of the utmost importance to a country which is economically dependent on others either for its imports (foodstuffs, raw materials) or its exports (foreign markets) or for the freedom of its communications in general, and failing which its equilibrium will be imperilled. As a rule, a country whose economic equilibrium depends on these factors tends to become a naval Power, and to interest itself in the freedom or command of the seas.

These same considerations will also apply to a country, even though it is not economically dependent on others, which lies on the main world trade-routes. Such a country may either be tempted to take advantage of its position in order to make extortionate demands (as was formerly done by countries which collected arbitrary and excessive toll-dues) or—what is more probable at the present time—it may feel that its position is endangered by the intervention of powerful interests utilizing the routes which, geographically, it is in a position to control, to obstruct, or even to close.

If the country owning the strait or isthmus is a strong country, it will itself regulate the conditions governing use. Its power may be exercised in war-time by stopping the traffic and in peace-time by imposing excessive or discriminatory tariffs, or by subjecting traffic to irksome conditions. If, on the other hand, the country owning the route is not the strongest, it will doubtless be tempted to act as if it were, but in such a case the principal user will be certain to interfere if it is not granted favourable conditions and will end by controlling, that is to say, by itself regulating in its own interests, the conditions governing the traffic. The chief user may even be tempted to seize the position and the surrounding land, either by conquest, the establishment of a protectorate, or by any other means affording it military control. If there are several Powers whose strength is more or less equal and who are jealous of each other, they will agree upon joint control; in this case the solution will differ only in appearance, because it will always be dictated by the strongest country or the strongest group.

This policy comprises certain principles which are nearly always adopted by Powers desirous of extending their activities to all parts of the world. Their primary aim is to make sure of benefiting by the freedom of communications and transit, whether for vessels, aircraft, commodities, men, or news to be transmitted by post, telegraph, or submarine cable; in particular, they desire the free use of international straits and channels. It is equally important for them to eliminate any factor likely to endanger the safety of the principal world routes or to take precautions in advance to deal with any such factors. In peace-time, the freedom of the routes may be sufficient for the purpose, and the Power concerned may be content with exercising what may be termed a 'negative' control; in war-time, however, the freedom of the seas will tend to assume the form of supreme control by that Power, i.e. the command of the seas.

Powers with a world-wide radius of action thus feel the
need for a large quantity of 'political apparatus'—naval
bases, coaling stations, and oil depots, landing grounds for
aircraft, submarine cables with control at the points at which
they come ashore, a wireless station, international channels.
A policy of this kind is not a peaceful policy, except in appearance, or at all events it is only negatively so. In actual fact, a
powerful country does not leave it to others to ensure and
guarantee the freedom and safety of its communications: it
always aims at controlling these itself. This does not mean
that it does not allow others to enjoy the safety and freedom
established by it; it means that such a country continues to
be the bestower. In these circumstances, there is a difference
between actual liberty, which may exist and even be freely
bestowed, and final control, the source of which is arbitrary,
because it is equivalent to the predominance of an individual
country.

If we could be certain that a country enjoying a strategical
position on world trade-routes would not take undue advantage of this position, or would not itself fall under the sway
of another country which would use its power to promote
its own exclusive interests, we should be right in thinking
that exclusive control by the chief user would no longer be
justified, and the latter might not even consider it necessary.

How is it possible to achieve this result ? By the internationalization of certain regions, which is the classic solution; by treaties between the principal parties concerned,
guaranteeing each other equitable conditions (for instance,
the Hay-Pauncefote Treaty concerning the Panama Canal);
by conventions in the application of which the principal
parties concerned have sufficient confidence, in time of war
as in time of peace, to refrain from taking *one-sided* action to

protect their interests; by the international acceptance of what might be called certain principles of international morality in regard to world routes: for instance, the guaranteeing of a right of passage for all, irrespective of nationality, or the guarantee that, in the application of tariffs, there shall be no discrimination in respect of the person or the destination (these two principles might now be regarded as generally accepted). From the purely economic standpoint, the solution would not need to be carried any farther in peace-time. Such a solution may, however, appear inadequate to the powerful interests concerned, because, on the one hand, they do not know what would happen in war-time and, on the other, they may be influenced by political as well as by economic considerations.

The traditional policy of the great countries concerned has been to undertake the task of supervision themselves, and it may be said that, as a rule, they have extended the benefits to all. Nevertheless, the precarious nature of such freedom cannot be denied. It is a peaceful solution only in the sense of being a *pax Romana*. At the same time, there may perhaps be no better substitute to-day. It is certain, however, that, if a recognized code of international rights and obligations in regard to communications were established, unfair treatment of the users of the main world routes would gradually become less frequent, and the temptations and pretexts to establish exclusive and unjust control would be continuously reduced.

iii. *Causes connected with the Expansion of Certain Countries.*

When a country has reached a certain stage of development, either as regards the number of its inhabitants, its industrial progress or the standard of living of its population, it naturally feels the need for economic expansion. It then ceases to be completely self-sustaining, because its territory or its natural resources become inadequate for its increased requirements, and it is forced to depend to some extent on other countries and, in one form or another, to obtain some part of its means of existence from abroad. Such a country then comes to take an interest in the affairs of the others. This may be conducive to peace, but it can also lead to war.

Expansion may take various forms. For instance, there may be an expansion of manufacturing manifested in the form of exports and efforts to secure foreign markets. Expansion may also take the form of the export of capital: foreign investments, development of foreign countries (by the establishment of undertakings in those countries), exploitation colonies, i.e. colonies regarded as places in which to invest capital and establish undertakings rather than as places in which to settle. Lastly, there may be an expansion of the population by emigration to foreign countries or by the settlement of territories which have no definite owner. A country may expand in all three directions simultaneously; if, however, expansion is not possible in one of these directions, it is proportionately increased in the other two; for instance, if an over-populated country cannot dispose of its surplus population by emigration, it will have to create industries and export manufactured products.

This gives rise to grave problems. To what extent should other countries be required to submit to the invasion of an expanding country? In actual fact, expansion is due to developments over which men have no control, even though they may believe they have. It is, we think, futile to consider whether this expansion is legitimate; it must be accepted as a fact, and efforts must be made to diminish its most dangerous consequences.

Experience shows that, even if it is pacific in appearance, the expansion of strong nations is based on force, and that expansion can only be resisted by force, even though, in this latter case, also, it is still pacific in appearance: for instance, immigration laws could doubtless not be maintained in the face of the protests of the countries which they exclude unless they were directly or indirectly supported by political or military strength. When expansion is enforced or checked by compulsion in this way, it is liable to be enforced or checked without any guarantee of moderation. However, in the case of a natural disequilibrium, for which a remedy is essential, it is always premature to suppose that the question has been finally settled by force: if the initial causes of the disequilibrium persist, natural equilibrium will always tend to be restored sooner or later, in one form or another. It is often difficult to say which is the more interesting—the country whose population is obliged to emigrate or the country which is striving to avoid taking these emigrants, the country which needs to expand or the country which fears the expansion of others. It may, perhaps, be said that, in general, expansion is in the interests of production, if it is not always in accordance with moral principles.

In these circumstances, and from an international standpoint, should these natural movements be opposed or encouraged? A satisfactory answer is impossible. Efforts might, however, be made to regulate such movements by subjecting them to certain conditions and providing safeguards for the country with a surplus population, the country receiving that population, and for other countries.

While exportation may be regarded as a necessity for

certain countries, this applies only to exports in general and not to exports to any particular market. It can hardly be maintained that one country has any right to export to a certain other country, because it is always possible, even though it may be difficult, to transfer sales from one set of customers to another. In these circumstances, the desire to export is hardly likely to lead to war. It may, however, cause friction and a strained situation may ensue.

We must distinguish between the exportation of raw products and of manufactured products: as a rule, the former are easily disposed of, and in many cases buyers are only too eager to obtain them (this brings us back to the difficulties concerning raw materials); on the other hand, manufactured products are difficult to place, and resistance to their importation is an obvious source of difficulties, which may lead to political crises.

General defensive measures, even if irksome, designed to prevent the importation of foreign commodities, are less dangerous than measures involving discrimination against any particular country. On the other hand, uniform Customs practices—for instance, those which conform to generally accepted international principles—will create a pacific atmosphere, even with a considerable amount of protectionism, if they counteract or eliminate any unfair treatment in individual cases. The work undertaken in this connexion by the Economic Committee of the League of Nations makes any comments on my part superfluous.

The expansion of capital may take many different forms: loans to States with a view to political domination (such cases, which are very frequent, are of a political rather than an economic nature, and consequently do not come within the scope of my subject); the investment of capital in a foreign country, either in the form of a private loan or to a foreign State, or of loans to private persons or companies in a foreign country; the management of undertakings by foreigners in a country and, in particular, *concessions* obtained from a State including the grant of special privileges. There are many fine gradations between investment pure and simple and concessions involving partial loss of sovereignty for the State granting the concession.

In the first case (political loans), these may easily lead to the establishment of a protectorate, *de facto* or *de iure*. In the second (investment of capital), pledges may often be demanded at a given moment, and these may sometimes involve an actual loss of sovereignty. But international opinion, mainly influenced by envious third parties (and not so much as a question of principle), is inclined to disapprove the taking of these pledges or, at all events, to demand that this should be done internationally. It cannot be denied, however, that very powerful countries, in regions which they regard as under their influence, refuse to permit this internationalization of their action. In the third case (undertakings and concessions), the final result is usually the establishment of an exploitation colony in a more or less open form. The foreign lender, investor, or owner of an undertaking will naturally be tempted to have recourse to political intervention (i.e. to urge his Government to exercise political pressure) if he does not feel certain of the security for his loan, if his operations are hampered or are in danger of being hampered by a revolution, by new legislation injurious to his interests, or by bullying or interference on the part of the local authority. On the other hand, this political intervention will be delayed or even avoided altogether if the undertaking can be carried on under stable conditions, pro-

vided, however, that the owner of the undertaking has no
ulterior political motive (in which case he could always find
some pretext or other for a complaint). Similarly, intervention will be avoided if the country in which the undertaking is being carried on is strong enough to resist or has
another Power behind it to back it up; this will also prove
to be the case if there are several owners of different nationalities, who are jealous of each other (unless they agree upon
joint intervention, in which case the independence of the
country in which their activities are being pursued is again
endangered, although in a different manner).

The most important problem raised in this connexion
concerns the right to exploit, the right not to exploit, the
duty to exploit, and the right to exploit in place of the
country which does not do so—for instance, if one State
does not work its resources, is another State entitled to do
so in its place? If one State has not the right, can this
wealth be exploited by a group of States? From a moral
standpoint, it would be hard to find an answer.

What actually happens is that *the will to produce*, which is
a form of *the will to live*, always conquers in the end. This
means that production will take place unless it is prevented
by a stronger Power. At the present time (we may ask
whether this has always been the case), it seems more difficult
to prevent production on the part of mankind than to promote it. If this is so, a wise country will not oppose what is
in fact a necessity, but will merely endeavour to safeguard its
independence in spite of this necessity. The solutions to be
adopted can thus be foreseen. In these circumstances, a
sovereign State cannot defend its rights, or, more correctly,
its existence, unless it refrains from insisting too strongly on
respect for all its rights; otherwise, sooner or later, its resis-

tance will be broken down by force or it will be corrupted by money; the vital impulse which urges humanity to produce is stronger than sovereign rights. The dangers resulting from this fact are obvious: there is a danger of servitude for the State which is forced to submit; for third parties, there is a danger that their interests may be injured if intervention benefits one party only. If servitude and the perils of servitude, both for the victim and for third parties, are to be avoided, the State making concessions (even against its will) must do so without any risk to its independence; the State making the application must respect the reasonable rights of third parties (can these, however, be defined ?); the State to which applications for concessions are made must feel that it is protected by international opinion; and the State applying for concessions must also feel that it is being watched by this opinion.

As we have already observed, supervision of this kind has always been exercised spontaneously through jealousy, but it should be made more dignified, more permanent, and more responsible. Principles should first be established, setting forth the attitude which each party is expected to adopt, demands which will be considered legitimate, guarantees which may be demanded and obtained. The rules of conduct based on these principles might develop into international practices. A complete policy might be built up in this way, for instance, with regard to international credits, undertakings in foreign countries whose sovereign rights might possibly need protection, &c. The mandate system, as it has been applied since the Treaty of Versailles, affords an example of intervention of this kind.

We now come to the question of expansion of population, and under it I will first touch on the problem of emigration.

We must distinguish between emigrants who can, and those who cannnot, be assimilated. If the emigrants belong to a race which can be assimilated by the new society in which they settle, they will probably be so assimilated, unless they arrive in sufficient numbers to impose the stamp of their race on the original inhabitants. If the emigrants belong to a non-assimilable race, they will only be able to settle in the country individually if their standard of living is higher than the average standard of the people among whom they establish themselves (they will then become the heads, the managers, or foremen of concerns). If, on the other hand, their standard of living is lower, then they will replace the lower strata of the original population.

What naturally happens in these two cases? In the first case (assuming, of course, that there is no political intervention), difficulties will rarely ensue. In the second case, the result will be the substitution, by surreptitious means as it were, of one civilization for another, rather than a political conquest; thus a former settlement-colony may gradually be converted into what is practically an exploitation or plantation colony. The former race will now exist merely as supervising personnel, while the character and race of the workers will have changed. This contingency has not escaped certain non-European countries, and this explains their uncompromising refusal to accept emigrants belonging to races which they do not consider assimilable.

In the case of emigration with an ulterior motive on the part of the emigrants' Government, emigrants, even if assimilable, endeavour to avoid assimilation by the new society in which they settle; their Government, at all events, desires them to remain separate. If this policy is successful, they intentionally and systematically form homo-

geneóus and separate groups; in some cases they claim special
political rights—rights which might possibly endanger the
political unity of the State in which they form a foreign
element. The result of immigration of this kind is eventually
to destroy the moral, and in some cases the political, unity
of the State. Force or war may be employed to support the
immigrants' claims, which are naturally resisted. If these
claims are finally conceded, the probable result will be the
de facto establishment of a colony.

As regards over-populated countries we must first consider to what extent a country needs to find outlets for part
of its population. As an alternative to emigration, the
country must export more goods, or possess exploitation
colonies (i.e. colonies for which it provides capital), or reduce
either its standard of living or the size of its population.
On the other hand, if the people emigrate, are they to go no
matter where? Obviously not, since only certain climates
will suit them. Again, they can only emigrate to sparsely
populated territories: if they emigrate to countries which
already have a large population, they will only be able to
settle among peoples whose standard of living is higher than,
or the same as, their own. Lastly, to what extent have
emigrants the right to refuse to be assimilated by the
country in which they settle? The individual may do what
he likes without attracting much attention. When the emigrants are considered collectively, however, especially when
they are definitely supported by their Government, the question assumes an entirely different aspect. If their number is
sufficiently large, if they possess sufficient moral and physical
strength and form a collective body, the immigrants can, either
entirely or to a very large extent, avoid assimilation by a
relatively weak society. If, on the other hand, they are

themselves weak while the other country is strong, they will not be able to hold out. But, apart from all political action, if they belong to a non-assimilable race and are more frugal in their habits than the people among whom they settle, they will end by securing their position, as it were, biologically.

To what extent are countries entitled to refuse immigrants? This refusal is, of course, strictly within their sovereign rights. In practice, however, they can only refuse if they are strong enough to do so, because, in reality, immigration laws are only maintained by military strength; otherwise those whose interests are thereby affected would use force to have them withdrawn. On the other hand, is it possible to discriminate between immigrants—that is to say, to refuse those who are non-assimilable or are so regarded, to discourage those whom it is difficult to assimilate, and to reject those who are not willing to be assimilated? Can exceptions be made, not only in respect of races, but in respect of countries? In short, is discrimination, which we are endeavouring to eliminate in regard to the exchange of commodities, to remain in the case of the exchange of population? The gravity of these problems will be recognized by all, especially as we have to ask ourselves to what extent these refusals are anything but political solutions. Experience shows that artificial barriers to prevent immigration may prove impossible to surmount. Nevertheless, can force be regarded as a final solution in the case of a permanent racial disequilibrium? It is well to remember that although this is a political, it is not a biological, solution.

In the long run, it is doubtless difficult and even impossible to fight against biological disequilibrium; if barriers are raised, they will last as long as a country is strong enough to maintain them, but the pressure will continue and will in all probability take other forms. Nevertheless, agreements can be drawn up between countries exchanging their inhabitants, especially as, in certain cases and subject to certain guarantees, immigrants may be welcomed and desired by the countries receiving them. There have been, and still are, a large number of treaties concerning the admission, refusal, and limitation of immigrants or labour; there is no reason why concessions and advantages should not be equitably granted by both parties to such treaties. In future, it may perhaps be possible to go farther and to determine or influence by agreement the actual size of populations— for instance, in order to reduce the international pressure of an over-populated country. Shall we one day witness an international conference for the limitation of births in certain countries or groups of countries? In the same spirit, we might inquire whether it will be possible, in regard to this same question of the exchange of population, to pass from the contractual to the international sphere. Can we devise principles of international value to be embodied in international conventions which would diminish the grave dangers resulting from the disequilibrium of populations? It is premature to attempt to answer this question. The problem is certainly one that can be studied and is deserving of study.

In this brief survey I have attempted to describe what appear to me the principal economic tendencies capable of making for war, and to indicate what are the possibilities of guiding these tendencies into channels that will instead promote the organization of peace through international agreement and action.

CHAPTER VI

WORLD PUBLIC HEALTH

Dr. F. G. BOUDREAU:

INSTEAD of describing the work of the Health Organization of the League in the usual way I propose to tell you
about some of its recent activities which will serve to illustrate its methods of work.

i. *The Eastern Bureau at Singapore.*

You will be interested, I am sure, in the work of our Eastern
Bureau at Singapore. It was founded in 1925 primarily for
the purpose of collecting and distributing as rapidly as possible all information available concerning the prevalence of the
most important epidemic diseases in the ports of the Far East.
Shipping plays a larger part in the life of the Far East than is
appreciated by those who have not travelled in that region.
Ports are numerous and the channels of shipping are densely
populated by all kinds of vessels. In addition to the transpor-
tation of freight there is a heavy passenger traffic, and much
movement of labour. For example ships plying between the
ports of Tsingtao and Dairen carry hundreds of thousands of
Chinese who desire to settle on the fertile plains of Manchuria.
Scores of thousands of Chinese sail from the ports of Swatow
and Amoy to the Netherlands East Indies, the Philippines,
and the Straits Settlements, and these are only examples of
the large movements of population in ships in the Far East.
The distance between ports of call in the East is comparatively short—for example, in returning from Shanghai
to Marseilles this year, a voyage of thirty days, four days was
the longest interval between ports of call. These factors

make of shipping an important potential source of disease—
on account of their human and animal cargo, and by animal
cargo I refer, of course, to rats which carry plague.

On this account it is necessary for port health authorities
to take certain precautions with ships arriving from other
countries, these precautions including the medical examination of passengers and crew, the disinfection of the holds to
destroy rats, and the destruction of material liable to be
infected.

The state of health of the passengers and consequently the
nature of the precautions taken by the port health authorities
depend upon the epidemic conditions at the port of embarka-
tion as well as at the port of call.

Naturally, as shipping is so important to the economic life
of the East, it is in the interest of the Eastern countries to
interrupt it as little as possible and to reduce the health
measures taken at ports to the minimum consistent with
safety.

When complete and recent information is available concerning the prevalence of epidemic diseases in the ports,
the task of the health authorities is relatively simple, while if
such information is not available their task is complicated, and
they must apply precautions often in excess of the real needs.

These facts furnish the background for the desire of the
Health Administrations in the Far East to have recent and
complete information concerning the epidemic situation in
the ports. This desire was never realized until the Eastern
Bureau of the Health Organization was founded at Singapore.

On 1 March 1925 this bureau began to function. Cables
were received giving information concerning epidemic diseases at thirty-five ports. This information was then sent to
Far Eastern Health Administrations by cable.

The authorities of the Singapore Bureau, looking into the future, decided that this part of their work would not be complete until they were in touch with at least 140 ports, this being the number of important ports in the Far East. I am glad to tell you that this figure was soon reached, and that the Bureau now receives all necessary information from more than 140 ports. Each week cables are received at Singapore giving the facts concerning the major epidemic diseases in each port—cholera, smallpox, plague, rat plague, typhus fever, dysentery, &c. At the end of the week this information, made into a message, is broadcasted from powerful wireless stations at Karachi, Malabar (Java), Nauen (Germany), Saignon, and Tananarive, so that it may be picked up by the various health administrations and ports. A network of less powerful wireless stations broadcast a simplified message for the benefit of ships at sea, so that the ships' officers may know, for example, whether the next port of call is infected. Should that port be infected, it does not mean that the ship will avoid calling—it means that the ships' officers may take the precautions necessary to protect the passengers and crew.

One example will serve to show the value of this service.

The wireless apparatus on a passenger steamer plying between ports in the Far East broke down and the operator was unable to pick up the message from the Singapore Bureau, which indicated that the next port of call was infected with cholera. Not knowing this, the officers permitted the through passengers to land for sightseeing purposes. Cholera later broke out among the passengers and the ship was subjected to the delays which are occasioned by the application of sanitary measures.

In some cases the Eastern Bureau is able also to inform the next port of call of the impending arrival of an infected ship.

That the Health Organization is a means of facilitating the co-operation of the different Governments in health matters is made evident by the work of the Singapore Bureau. This Bureau had behind it no international law requiring the Health Administrations to send it reports. All the cables received were the voluntary offerings of the Health Administrations, sent at their own expense. The wireless stations were also placed at the disposal of the Singapore Bureau by the different Governments. Both of these facts show that the Health Administrations are eager to collaborate in the field of international health when proper machinery is available.

While I have emphasized this part of the work of the Eastern Bureau of our Organization, I do not wish to imply that it is the only important activity. As a matter of fact the Bureau undertakes the co-ordination of national research in such questions as plague and vaccination against cholera, is making a study of quarantine stations, and has taken an important part in the general work of the Health Organization in China, which I now propose to describe to you.

ii. *Co-operation of the Health Organization with the Government of China.*

In 1929 the Secretary-General of the League received a request from the National Government of China, asking that a mission from the Health Organization should be sent to China to advise the Government on port quarantine. On arrival in China we were asked by the Minister of Health to make a study of other health matters as well, so that we were given opportunities of studying the organization and plans of the Ministry of Health, the plans for provincial health work, the municipal health services, medical schools, demonstrations, and health centres, in addition to the health work of the principal ports.

Before we left China the Government adopted a number of proposals for collaboration with the League in health matters, and these proposals, after being considered and approved. by the Health Committee, were adopted by the Council of the League.

These proposals may be summarized as follows:

1. That the Health Organization should assist the Ministry of Health in China in the reorganization of China's port health services. The so-called Treaty Ports are the most important ports in China, and not infrequently port health work was begun by the authorities in the foreign concessions. More recently, this work has been assigned to the Customs' services, and now that Customs are in the hands of the Government of China this service has been placed under the Ministry of Finance. It is the Government's plan to transfer this work to the Ministry of Health, and, in so transferring it, to reorganize and strengthen it. Now port health work is very expensive in some countries and quite economical in others; the practice differs so much that the Ministry of Health, wishing to adopt the best, and to profit by the experience of other countries, called upon the Health Organization for help.

This help was afforded first by making a detailed survey of the most important Chinese ports in order to secure a knowledge of their conditions and needs, second by setting up a Committee of representatives of the Health Administrations of the most important maritime countries, and third, by providing facilities for training abroad Chinese medical officers selected for work in the new port health services.

The sub-committee of the Health Committee mentioned

above will make a study of the detailed survey of Chinese ports, and on that basis will draw up a scheme of organization for the new health services. Thus the Government of China will have the benefit of the experience of the most important maritime countries in this field, and the scheme will have the approval of the authorities of those countries. How important that approval will be is evident when one remembers that it will be the duty of the Chinese port health officers to board, examine, and perhaps quarantine foreign ships.

Just one example of the manner in which the Health Organization is able to assist in the training of medical officers appointed to posts in the new port health services: a programme was made for such an officer by the Health Organization, which asked the Health Administrations concerned to facilitate his studies. As a result this officer was enabled to spend several months at the important ports of Hamburg and Bremerhaven in Germany, London and Liverpool in England, New York and New Orleans in the United States of America. At each of these ports this officer followed the routine work of the port health officer or one of his assistants, boarding ships, observing the examination of passengers and crew, assisting in the disinfection of vessels, and securing an exact idea of the routine of port health work in these progressive ports.

Having gained such an intimate knowledge of the practice of port health work in these countries, he will be in a position to apply his knowledge to the best advantage in his new work in China.

2. The Chinese Government asked for the assistance of the Health Organization in its study of medical education, one of the most difficult problems it will have to solve. There are said to be four thousand practitioners of modern medicine

in China, a country of over three hundred millions. The small number of medical schools in the country will take years to graduate the number of physicians required to satisfy the country's needs. Moreover, a certain proportion of these schools are so badly equipped and inadequately staffed that the Ministry of Education has ordered them to close. While quite a number of Chinese are trained in medical schools abroad, the number is relatively small in comparison with the needs.

Obviously any health programme must have as a basis an adequate supply of properly trained physicians, so that the Government must take steps to deal promptly with this problem.

There are two schools of thought with regard to medical education in China. The first believes that a large number of medical schools should be established, to give short courses, lasting, say, three to four years, to the end that a large supply of second-rate physicians may be graduated. These men, according to this school, would be more apt than better trained men to settle down in villages and rural districts.

The second school believes that only the best type of medical education should be tolerated, for the finest schools will produce a sufficient supply of mediocre physicians.

This is the problem in a nutshell. In presenting it to you in so few words I have over-simplified it, but this presentation will suffice for our present purpose.

It was naturally impossible for any temporary visitor to China to deliver judgement in this matter. But the Health Organization of the League has certain facilities at its disposal, and these facilities were freely offered to the Government of China, with the unanimous approval of the Council of the League.

First, the Health Organization agreed to draw up a

memorandum on the evolution and present situation of medical education in the most advanced Western countries. This would be, in fact, a description of the methods used in other countries to solve some of the problems in this field facing China to-day.

Second, the Health Organization has sent to China, to work with the Government's Committee on Medical Education, a distinguished medical educator from Denmark.

Third, a committee on medical education will be set up by the Health Organization, consisting of the experts who have been studying this subject in the different countries. As a matter of fact, many authorities consider that the time is ripe for the work such an international commission may be able to do, but I shall confine myself to what the commission might do in connexion with the Chinese problem.

The information collected in China by the expert from Denmark will be considered by the commission on medical education in the light of its knowledge of the experience in other countries. In this way the best possible advice will be available to China in her struggle with this fundamental social problem.

3. The third proposal of the Chinese Government was that the Health Organization should assist in organizing what will be called a Central Field Health Station.

In order to make this clear I must explain the situation which faces the Chinese Ministry of Health from the purely public health point of view. If in China there are only a handful of doctors with modern training in clinical medicine, there are still fewer with a modern training in hygiene and public health. The Government desires to use these few to the best advantage. Obviously, one of the ways in which they can best be used is in the training of others.

Again, no one knows what are the real public health problems of China to-day, or, to put it more correctly, what is
the magnitude of the various problems. Now any Ministry
of Health must have a more or less exact idea of the varying
importance of the health problems it is called upon to solve,
in order to draw up a logical and economical programme; in
order to utilize its slender resources to the best possible advantage. This is not known in China because there are not
sufficient doctors, for example, to give death certificates. As
a friend of mine said wittily, 'Hundreds of thousands of
Chinese die without medical assistance'.

The purpose of the Central Field Health Station is three-
fold: first to train health officers, second to study the problems of public health, to find out their relative importance
by intensive study in small selected areas.

The third purpose of the Central Field Health Station will
be to make experiments in health administration in restricted
areas in order to find the system most suited to the Chinese
conditions.

The Ministry of Health proposes to transfer all its technical
officers to this station, and has asked the assistance of the
League's Health Organization in organizing and operating it.

Now there are in Central and Eastern Europe a number of
similar institutions, established to meet conditions resembling
somewhat those found in China. These are known as institutes of hygiene, and, unlike the older form of such institutes,
they include schools for the training of public health officers
and have control of certain areas in which health problems are
investigated and experiments made with different methods
of health administration.

Here again the Health Organization was able to assist
China by means of the experience acquired in other coun-

tries, for the director of one of these Institutes (Zagreb, in Yugoslavia) was sent to advise the Ministry of Health on the organization and administration of the Central Field Health Station on behalf of the Health Organization of the League.

The plan of organization of the Central Field Health Station was submitted to a group of directors of schools and institutes of hygiene convened by the League for other purposes.

Finally, the League will arrange for the training abroad of Chinese Medical Officers selected to direct the station and its various divisions.

4. If the medical situation in China as regards practising physicians is difficult, so is the situation as regards hospitals.

There are only a few hundred of these in a country requiring thousands. In England there is said to be one hospital bed for every 600 people, while in Fukien Province, where the proportion is highest, there is one bed to 9,210 people. In Kiangsi and Yunnan Provinces the figures are one to 151,600 and one to 246,490.

In addition, a majority of the hospitals are controlled by foreigners, and very few Chinese doctors have been able to learn by experience the difficult technique of hospital administration.

The Ministry of Health realizes that hospitals must be built and administered by its own people if the needs of China in this respect are to be met, and has decided to begin by building two large institutions, one in Nanking, to be known as the 'First National Hospital', the second in Hangchow, in collaboration with the Government of the Province of Chekiang.

The Health Organization is asked for assistance in planning these hospitals and in training their medical superintendents.

The League's Health Organization has arranged to provide training for these superintendents in European countries. One of them will spend several months with the superintendent of a very large hospital in Vienna, as the first stage in his studies abroad.

The hospital at Hangchow is to be the centre for all medical and public health work in the Province, and will be the head-quarters of the Provincial Health Commissioner, the Provincial Hygienic Laboratory, &c.

The Health Organization is asked to assist in planning these hospitals as well as in training their personnel, and you are familiar enough now with our methods to know how these requests will be met.

iii. *The Province of Chekiang.*

You will, I am sure, be interested to hear something of this Province with its population of twenty-five millions. It is situated on the sea-coast south of Shanghai. Its capital, Hangchow, is about five hours by train from that city.

This city, the southern terminus of the Grand Canal, is famed in Chinese poetry, and has been the Mecca of poets and writers from all over China for ages. It is a Mecca in the true sense as well, for pilgrims from all parts of China come in thousands to visit its many beautiful temples.

Marco Polo visited Hangchow and wrote a glowing description which it would well repay you to read. The last Empress of China thought so highly of its beautiful lake with its quaint bridges and picturesque surroundings that she planned the Summer Palace near Peiping along similar lines, excavating for a lake, building bridges like those at Hangchow, and throwing up embankments to resemble the hills bordering West Lake.

The Province, too, is beautiful, with its whitewashed villages, its well-kept farms, and its wooded hills, the last an unusual sight in China, where poverty has resulted in the destruction of forests, which are used for fuel.

This beautiful province has been left practically unmolested by the civil wars which have wrought so much havoc in many parts of China.

Chekiang also enjoys a progressive Government. The Chairman or Governor is the leader of the reconstruction movement in China. The Director of the Provincial Bureau of Civil Affairs has wide humanitarian interests and a real appreciation of the social needs of the people. When we were in Chekiang, sixteen thousand elementary schools were functioning, there was a good normal school with more than a thousand teachers in training, a well attended modern university, and a school for local Government officials attended by some three hundred carefully selected candidates from the Province.

The Provincial Health Commissioner has prepared an excellent public health programme which the Government intends to apply as rapidly as possible. This programme includes the building of a large central hospital at Hangchow, the training of doctors in hygiene, the education of midwives, provision of pure water supplies in the principal cities, the establishment of a provincial hygienic laboratory, a study of malaria, &c. This programme is being applied as rapidly as possible, and no one can question the earnestness of the Government, which has given many proofs of its firm intention in this respect.

The provincial health commissioner is being trained abroad under the auspices of the Health Organization of the League. He has studied in Yugoslavia, Hungary, Austria, Germany,

Poland, and Denmark. When his European studies are complete he will be in a position to apply the experience he has acquired abroad in the Province of Chekiang. I have already described the facilities offered to the Chinese doctor who will direct the work of the new provincial hospital at Hangchow.

This brief description by no means exhausts the scope of our co-operation in China with the Ministry of Health, but I have said enough to give you an idea of the methods of work employed by the Health Organization.

All of us who have visited China have the highest admiration and sympathy for the intelligent and energetic efforts being exerted by the Chinese in the field of health. The results of these efforts will redound to the benefit of the Far East as well as to China herself. In co-operating with the Government of China through the League, the health administrations of other countries will not only be fulfilling the obligation assumed by their Governments when the latter subscribed to the Covenant, but will be helping to make the world in general more healthful.

iv. *Co-operation with the Government of Greece.*

China is not the only country which has sought the co-operation of the League in health matters. A whole series of countries have asked for collaboration in regard to special subjects, such as malaria, syphilis, infant mortality, &c. In 1928 the Government of Greece asked for the assistance of the League in the reorganization of its sanitary services. An international group of expert health officers, including Americans, Australians, English, and Yugoslavs, made a survey of selected parts of Greece, and the League's Health Committee, on the basis of that survey, advised the Greek Government concerning the plan of sanitary reorganization. This plan is now being applied by the Greek Government, with which the League is still co-operating. A new school at Athens for training public health officers will open its doors in January 1931. Public health nurses and visiting aids are also being trained. A large national health centre is being established in Athens. Studies of malaria are being carried on and many other fields of health are being explored. Within the limits of the time available it is impossible for me to give you more than the briefest sketch of this work, but those who are interested may find fuller details in the official reports.

The Government of the Republic of Bolivia has also asked for the assistance of the Health Organization in the re-organization of her sanitary services. Two representatives of the Health Organization have just completed a preliminary survey of Bolivia's health problems, on the basis of which a plan of co-operation will be discussed by the Health Committee in 1931.

v. *Development of the Health Organization's Programme.*

The work which I have been describing to you is of comparatively recent date, and it must be remembered that the Health Organization of the League has been in existence for nearly ten years. Its early years were devoted to a few fundamental activities which have had a normal and useful development.

The Service of Epidemiological Intelligence is perhaps the most important of these. I have already described to you the work of our Eastern Bureau at Singapore, an outgrowth of this Service at Geneva.

In the attempt to keep all Health Administrations informed

concerning the movement and prevalence of epidemic disease, the Health Organization issues daily, weekly, monthly, and annual bulletins from Geneva, which supplement the infor mation collected and broadcasted at Singapore.

This service is as complete as it is possible to make it, in view of the fact that in a number of countries the public health and medical services are not sufficiently well organized to ensure complete and reliable reports.

Another of the fundamental activities of the Health Organization was the attempt to standardize the units of sera, vaccines, and certain other biological products, the dosage of which is determined, not by weight and measure, but by biological methods.

Diphtheria antitoxin is a good example. Without international standardization the diphtheria antitoxin unit would probably differ in every manufacturing country, for it is a purely arbitrary matter. During the war, when there was so much tetanus, English and American doctors in France were given French tetanus antitoxin to use, which differed materially in unit strength from the antitoxin to which they were accustomed.

It is of the greatest importance that these biological preparations should be standardized internationally, for the protection of the patient, as well as for the benefit of the physician. The patient benefits because the preparation used in his treatment has been compared to an international standard which the greatest authorities agree is the proper and most effective standard.

The doctor benefits because he can profit from the experience of physicians in other countries by reading reports of their work in the medical literature. When a unit of antitoxin means the same thing in all the medical world, is not that the beginning of a universal language in respect of sera ?

Finally, there are many countries which do not manufacture these products, and it is to their advantage to know that the products bought from neighbouring countries are identical, have similar dosage, and have been brought up to the standard laid down as most suitable by an international body of experts.

Work on this subject is going on constantly. The preparations dealt with comprise many sera such as diphtheria, tetanus, and dysentery, many drugs such as digitalis and strophanthus; many specifics such as the whole group of salvarsans. This work is carried on in various national laboratories under the auspices of the Health Organization.

When it is considered desirable to take up the standardization of a particular preparation, the experts most concerned from the various countries are called together. In the first discussion technical difficulties arise, which can only be overcome by comparative studies in the various national laboratories. This work goes on for months, perhaps for years, the workers being kept in touch with each other by means of the Health Section of the League.

Finally, the preliminary work is completed; the time is ripe for agreement. The experts are again convened, an international standard is adopted, and one more chapter in this work is complete.

But it is necessary to devise some method of preparing and preserving the international standard, of sending samples of it out to national laboratories, and of comparing national standards with the international standard from time to time.

As the Health Organization of the League has no laboratory, certain national laboratories are selected for this work.

For example, the Danish State Serum Institute acts for the Health Organization of the League in regard to nearly all the sera, while the Medical Research Institute at Hampstead (England) acts similarly in respect of a number of other biological preparations. National Laboratories in Germany, France, &c., also prepare and distribute certain preparations, in addition to making the comparisons necessary to insure that national standards are identical with the international standard.

This work of standardization is a particularly good example of the Health Organization's methods, for instead of establishing an international laboratory, which might be subject to severe criticism, it acts through national laboratories, and is thus a method for the co-operation of national laboratories in the international field.

The limits of my time do not permit me to describe the other branches of the Health Organization's work. I should like to tell you, if time permitted, all about our system of collective studies and interchanges whereby the health officers of many countries are given opportunities of studying the development of health work abroad. More than five hundred medical and sanitary officers have already benefited from this system, which has not only resulted in an effective interchange of information and experience in technical health matters, but has developed an *esprit de corps* among the health administrations of the various Governments.

You would be interested, I am sure, in the infant mortality inquiries carried on in seven European and four Latin American countries under the auspices of the Health Organization, inquiries which have brought to light the relative importance of various causes of infant death, and have aroused so much interest in this subject that five

Governments have asked the Health Organization to assist them in carrying on similar inquiries.

Nor could you fail to be interested in the malaria work of the Health Organization, which has resulted in international agreement on the methods and principles which should govern the fight against malaria.

The work of the Health Organization comprises, in addition to those mentioned, studies and investigations of leprosy, syphilis, cancer, tuberculosis, fumigation of ships, and many others in which international work of this kind is desirable.

In view, however, of the limits of time and space, I propose to close with a short description of the organization of this international health work.

vi. *How the Health Organization is organized.*

Like the League itself, the Health Organization consists of three bodies:

1. An Advisory Council.
2. An Expert Committee.
3. A Health Section.

The Advisory Organ is the permanent committee of the Office International d'Hygiène Publique (International Public Health Office), an intergovernmental health organization founded in Paris in 1908 as the result of the Rome Agreement of 1907.

Delegates from the Health Administrations of more than forty-five States sit on that committee, which meets twice a year in Paris, and the constitution of the League's Health Organization provides that the League may refer health questions to that body for advice and report. Advantage is taken of that provision in Articles VIII and X of the 1925 International Opium Convention, these articles setting out the procedure for including or excluding from the Convention preparations containing opium or cocaine.

The Health Committee, which meets usually twice a year at Geneva, consists of twenty-four health experts from various countries. As the members of this committee are selected as experts and not as delegates of their Health Administrations, such experts may be citizens of countries not members of the League, and, as a matter of fact, its membership has always included persons from the U.S.A.

It is the business of the Health Committee to advise the Assembly and the Council on all health matters.

Finally, the Health Section, an integral part of the General Secretariat of the League, consists of some seventeen full-time medical officers with the necessary clerical assistants, and has an office at Singapore as well as at Geneva.

The Health Committee has set up many sub-committees, and many health experts are co-opted for particular purposes by the Health Organization, so that scores of the world's foremost medical officers of health are constantly or occasionally at work for the League in health matters.

It is due to the unselfish and disinterested co-operation of these experts that the Health Organization has been able to make so much progress in the course of its short life.

Any description of the work of the Health Organization would be incomplete did it not take into serious consideration the importance of its relations with the various organs of the League.

Every proposal for new work must be approved by the Council of the League, and all its work is reviewed seriously by the Assembly.

It is in relationship with the two other technical organizations of the League (Transit and Communications, Financial and Economic) in regard to subjects of mutual interest, such as the establishment of refugees and port health work. Joint committees have been set up by the Labour Office and the Health Organization to deal with the medical aspects of social insurance and the disinfection of hides to prevent tetanus.

Those of my audience who have studied the development of international co-operation before and after the war, will realize that the Health Organization, constitutionally and otherwise, is well fitted to act to-day as a medium for the fruitful collaboration of Health Administrations in the field of international public health.

CHAPTER VII

COLONIAL ADMINISTRATION AS AN
INTERNATIONAL TRUST

Dr. KASTL:

i. *Historic Evolution of the Political Mandate.*

THE international mandate as defined in Article XXII of the Covenant of the League is a novelty, although similar conditions have frequently prevailed in the history of the European States during recent centuries. The State contracts concluded with the charter companies in the seventeenth and eighteenth centuries, despite the selfish commercial policy of these companies, also deserve mention, while, in the closing decades of the nineteenth century, the international mandate met with a certain amount of favour as an instrument of international policy in difficult circumstances. I may quote as examples the British administration of the Ionian Islands under a mandate of the Powers, the Conference of Washington (1878) at which the administration of Samoa by Germany, Great Britain, and the U.S.A. was discussed, and the Austrian occupation of Bosnia and Herzegovina in virtue of a decision of the Berlin Congress. The Berlin Congo Act of 1885 contained some stipulations which no longer aimed simply at furthering the capitalistic interests of the European owner States but at promoting the welfare of the colonial territory and its population. The idea of the 'open door policy' and of 'economic equality' was subsequently suggested for the first time by America in connexion with the discussions concerning a common Franco-Spanish 'mandate' as a solution of the Morocco conflict.

Towards the end of the war, General Smuts, when a

member of the British War Cabinet, drafted a scheme for the creation of a League of Nations containing articles on a proposed mandate system; shortly afterwards, President Wilson drew up his well-known League of Nations scheme, in which extensive use was made of General Smuts's proposals.

That, despite the unavoidable collision at the Paris Peace Conference between imperialistic views and Wilson's proposals, the new conception of trusteeship under international control gained at any rate partial recognition is certainly true. Nevertheless, owing to its one-sided application to the German colonies, it failed to provide a generally applicable solution. It bears too noticeably the character of a substitute for the desired annexation. The mandates system was 'invented', I may be allowed to say, and its value as a new step forward in colonial development 'urged' upon the President in order to gain for it his support. Nor should it be forgotten that this solution yielded only substantial advantages for the victor States; especially Great Britain and its dominions and France. Lansing, in his book, *The Peace Negotiations*, calls attention to the fact that, by the mandates system, Germany lost her claims to compensation for her colonies. Moreover, it gave *inter alia* Great Britain an opportunity for fulfilling, in some degree, her promises towards the Arabs of the ceded Turkish territory in regard to autonomy, although, in the selection of the Mandatory, the wishes of the population under the A mandates were in general ignored, in spite of Article XXII of the Covenant.

ii. *The League of Nations Mandate.*

Legal Sources. As shown quite indisputably by what has been stated above, the present mandates system is, both in origin and structure, a political matter. Hence an inquiry on formally legal lines appears in general superfluous, especially as it might easily lead to false conclusions.

The legal sources for this group of questions are primarily the peace treaties regulating Germany's renunciation of her colonies and Turkey's renunciation of her Arabian provinces of Syria, Palestine, and Iraq, namely, Articles 118 to 127 of the Treaty of Versailles and—in place of the Sèvres peace treaty, not ratified by Turkey—the Treaty of Lausanne signed on 24 July 1923; in addition, there is Article XXII of the Covenant regulating the mandates arrangement.

The agreements between the Allied and Associated Powers on the one side and the various Mandatory States on the other, in regard to the lines to be followed in administering the mandated territories, are instruments implementing the treaty texts on which the system is based. The same may be said of the provisions as to the exercise of control by the League of Nations—for instance, the Statute of the Permanent Mandates Commission.

This leads to a deduction not unimportant—for instance, in connexion with the question of the 'East African Dominion' —namely, that the constitutions of mandated areas must harmonize with the standards laid down in Article XXII of the Covenant. If, therefore, they are in any way contrary to the principles or spirit of this Article—for instance, in the mandate for Tanganyika—their legal validity becomes doubtful.

Application of the Legal Sources. On the basis of Article IV, para. 4,[1] of the Covenant, the Council of the League of

---

[1] Art. 4, par. 4, 'The Council may deal at its meetings with any matter within the sphere of action of the League or affecting the peace of the world.'

Nations has reserved to itself, by the interpretation of Article XXII [1] of the Covenant, the right of decision in all mandates questions; it faced the first Assembly of the League of Nations with an accomplished fact and has not altered its attitude in spite of the energetic protest of the Assembly—on the ground, doubtless, of Article III, para. 3, of the Covenant, according to which the Assembly 'may deal at its meetings with any matter within the sphere of action of the League or affecting the peace of the world'.

Consequently, *de facto* the Council not only determines the mandates policy of the League; in addition, it decides as to the interpretation of numerous vague points in Article XXII. True, in practice, it generally confines itself to taking cognizance of the attitude adopted by, and to accepting the conclusions of, the Permanent Mandates Commission, and, through the instrumentality of its secretariat, to handing on to the mandatories the decisions recommended by that Commission. In these circumstances, its technical advisory authority—the Mandates Commission—may claim recognition for having frequently and successfully maintained the principles of the mandates system in opposition to some contrary wishes of the mandatories.

All that remains, therefore, to the Plenary Assembly— whose working organ is the sixth Committee—is simply to

[1] The relevant paragraphs of Article XXII read :—
'7. In every case of mandate, the Mandatory shall render to the Council an annual report in reference to the territory committed to its charge.'
'8. The degree of authority, control, or administration to be exercised by the Mandatory shall, if not previously agreed upon by the Members of the League, be explicitly defined in each case by the Council.'
'9. A permanent Commission shall be constituted to receive and examine the annual reports of the Mandatories and to advise the Council on all matters relating to the observance of the mandates.'

register or discuss the resolutions of the Council, its advice being, as Lord Balfour unequivocally pointed out in 1920, without any binding effect upon the Council.

The League Secretariat, which as regards mandatory questions conducts the secretarial work of the three bodies, presents an annual report on the activities of the Permanent Mandates Commission and the Council to the Assembly.

From what has been said it becomes clear that practically all rights are vested in the Council. On the ground of this procedure, the Council, with its lack of actual and effective powers, may be placed before exceedingly awkward problems, and the future will reveal the wisdom or unwisdom of such an arrangement.

The idea of a theoretically satisfactory solution is contained in Article XIV of the Covenant with its reference to 'the establishment of a Permanent Court of International Justice' which 'may also give an advisory opinion upon any dispute or question referred to it by the Council or by the Assembly'. This decisive judicial function accorded to the Permanent Court has already, on one occasion, taken concrete form in the decision given concerning the Mavromatis concession in Palestine.

Moreover, there are, in the constitutions of all the mandates, provisions according to which disputes between a Mandatory and another member of the League concerning the application or interpretation of the provisions of the mandate shall be submitted to the Permanent Court of International Justice in the event of its proving impossible to reach a settlement by negotiation.

Definition of League Mandate. That the vagueness of Article XXII of the Covenant renders difficult an interpretation of the word 'mandate' is obvious.

People speak nowadays of 'colonial mandates', 'international mandates', and so on, and these phrases are undoubtedly always intended to mean the same thing, although the ideas they really express are anything but identical.

Nor has any clear definition of the word 'mandate' been given. Of the definitions known to me, I like Strupp's best; it runs as follows:

> 'Mandates are territories inhabited by peoples not yet mature for self-government—territories which, by virtue of the treaties of Versailles and Lausanne have been ceded by Germany and Turkey and—being placed under the League of Nations—have, in third-party interests, namely, in the interests of the inhabitants of the mandated territory, been transferred by it on various principles to Mandatory States by whom they are administered on behalf of the League of Nations and under its supervision.'

This definition distinguishes between the mandate and such similar institutions known to international law as protectorates, which lack international control, and colonies having a sovereignty in common with their mother-country.

iii. *Article XXII of the Covenant.*

Content. In the initial history of the present League mandates, it is particularly striking that Wilson's suggestions have, to a certain degree, carried the day against the strong desires of annexation in the full sense.

The one Article (XXII) dealing with the mandates question in the Covenant contains the following instructions:

I. (*a*) Instructions referring to

(1) the former German colonies 'which are inhabited by peoples not yet able to stand by themselves',

(2) certain former Turkish territories which, in consequence of the war, are no longer subject to the sovereignty under which they stood.

(b) The well-being and development of these peoples is aimed at.

II. (a) For this purpose the tutelage of the peoples mentioned in item I is transferred to advanced nations suitable for the task and 'willing to accept it'.

(b) The guardianship is to be conducted as a mandate of the League of Nations and on its behalf.

III. The character of the mandate is determined by:

(a) the stage of development of the people,

(b) the geographical situation of the territory,

(c) the economic conditions of the people,

(d) other circumstances of the same nature.

IV. (a) In consequence of this stage of development, certain formerly Turkish communities can be provisionally recognized as independent nations,

(b) provided they have 'the advice and assistance of a Mandatory until such time as they are able to stand alone.'

(c) In the selection of a Mandatory, the wishes of these communities must be a principal consideration.

V. The stage of development of the peoples of Central Africa is such 'that the Mandatory must be responsible for the administration of the territory' under the following conditions:

(a) the prohibition of abuses such as slavery, the arms traffic, and the liquor traffic,

(b) that freedom of conscience and religion be guaranteed, subject to the maintenance of public order and morals,

(c) prohibition of military and naval bases,

(d) prohibition of military training of the natives for other than police purposes and the defence of the territory,

(e) that equal opportunities be secured for the trade and commerce of other members of the League.

VI. Territories such as South-West Africa and the South Pacific Islands may be administered

(*a*) under the laws of the Mandatory,

(*b*) as integral portions of its territory,

(*c*) subject to the safeguards above mentioned in the interests of the indigenous population.

VII. An annual report must be lodged with the Council.

VIII. If not previously agreed upon by the members of the League, the degree of authority, control, or administration to be exercised by the Mandatory shall be explicitly defined by the Council.

IX. A permanent commission has to

(*a*) receive the annual reports of the Mandatories,

(*b*) examine them, and

(*c*) advise the Council on all matters relating to the observance of the mandates.

A Vague Compromise. These vague and even to some extent contradictory stipulations have been subjected by writers to not altogether favourable criticism. J. Stojanowsky, for example, writes concerning them in his monograph, *La Théorie générale des Mandats nationaux*:

' . . . son vague intentionel s'explique par le désir de ses rédacteurs de voiler les divergences de vues des diverses Puissances et de laisser à l'avenir et à l'expérience le soin de décider de certains principes fondamentaux.'

Again, one of the best authorities on the mandates system, van Rees, the vice-president of the Mandates Commission, calls attention in his exhaustive work, *Les Mandats Internationaux*, not only to the 'lack of a proper definition of the highly important juridical concepts of the mandates system', but also to the not over-careful drafting ('rédaction peu soignée'), and adds that Article XXII is the only article drafted by the authors themselves and incorporated in the

Covenant without examination by a competent drafting committee.

iv. *The Chief Principles of the League.*

Mandates. Two main principles of Article XXII are, indeed, strikingly worked out. One is, above all, the duty of advanced nations to develop the less civilized; secondly, that the resources of areas not yet exploited be placed at the disposal of the whole world, i.e. the members of the League. But how these tasks are to be carried out by the instrumentality of the three types of mandate, what legal relations exist between the new organizations and what are the characteristics of a mandate—all this and much else the Committee of Ten has left the future to elucidate.

'No Annexation.' It is, for example, an established fact that 'mandate' and 'annexation' are contrary terms. But it is at present impossible to predict how the mandates will develop theoretically under the interpretation of the Mandates Commission and of the Council or in the practice adopted by the Mandatories. In regard to the activities of the Mandates Commission, let me quote the instructive, though perhaps exaggerated views of van Maanen-Helmer, who writes:

'In the opinion of the author, had there been no Permanent Mandates Commission the disposition of the former German Colonies would so unquestionably have been equivalent to annexation that the mandates system would no longer be heard of.'

According to van Rees, the 'no annexation' principle gives rise to the following postulates:

(1) The mandated area is distinct from the territory of the Mandatory;
(2) The Mandatory must strictly observe the inviolability of the mandated area;

(3) The nationality of the inhabitants is not that of the Mandatory power;

(4) Inter-Mandatory agreements have no force as regards the mandated territories unless this is expressly stated.

These postulates are somewhat contrary to the charters of the B and C mandates, since in Articles IX and X of the B mandates and in Article II of the C mandates the right is accorded to the Mandatories to administer their mandates 'as an integral part of their own territories' though certainly 'subject to the provisions of the mandate'. As an example of the care with which the Mandates Commission works, I would point out that, during the fifth session of that Commission, Lord Lugard raised objection to observations in the report on the Cameroons under British mandate because these observations stated various districts to have become an 'integral part of Northern Nigeria'. In his opinion, Article IX of the Charter only justified reference to *administration* as an 'integral part'. The territories must remain separate entities.

It is naturally very difficult for the Mandates Commission to perform its task adequately when—as in the case of the Gold Coast and a certain part of Togo—independent administration of mandated territory is stultified by extremely close administrative connexion with neighbouring colonies.

The Mandates Commission has questioned the employment of the expression 'province of a colony' by the Belgian Government in the 'Act of August 21st, 1925, concerning the Administrative Union of the Congo and Ruanda-Urundi', the phrase being used in connexion with the latter territory. No reply has been received from the Belgian Government.

Similar questions will probably be raised in connexion with

the desire of the British Government for 'closer union' of Uganda and Kenya with the mandated territory of Tanganyika. The statement of the British Government on this point is at present before a joint committee of both houses of Parliament; the British Government will doubtless submit it to the Mandates Commission for consideration, and the report of the Parliamentary Committee may perhaps be discussed later at Geneva—above all as to whether the intentions of the British Government as regards Tanganyika are in conformity with the provisions of the mandate.

Any solution which does not seem to be consistent with the principles of the Mandate, especially of Article XXII of the Covenant, should be strictly prohibited. The Mandates Commission must maintain the integrity of the mandated territories in any way it can and must do everything in its power to ensure that the mandated territories remain 'separate entities'.

It is typical of the present situation that, in response to the repeated injunctions of the Mandates Commission, the Government of the Union of South Africa has, at last, submitted to the League Council an amendment to the Act concerning Railways and Harbours of the year 1922, the purpose being to adjust that Act to the requirements of the mandate. The claim to sovereignty over railways and harbours in the mandated territory of South-West Africa hitherto maintained by the Union was in contradiction to the 'no annexation' principle and was therefore legally untenable.

Sovereignty. The views of the various mouthpieces of the League as to who has sovereignty over the mandated territories—a question closely connected with the 'no annexation' principle—are reflected in two statements made in the Council at an interval of nine years.

In 1920 M. Hymans said at San Sebastian:

'Nous nous trouvons en présence d'une institution nouvelle. La science décidera dans quelle mesure on peut lui appliquer les anciennes notions juridiques.'

In 1929 Procopé amplified this pronouncement of M. Hymans by a further statement in the Council which ran:

'I think all my colleagues will agree with me that there is no reason to modify, in any way, this opinion, which states implicitly that sovereignty, in the traditional sense of the word, does not reside in the Mandatory Power.'

A more comprehensive decision on the part of the Council, in particular as to who has sovereignty, has not been made and is scarcely to be expected in the near future. These views of the League Council which—though only provisionally—are adopted to meet practical political requirements, have persisted as against the Mandatories and otherwise. Even the originally very dissatisfied Union of South Africa has shifted its standpoint in respect of the well-known decision of its Supreme Court, namely,

'That the Union had "full powers of administration, only limited in certain definite respects by the mandate".'

As a result of this change of attitude, the South African Government forwarded, on 12 December 1929, a telegram withdrawing their opposition to the standpoint of the League Council.

At present four different schools exist as to the allotment of sovereignty. One school, of which Schneider and Freytagh-Loringhoven are representatives, ascribe joint sovereignty to the League and the Allied and Associated Powers. Fauchille and, virtually, Rougier, divide the sovereignty over the A mandates between the mandated territory and the Mandatory, while they attribute full sovereignty to the Mandatories over the B and C territories. Another theory, held *inter alios* by Rolin, subjects all mandates to the sovereignty of the Mandatory. Schücking, Wehberg, and their supporters, on the other hand, vest sovereignty exclusively in the League of Nations. There remains one claimant, namely, the population of the mandated territories, championed by Millot and Stojanowsky. Finally, there is the interesting opinion of Pahl, who considers the mandated territory to be the holder of momentarily latent sovereignty the exercise of which has been temporarily transferred, in part to the community itself, in part to the mandatory, and in chief part to the League of Nations.

Personally I share the opinion of Schücking and Wehberg. Sovereignty over the mandated territories can vest only in the League of Nations, this being the institution which—uninfluenced by any outside pressure—has to pronounce final decisions in matters regarding these territories.

Duration of the Mandate. Just as uncertain as the rest is the duration of the mandate.

Leaving aside what, for the moment, are highly theoretical questions, such as the position in the event of a dissolution of the League, or a resignation of membership by a Mandatory, or as a consequence of belligerent hostilities, the one practical problem remaining is the termination of the mandate—a question on which, whether regarded juridically or politically, there exists no agreed opinion. The standpoint of Rolin and other authorities—a standpoint shared by Hammerschlag as concerns B and C mandates—is that the allotment of a colonial mandate is, by its nature, final. Such a view cannot be reconciled with Article XXII, since that article applies the mandates system to 'colonies and territories . . . not yet able to stand by themselves'. The logical conclusion from this is that we have here a transitional stage in the political development of certain peoples. Being transitional it must, sooner or later, come to an end; the mandated people will outgrow their tutelage and the trusteeship, having lost its meaning, will (? must) cease to exist.

As long ago as 1920, the Council, in approving the constitutions for Palestine (Article XXVIII) and Syria (Article XIX), expressly referred to the termination of the mandate; while, five years later, in the financial resolution I have already referred to, it also took into consideration the possibility of the cession or transfer of a mandate.

Concerning this termination of mandates, statements have also been made by representatives of the mandatories. Thus, during the deliberations on the A mandate for Syria, in March 1926, the French delegate stated before the Mandates Commission that the mandate was 'a provisional régime and served to educate peoples not sufficiently developed in a political sense in such a way that they might some day arrive at complete self-government'. So, too, as recently as January last, the Prime Minister of the Union of South Africa, in dealing with the C mandate over South-West Africa, stated that 'the time must come when the mandate will have to cease'. That he drew deductions irreconcilable with the mandates system does not affect my argument as to the temporary character of the mandate. His idea is that South-West Africa is a province of the Union of South Africa, which means annexation.

The first practical solution—affecting, it is true, an A mandate—has been decided upon by Great Britain. On

4 November 1929, the British Government informed the League Council that they would, in 1932, recommend the accession of Iraq to the League of Nations.

Greater difficulty is involved in the solution of the B mandates, as it is not possible to foresee when their populations will reach a stage of development enabling them to govern themselves.

What view Great Britain, as a Mandatory, takes of this question is not known. In any case, two pronouncements made by prominent English politicians may be of interest— pronouncements which refer to Tanganyika, this spot having been brought into the limelight by the East African Dominion scheme of the British Government.

The Colonial Under-Secretary of State, speaking at an East African banquet on 25 June 1925, said:

> 'I wish to correct the idea that there is something transient in our hold upon Tanganyika. It is as essentially part of the British framework as any other Protectorate.'

Four years later, Sir Austen Chamberlain, in addressing the House of Commons on 22 April 1929, stated that:

> 'The Mandates over the former German colonial territory (which derived from the Treaty of Versailles and not from the League of Nations) were definitely allotted to the existing holders and there has never, so far as I am aware, been any suggestion that any of the existing mandatories desired to be relieved of its responsibilities.'

Extremely interesting in this connexion was the naturally abortive discussion on the determination of the mandates in the sixth Committee of the Assembly in September 1929. A sharp antithesis of views was here observable between the 'provisionalists' and the 'permanentists'. While the

Italian representative, Count Bonin Longare, and the members of the Mandates Commission, Rappard and Palacios, stressed the provisional character of the mandate, others— above all Sir James Parr, the accredited representative of New Zealand in the Mandates Commission for many years (Samoa is a C mandate), supported by the French representative as regards B and C mandates—expressed an absolutely contrary opinion.

Sir James Parr's words are characteristic. He is reported to have said:

'Great Britain would not hand back the mandates nor would her Dominions; he could assure the Committee of that.'

Finally, it may be mentioned that, according to Rappard, a transfer or return of the mandate is only feasible if, in addition to the wish of the mandatory and the unanimous assent of the League Council, the United States of America— as one of the pentarchy referred to in Article 119 of the Peace Treaty—has been heard.

As already argued, there can, in my opinion, exist no doubt as to the transferability of all mandates or as to their having to cease so soon as the respective territories have reached the requisite stage of development. Attempts to undermine this thesis seriously jeopardize the very basis of the mandates system and, indeed, the basis of the mandates themselves.

It is not impossible that these considerations may some day acquire practical value, inasmuch as the allotment of the mandates by the Allied and Associated Powers unquestionably failed to take due account of many an expressed wish of a certainly no less valid nature.

Status of Inhabitants. Obliged thereto by measures of

certain Mandatory Governments, the competent organs have exhaustively discussed the nationality of the inhabitants of the B and C mandated areas. In contradistinction to the inhabitants of territories under A mandate—who, quite irrespective of the provisions of the Treaty of Lausanne, possessed nationality as citizens of states of legally established standing—the national status of the B and C mandate inhabitants was not regulated in Article XXII of the Covenant.

It is not uninteresting, in this connexion, to read the rather negative decision adopted on 23 April 1923 by the League Council. It runs:

'1. The status of the native inhabitants of a mandated territory is distinct from that of the nationals of the Mandatory Power and cannot be identified therewith by any process having general application.

'2. The native inhabitants of a mandated territory are not invested with the nationality of the Mandatory Power by reason of the protection extended to them.

'3. It is not inconsistent with paragraphs 1 and 2 above that individual inhabitants of the mandated territory should voluntarily obtain naturalization from the Mandatory Power in accordance with arrangements which it is open to such Power to make, with this object, under its own law.

'4. It is desirable that native inhabitants who receive the protection of the Mandatory Power should in each case be designated by some form of descriptive title which will specify their status under the mandate.'

Five years later, as a result of certain special incidents, the Mandatory Powers were requested to supply information as to the manner in which they had put this decision of the Council into practice. The exhaustive replies showed that, in various territories, the inhabitants could already acquire a specific nationality whereas, in others, it would soon become possible for them to be naturalized.

From further information requested as to the national status of natives it was learned that the natives of mandated areas were designated as follows:

'British protected person, native of the mandated territory of Togoland, Cameroons, or Tanganyika.'

'Natives of Togoland (or of Cameroons) protected under French Mandate.'

'Nationals (ressortissants) of Ruanda-Urundi.'

'Native inhabitant of South-West Africa under the protection of the Union of South Africa in its capacity as mandatory of South-West Africa.'

'British protected person, native of the mandated territory of New Guinea or Nauru.'

'British protected person—Native Samoan.'

'Inhabitants of the islands.' (Japanese South Sea Islands).

Special conditions not affected by the foregoing prevail in South-West Africa, inasmuch as in that country there has existed, side by side with the native population, a continually growing white element now numbering upwards of 30,000 souls.

The Union of South Africa, desiring—as she stated—for administrative reasons to give these whites as far as feasible one and the same nationality, applied—with partial success— to the League Council for release from the rule forbidding collective naturalization. In justification, it was explained that, in reality, there existed no distinction between such collective naturalization and the permitted individual naturalization, provided only that the persons affected were allowed individually to decline the naturalization. In virtue of the Union law promulgated in 1924, the greater part of the white population of the territory acquired British nationality, while, in the year 1928, a further *en bloc* law made them all nationals of the Union, but in the latter case without allowing them individually to decline to become Union nationals.

Accordingly, almost the entire mass of the non-native population of South-West Africa in possession of civil rights has forcibly accepted the nationality of the Mandatory Power. In this way the prescribed nationality distinction between the inhabitants of the mandated country and nationals of the Mandatory Power has been almost completely obliterated.

The Mandates Commission, which dealt with the matter during the autumn session of 1928, referred the Mandatory Power to the Court of International Justice. Against this, in January 1930, a Member of the Council raised a sharp protest, stating that, neither from a political nor a practical point of view, had the problem been adequately gone into to permit a purely juridical treatment. At least, according to the view of this Member, the entire question must be reserved for further examination by the instruments of the League.

v. *Mandates Treaties.*

Origin. In order to put the provisions of Article XXII into practice it was necessary to allot the mandates and to provide the Mandatories with executory rules.

But the allotment of the territories and the delimitation of the frontiers was announced on 7 May 1919, while, in the summer of that same year, a Committee of the Chief Powers met in London under the chairmanship of Lord

Milner to draft the mandatory provisions for the former German colonies (B and C mandates).

According to an interpretation of paragraph 8 of Article XXII, formulated by M. Hymans,

> 'If the degree of authority to be exercised by the Mandatory has not already been made the object of previous agreement among the members of the League, the Council gives an express decision on the matter.'

On the ground of this not uninteresting interpretation, the League Council, at its sitting of 5 August 1920, resolved that the articles drafted by the Chief Powers were to be examined and approved by it.

The Plenary Assembly, to which this resolution was communicated, approved of the arrangement, in spite of the opposition of certain prominent members such as Lord Cecil, and thus divested itself of the right of decision indisputably pertaining to it in virtue of paragraph 8 of Article XXII.[1]

By December 1920 it was possible to ratify the C-mandate articles drafted by the Chief Powers in pursuance of the resolution of the Council, whereas those for the A and B mandates had to wait till the middle of 1922 because serious intervening difficulties of a political nature had first to be overcome.

The numerous secret treaties entered into by the Allied and Associated Powers during the war had to be liquidated and consideration given to the claims of the United States as a non-member of the League of Nations, inasmuch as that country claimed a voice in the settlement of the mandates.

[1] Art. 22, par. 8, 'The degree of authority, control, or administration to be exercised by the Mandatory shall, if not previously agreed upon by the Members of the League, be explicitly defined in each case by the Council.'

Fourteen mandated territories required attention. Thirteen of these were dealt with in charters (mandates). The fourteenth was Iraq, in regard to which Great Britain, on 10 October 1922, concluded with King Faisal an agreement called in the preamble a treaty of alliance; this treaty was approved by the Council in September 1924, and again, in March 1926, on the basis of a communication from the British Government to the effect that it was in harmony with Article XXII of the Covenant. Thus Iraq, while recognized as an independent State, remains subject to the mandates system until its accession to the League of Nations.

The preamble and seven articles uniformly drafted for the existing C mandates and the nearly identical twelve articles of the B mandates differ very considerably from the far more detailed articles (in one case twenty and in the other twenty-eight) drafted for Palestine plus Transjordania and for Syria plus Lebanon, since these States were already recognized provisionally as independent and, moreover, in the case of Palestine, the fulfilment of the Balfour declaration was to be ensured.

However, the articles of all mandates are based on certain notions common to them all.

Protection of Natives. The long since recognized need—recognized at least by progressive Powers—for colonial administration to make due provision for the development of natives has become a binding international duty under the mandates system.

In accord with the provisions of Article XXII, the protection of the natives is expressly prescribed in all fourteen mandates, though the details naturally differ between the three groups.

The most detailed provisions are those 'concerning the

material and moral welfare as well as the social progress' in
the B mandated territories whose inhabitants are in greater
need of protection. The slave trade is to be suppressed,
forced labour restricted to public works and to be paid for,
and labour contracts and the enlistment of labourers controlled. In fixing the regulations concerning the ownership
of real property, the rights of the natives are to be protected;
the transfer of real property is to be controlled by the public
authorities; freedom of conscience and the free exercise of
religion are to be guaranteed. Military exploitation of the
mandated territory, except to the extent requisite for defence
of the country, is prohibited, and the traffic in arms and
intoxicating liquors is to be controlled.

Far less exhaustive are the provisions concerning the
C mandates, doubtless because these territories may be
administered as integral parts of the Mandatory country and
according to its laws. Still they comprise much stricter
stipulations as to the slave trade as well as instructions concerning forced labour, particulars referring to the control
of the traffic in arms, and a prohibition of the supply of
spirituous liquors to natives. Further, the provisions concerning military and religious matters are repeated.

A further important responsibility, not clearly stated in the
charters, is the relation between natives and whites. The
regulation of this matter must necessarily differ in the various
countries, owing to the different circumstances of each.

A closely connected point is the effort made by the
Mandatories to give the natives a growing share in the
administration of the country. Mention may here be made
of the systematic endeavour on the part of the British
authorities to cultivate 'indirect rule', whereas the French
tend more towards direct leadership by white officials.

Economic Equality. Like 'protection for the natives', the second point in the A and B mandates, namely, 'economic equality' for the Members of the League, is a valuable administrative rule long recognized by colonial States.

The complete fiscal and economic equality of all States Members of the League is prescribed. Every customs discrimination in the treatment of goods, whether as regards origin or destination, is forbidden. Moreover, in the B mandates the right of settlement is guaranteed to nationals of all League States.

Though on decisive points they do not always meet with success, the League Council and the Mandates Commission endeavour to see that these standards are duly maintained. The Council, for instance, has decided that the provisions entitling the B Mandatories to conclude customs unions between mandated territories and neighbouring countries must not be interpreted as permitting, in any way, a restriction of economic equality.

Further, on the occasion of its September session in 1928, the Council requested the A and B Mandatories to submit information concerning the provisions for procuring material and supplies by the government authorities of the mandated territories. As the replies received were inadequate, the Council had a questionnaire drafted and forwarded in 1929 to the different Governments.

Closely connected with the foregoing are the deliberations of the Mandates Commission concerning postal tariff discrimination in certain A and B mandates. As the matter was one of slighter financial importance and, in the opinion of the majority of the members, had nothing to do with economic equality, it was ultimately decided not to present any proposals to the Council; nevertheless, it is interesting to note that, taking a contrary view to the majority of the Mandates Commission, a member of the Council put in, at its January session in 1930, a formal protest in which he stated that, at least indirectly, the matter *did* affect the question of economic equality.

On similar principles, the Mandates Commission has frequently discussed the admission and appointment of qualified medical practitioners of any League State; indeed, under instructions from the Council, it recently forwarded a detailed questionnaire on the subject to the mandatory States.

Although discussed for many years, this question, unfortunately, is not settled. I think it is absolutely clear that the humanitarian work of a medical practitioner, or of all people belonging to a normal medical staff or hospital, has not the slightest contact with political considerations. There, nationals of all States Members of the League should be admitted on an equal footing to improve the sanitary conditions in the mandated territories, conditions at present not at all satisfactory on account of lack of personnel. Further— likewise in the interests of economic equality—the Commission examined, in 1928, the prolongation of the ninety-nine years' agreement concluded with the Anglo-Persian Oil Company. So, too, a year later it inquired thoroughly into the granting of the Dead Sea Concession and the allotment of orders for the enlargement of the Harbour of Haifa, interviewing for that purpose representatives of the Mandatory Powers.

Disinterestedness. Closely connected with the principle of 'no annexation' is the disinterestedness of the guardian in matters concerning his ward, as Professor Rappard put it on the occasion of the ninth session of the Mandates Commission.

According to Mr. van Rees, the mandated territory has, in virtue of this principle, a claim to the ownership of its revenues.

The fiscal affairs of the Mandatory and of the mandated territory must be kept quite distinct and separate. It is particularly difficult to meet this requirement in the case of such territories as Togoland and the Cameroons under British mandate, which are respectively administered as portions of the adjoining provinces of the Gold Coast and of Nigeria.

Again, upon the 'no annexation' principle is based the view that credits granted to mandated territories may be jeopardized by certain circumstances. This idea led, in the year 1925, to the adoption by the Council of the following, and for various reasons interesting, resolution:

'The Council . . . .

(1) Declares that the validity of financial obligations assumed by a Mandatory Power on behalf of a mandated territory in conformity with the provisions of the mandate and all rights regularly acquired under the mandatory régime are in no way impaired by the fact that the territory is administered under mandate;

(2) Agrees on the following principles:

(*a*) That the cessation or transfer of a mandate cannot take place unless the Council has been assured in advance that the financial obligations regularly assumed by the former Mandatory Power will be carried out and that all rights regularly acquired under the administration of the former Mandatory Power shall be respected; and

(*b*) That when this change has been effected the Council will continue to use all its influence to ensure the fulfilment of these obligations.'

Interesting, again, is the conclusion come to by the Mandates Commission when dealing with the question of phosphate exploitation in Nauru by the Mandatory State. The matter was discussed during the third session of the Commission and it was decided that it was irreconcilable with the principle of disinterestedness for a Mandatory State to carry on enterprises for its own benefit in the mandated territory.

vi. Mandates Commission.

Constitution. In pursuance of paragraphs 7 and 9 of Article XXII, which prescribe the constitution of a permanent Commission to receive and examine the annual reports of the Mandatories and to advise the Council on all matters relating to the observance of the mandates, the Council published on 29 November 1920 the *'Constitution of the Permanent Mandates Commission'*; it contains the provisions still, in general, valid concerning the organization and procedure of the Mandates Commission and its relations to the Council and the Plenary Assembly.

The Commission was to consist of nine (since increased to ten) members appointed by the Council; they must not hold any public post nor may the majority of them be nationals of Mandatory States.

In addition, there may be a technical member of the International Labour Office, to advise on native labour questions.

The 'Constitution' defines the methods to be pursued in examining the annual reports of the Mandatories; it provides for the co-operation of the representatives of the Mandatories in exercising this supervision and for the presentation of the views of the two parties to the Council, which is required to publish the report submitted to it.

Formal matters, such as the procedure and head-quarters of the Commission, financial questions, &c., are regulated.

The Commission is to have its seat in Geneva and to draft its own standing orders; it may co-opt technical members in an advisory capacity.

Standing Orders. The rules of procedure of the Permanent Mandates Commission, subsequently drawn up, were approved by the Council on 10 January 1922. In its present twice-amended form, it regulates in detail the procedure to be followed.

Under Article I, the Mandates Commission meets in June and November every year for a session of about twenty days each time. Extraordinary sessions may be held as was the case this year in connexion with the regrettable incidents in Palestine.

Article II fixes the number of members. Now that it contains a German member—appointed on 9 September 1927—the Commission comprises a national of each of the following countries:

Belgium,	Italy,
France,	Japan,
Germany,	Norway,
Great Britain,	Portugal,
Holland,	Spain,

Switzerland.

It will be seen that there are four delegates from Mandatory States; Professor Rappard, the Swiss member, was formerly Director of the Mandates Section of the League Secretariat, and so is intimately acquainted with all mandates questions. There is also an advisory member from the International Labour Office as already mentioned.

The provision requiring a quorum of six members is irreconcilable with the provision of the Constitution that the majority of the members must always consist of nationals of non-Mandatory countries. Proposals as to the removal of this difficulty have been made by van Rees in his book entitled *Les mandats internationaux.*

Resolutions pass by a simple majority; but a minority may put their views before the Council accompanied by a detailed account of the reasons for their conclusions.

The provision that the president and vice-president are to be elected annually by secret ballot has, in practice, resulted in the regular appointment, year by year, of the same gentlemen, namely, the former Under-Secretary of State in the Italian Colonial Ministry, Marquis Theodoli—who invariably conducts the deliberations with great dexterity—and the former vice-president of the Netherlands East India Council, M. van Rees.

Arrangements based on the provisions of the Constitution are then made for dealing with the annual reports of the Mandatory States. The examination of these reports requires the presence of the authorized representative of the Mandatory Power concerned, but the Commission's conclusions are framed without him and forwarded to him for any comment he may care to make. The report of the Commission, accompanied by any comments received, is then communicated to the Council.

Whether sittings are open to the public is left to the decision of the Commission. It has become the custom to throw open only the first sitting of each session, as it is considered that the discussions with the representatives of the Mandatory Powers can be successfully conducted only if uninfluenced by the need to consider their repercussions on public opinion. However, as the very detailed minutes are published about six weeks after the close of each session, all parties interested—including the Press—have an early opportunity of becoming acquainted with the proceedings.

The Standing Orders also contain provisions of no general interest as to the obligations of the League Secretariat, the formal conduct of the sittings, the duties of the President, the languages to be used, the head-quarters of the Commission, the attendance of experts, &c.

Activities of the Mandates Commission. Yearly Reports. It is exceedingly interesting to observe how the Mandates Commission, which, since its inception, has held eighteen sessions aggregating more than 300 days' sittings, has tried again and again to establish, over and above the annual reports rendered to it, a basis upon which to make its supervision of the mandated territories really effective.

Naturally the foundation is, and must remain, the examination of the annual reports as carefully provided for in the Constitution. As already mentioned, accredited representatives of the Mandatory Powers participate in the examination and are obliged to give any information desired. The discussions are, of course, conducted in a conciliatory form and have scarcely ever given rise to any difficulty worth mentioning.

Recognizing that the annual reports only provided a possibility of adequate supervision if commented upon by thoroughly informed persons—that is to say, persons holding leading positions in the mandated territories—the Commission, acting through the Council, suggested to the Mandatory Powers that they should appoint as representatives at the discussions only administrative officials of higher rank in the mandated territories. The result was satisfactory. In the next session of the Commission, the majority of the reports could be examined in the presence of responsible leading officials of the mandated territories. It may, without exaggeration, be stated that, at the present time, every administrator or governor lays store upon personally representing his territory at least on one occasion at the sessions of the Mandates Commission.

The discussions—which, together with the reports, are published and thus subjected to public criticism—have not merely led to the members of the Commission gradually acquiring an exceptionally extensive knowledge of the conditions obtaining in the mandated territories; another result is that the quality of the reports has, with the passing of time, strikingly improved. But it would be going too far to say that these reports enable the events in the mandated territories to be accurately followed.

The reports suffer by the fact that they are official reports to be published and that naturally the tendency prevails and is bound to prevail of avoiding so far as possible difficulties in connexion with public criticism.

Petitions. Notwithstanding the detailed character of these after all unilateral reports, it is only natural that the Commission endeavours to supplement them by getting into touch with the inhabitants of the mandated territories. Its unofficial suggestion that petitions should be permitted was, on a British motion, ultimately agreed to by the Council on 31 January 1923.

Under the Standing Orders, petitions may be presented to the Mandates Commission both by the population and by others. Whatever the source of the petition, the Mandatory Power must give its views on the matter. But, while petitions originating with the inhabitants of the mandated

M

territory must, in all cases, receive the attention of the Commission, those lodged by other persons may be turned down by the President of the Commission if he regards them as unsuitable for consideration.

The Mandates Commission may also reject the reports presented to it or may hand them on to the Council accompanied by a statement of its own views. As a rule the Council then instructs the Secretary-General of the League to forward the observations of the Mandates Commission and his decision to the petitioners.

Hearing of Petitioners. When success had been achieved with this very gingerly dealt with procedure for petitions, the Mandates Commission went a step farther and presented to the Council an application that it be permitted to hear petitioners in person. This demand, which undoubtedly seemed very disagreeable to the Mandatory Powers, at once met with keen opposition in the Council. The prevailing view was that 'An oral hearing of petitioners would undermine the authority of the Mandatories', with the result that, after obtaining the views of the Powers represented in the Council, the Mandates Commission was informed on 7 March 1927, without discussion, that no benefit would accrue from an alteration of the petition procedure hitherto observed by the Mandates Commission.

This does not, of course, detract from the right of individual members of the Mandates Commission to receive petitioners personally in an unofficial capacity. But I myself regret very much that the second suggestion of the Permanent Mandates Commission did not succeed.

Special Reports. It has become the custom to have special events occurring in mandated territories inquired into by special delegations of the Mandatories and for the reports of those delegations to be submitted to the Mandates Commission; for instance, the insurrection of the Bondels-warts, a largely mulatto community in South-West Africa, the happenings in Syria, Samoa, and Palestine, &c., were dealt with in this way.

Questionnaires. The desire of the Mandates Commission to facilitate the examination of the reports led to the demand that the annual reports of the Mandatories should be drafted in detail and on a common plan, and to small questionnaires being framed as a guide. Those for the B and C mandates were the first to be worked out, but they were soon followed by one for the A mandates, approved by the Council on 10 October 1921. These questionnaires contained alto-gether forty-nine questions; but they soon proved inadequate and the Commission consequently prepared a fresh B and C Mandate questionnaire containing 118 questions. This was submitted to the Council in June 1926; but it unfortunately met with the disapproval of that body, as several of the Great Powers represented therein objected strongly. Sir Austen Chamberlain, in particular, pointed out

'that the Commission showed a certain tendency to extend its powers; matters would ultimately go so far that, not the Man-datory Powers, but the Mandates Commission would administer the mandated territories.'

In this case again—the Mandates Commission persisting in its proposal—representations were made to the Mandatory Powers, but, so far as I have been able to ascertain, no reply has been forthcoming.

I do not pretend that it would be absolutely necessary to have a questionnaire of 118 questions in all cases, but the rejection of the Commission's proposal by the Council is symptomatic of the fact that in the eyes of many of the interested parties the international supervision of the Mandates Commission must stop at the point where it becomes inconvenient to the Mandatory Powers.

League of Nations Secretariat. We must not forget the activities of the Mandates Section of the League Secretariat. This department handles all League matters concerning mandates.

As a former member of the Mandates Commission, I may state on this occasion that the task of the Mandates Section is a very difficult one and requires thorough knowledge, great capacity, and tact. The Mandates Section deserves full acknowledgement for the manner in which it performs its duty.

Inquiries in Mandated Territories. At the suggestion of its Spanish member, Señor Palacios, the Mandates Commission during its seventh session discussed the possibility of instituting inquiries on the spot in the mandated territories. However, in view of the known attitude of the Council, the Commission decided not to submit any proposal on the subject.

That, because of this attitude, all specifically political negotiations concerning the competence of the Mandates Commission were bound to result in a compromise was obvious. In any case, it would be difficult to contend that the Council—and, in particular, the Mandatory Powers represented in it—have granted the Mandates Commission all the rights which, within the limits of what is politically feasible, are required to provide a full possibility of successful work.

vii. *Conclusion.*

Prospect. If now, in conclusion, we endeavour to strike a balance between success and failure in regard to the labours of the Mandates Commission, especially if considered from the negative standpoint of what would have been the development of the mandates but for the existence of the Commission, one must admit that those labours have met with no inconsiderable success. Possessing no tangible means of enforcing its decisions, the Commission was obliged to rely solely upon public opinion for support; but, doing so, it has undoubtedly succeeded in developing definite ideas in regard to the meaning, purpose, and possibilities of the mandates system. Beyond this it has, by means of its expert advice, done everything possible to promote the evolution of the mandated territories and their inhabitants and it has, in this way, demonstrated that the Imperialistic colonization methods are perhaps not always the wisest.

Whether it will prove possible for the mandates system to develop further—whether, among other things, it will, as some optimists believe, ultimately extend to at least the non-mandated colonies of Central Africa—cannot yet be determined. As M. Orts, Belgian member of the Commission, said on a certain occasion: 'It is probably too early to form an opinion.'

The Mandates Commission draws its ultimate *raison d'être* from the League of Nations, an institution which, according to a widespread conviction, was created as a means of guaranteeing the results of the World War. The League is to a certain extent endeavouring to emancipate itself from that tendency and to cure its defect of birth, but the success within the last ten years is not promising. Only if a widespread international basis for that institution can be found which excludes the application of physical force and a policy of alliances, and creates in the political world equality and an atmosphere of peace and mutual toleration, will it, perhaps, become possible to make secure the at present very uncertain existence of the Mandates Commission and to establish the ideas for which it stands.

If international peace is achieved and confirmed in every sense and if, as a result, the League of Nations, as the organ of international solidarity, acquires greater authority, the mandates system will have some chance of fulfilling its purpose. But the system must in the meantime prove itself superior to the former colonial policy both from the standpoint of the colonizing country and that of the colonized.

On the other hand, if the present mandates system remains what it is considered by a very large number of people to be, namely, a way to camouflage and conceal the confiscation of certain provinces and colonies from their former owners, and if the undeniable desire of certain Mandatory Powers to annex or at least to prepare the annexation of the territories entrusted to them persists, the mandates system will certainly lead to failure and the world's solidarity will suffer a grievous blow.

The mandates system will in the near future undergo, as I have mentioned above, a very severe test of its validity, in connexion with the East African question. I hope that the public opinion of the world will be able to declare that the Mandates Commission and the Council have done their duty in preventing every, even the slightest, violation of the principles of the Mandate.

CHAPTER VIII

NATIONAL TOLERANCE AS AN INTERNATIONAL OBLIGATION

Professor GILBERT MURRAY:

THE subject of my lecture is the question of Minorities, and the treatment of the ethnic religious or cultural minorities in various European States. There are, I believe, forty million people in Europe now living under alien Governments. There is nothing very serious in that. I wonder how many people there are living in the rest of the world under alien Governments. There must be millions in America, mostly not at all uncomfortable; there are the Welsh in Great Britain; if you like, there are also the Scotch. They are a minority, and I notice that the idea of the Scotch being oppressed arouses your open ridicule. That is to say, there is no reason why, in any given nation, there should not be a minority, speaking possibly a different language, having different blood, having different national customs from the majority of the people round them. It does not necessarily lead to oppression.

i. *The Persecution of Minorities.*

Let me now take a concrete instance to illustrate the sort of difficulty you have to deal with in certain regions. I take a particular instance, a case that I know of, I may say, at first hand; but, in order not to attack any particular Government or nation, I won't mention the geographical details. This was a little boy in Macedonia who went to school and pronounced some word or other with a Bulgarian accent, which he ought not to have done. He was scolded and he did it again. Then he reformed himself. Then he came back another day and accidentally repeated the same word with the same Bulgarian accent, whereupon the schoolmaster took a curry-comb (the thing with which you comb horses), scarified both the boy's cheeks several times, then rubbed his face in the dust. A friend of mine was told this by the boy's father and he also saw the boy. My friend asked the boy's father why he did not at once go to the police. The boy's father said, 'What would be the good? They would only beat me.' My friend said, 'Why do you not appeal to the League of Nations?' 'Why,' was the reply, 'I should be murdered.' That is the sort of problem, in an extreme isolated form, that you have to deal with.

Now let us consider one point. Why do people persecute minorities, or persecute other people in general? It seems an odd taste. Why should Catholics have burned Protestants, and Protestants have burned Catholics? Earlier than that, why in the early Christian Church should the most violent and permanent and furious passions have been raised because people differed on the point whether the third Person of the Trinity proceeded from the Father through the Son, or from the Father and the Son? It seems at first sight a point on which nobody had any information and which could not possibly affect the interests of anyone in the world. Why did you have 3,000 people murdered in one day in Constantinople because the people who favoured the green jockeys in the horse races had such strong feelings against the people who favoured the blue jockeys? Of course, there may have been bets concerned there, and bets do rouse a good deal of emotion.

Man is a very cruel animal. We have got to remember that; I suppose he is the most cruel animal that exists, but still he is not as cruel as all that. We do not really go about, whenever we get a chance, torturing or beating a fellow creature. The explanation of wanton cruelty only carries one a very little way. I think you will find that the main reason in every case is fear. That is to say, Protestants murdered Catholics or burned Catholics because they were afraid of Catholics; Catholics burned Protestants for exactly the same reason; and the reason they have stopped burning each other is that, owing to political changes, say in Great Britain, we are neither of us afraid. A little bit ago people felt that, if the Catholics got into power, they would turn out the king, they would dispossess all the Protestant nobles, and remove all the Protestants from office. Everybody would lose his job. The mere suggestion of that prospect naturally roused the strongest passions. The current phrase in Ulster, where the anti-Catholic feeling is very strong, is that if you don't look out, or something goes wrong, or such and such policy is carried out, 'the Papists will murder us in our beds'. Of course we all hate anybody who would murder us in our beds. It isn't in the least his opinion about the Pope that matters; it is that the horrid fellow wants to murder us in our beds. Similarly with the blue and green jockeys. It wasn't just preference for colour, or preference for particular jockeys; it was that, if the green faction got on top, the blue faction would lose their jobs, and be persecuted; similarly, if the blue faction got on top, the same thing would happen to the green. I think you will find that, at the root of all persecution, the main cause is fear.

But do not let us exaggerate. Fear is mixed up with many other elements. There may be revenge. Take the case of the schoolmaster I have already quoted. The reason why that schoolmaster was infuriated by the Bulgarian accent was probably that people with that accent had done terrible things to him and his family, things which he remembered with a sort of burning rage; and further, that he knew that people with that accent might, if something went wrong, do the same sort of thing again. You generally have revenge connected with fear. One must remember, then—without going into details—that all sorts of other psychological causes will co-operate, and that the association of ideas will produce the most curious results. I remember, for instance, a man from one of the States of Eastern Europe, speaking to me with passion of his hatred of Jews, which he attributed to his devotion to Jesus. It seemed to be the only way he had of showing that devotion; and, of course, he had to show it very strongly. All sorts of motives and pretences like that come in; covetousness comes in. If the person you can persecute is rich and there is a chance of plundering him, the motives are stronger. But the centre is fear: the feeling that the people with that characteristic have done you and yours some terrible wrong and are likely to do it again.

I think that is the first point from which we should start in order to understand the psychological side of the problem.

ii. *The International Guarantee given to Minorities.*

As I said, in Europe there are some forty million people living under alien Governments, and their situation is made dangerous by this particular fact: that the people who are now subject are in most cases the old enemies, the people who were on the other side in the Great War. Consequently, the people who are now subject are the people who used to be on top, so that there is a special motive of revenge, of getting your own back against them. In a good many cases the people who are now subject are on the whole the richer class, and, as the other changes in Europe have largely been accompanied by a sort of social revolution, the motive of plundering the rich comes in as well. That, I think, was recognized by everybody at the end of the war. I cannot do better than quote Professor Rappard's words on the subject:

'At the end of the war the victors had been led partly by irresistible external circumstances, and partly by internal circumstances which they have not resisted, to violate the precepts of the self-determination gospel. They now offered as a palliative, and in lieu of self-determination, a form of international protection by which they hoped that the victims of these violations would be more readily reconciled to their new position.'

That was expressed in an exceedingly good and interesting letter by M. Clemenceau, from which I just quote one sentence: he proposes the arrangements of what are called the Minority Treaties in these words:

'For the sake of peace and harmony and the very spirit of peace within and without the States, and also for the reconciliation of nations, it is necessary to assure to national minorities certain rights which, moreover, are not in opposition to the sovereignty of the State.'

You can see from that phrase the beginning of a difficulty that was likely to arise. M. Clemenceau is giving certain international guarantees to the minorities against oppression, and he has an uncomfortable feeling that some people, at any rate, will say that that is a violation of the sovereignty of the States. Of course they did. I will speak in a moment of the method that was followed, but I would first just make a few obvious criticisms of principle.

This was an international guarantee that was given. But the wrong against which the treaties were intended to guard was not an international thing at all; it was a case of what are called ordinary 'humanity rights'. Certain groups of individuals were being badly treated or oppressed, or in danger of being so. The remedy suggested was an international remedy. That means that it does not exactly touch the spot, and also that it implies much too heavy artillery. Take the case of that little boy I was speaking of. The wrong that had been done to that boy was not an international affair, and there is something a little disproportionate in putting in motion a great international organization for the sake of correcting an offence that ought to be corrected on the spot by the nearest authority.

iii. *States not bound by Minority Treaties.*

Another very obvious difficulty was this. It was possible in the Peace Treaties to put in special clauses for the protection of minorities in the case of certain nations, namely the new nations that were being created or the nations to which great grants of new territory were given, because then the grant was accompanied by a certain condition. But the result was that the new nations found themselves all bound by these Minority Treaties while they were surrounded by a number of older nations who were not bound at all but could do anything they liked to their minorities, and that produced a feeling of injustice.

On the point of the other States not being bound, it is worth while recalling a resolution which I proposed in the Assembly in 1922, and which was accepted. It was quite impossible to get the other nations to accept a legal obligation to the Council of the League for the proper treatment of their minorities, but we did get a unanimous vote of the Assembly expressing the 'hope that the States which are not bound by any legal obligation to the League with respect to minorities will, nevertheless, observe in the treatment of their own racial, religious, or linguistic minorities, at least as high a standard of justice and toleration as is required by any of the Treaties, or by the ordinary procedure of the Council.' [1]

I ought to say that in the Treaties—it has nothing to do with the Covenant—in the Treaties constituting the new nations the duty is laid upon the Council of the League of Nations to protect the rights of minorities in a number of different ways which I have not time to go into. They are to be protected in their culture, education, religion, civil rights, and so on. How was the Council to do this? They decided to proceed, and I think it was a very good decision, by means of petitions. That is to say, if a wrong was being done, if the Treaties were being broken, a petition was to be addressed to the Council.

iv. *Procedure in dealing with Petitions.*

The first question that arose was—who had the right to send a petition? In that, the Council took an exceedingly liberal position: that a petition might come from anybody, from any corporation or any individual. That was an exceedingly wise and generous provision to make. For instance, if you or I had seen that little boy being maltreated we could have sent information, and our information would not have been rejected on the ground that we were not duly accredited delegates. The next question was, how the petition was to be received, because, naturally, it would hardly do to have the Council of the League snowed under by irresponsible petitions sent in by any lunatic who liked to send them. The general principle is that petitions first of all

---

[1] Curiously enough, a very great authority on this subject, Mr. Lucien Wolfe, has always considered that the situation was peculiar to certain areas and ought not to be generalized.

have to satisfy certain conditions: they have to be couched in reasonable language; they have to be about some subject that has not just been settled, and so on. A number of elementary considerations of that sort are laid down. Then they are sent to the Secretary-General, that is to the Secretariat, who can see if they fulfil these conditions and are 'receivable'. If they are receivable, they are passed on.

Where are they passed on to? The first idea was to pass them on to the President of the Council, and here comes the snag which has really stood in the way of any satisfactory procedure. It was felt that if the President of the Council had to take action on these petitions he would be concentrating on himself and his country all the unpopularity which would naturally result. I mean, supposing we consider that Poland or Rumania has maltreated a minority, and let us suppose that a Frenchman is the President of the Council, then the Frenchman is constantly in the position of making bad blood between France and Rumania or France and Poland; and, if he is human, he generally will prefer to allow a little irregularity about a Minority Treaty to go on rather than make a quarrel between his country and another. That is an exceedingly strong motive with all politicians and diplomats. Politicians and diplomats do not seek quarrels; rather they evade their duties in order to avoid quarrels.

The way out of that danger was to appoint a Committee of three so that the unpopularity would at least be divided. The Committee of three were to look at the petition and then consider what was to be done. They have been in action now for some seven years. In a good many cases they have thought that nothing could be done; in a good many cases, it is impossible to say how many, they have followed a procedure which was not contemplated in the Treaties but which does seem to have been exceedingly useful. They have called the attention of the Minorities Section of the Secretariat to the thing that had gone wrong, and one of the members of the Secretariat has taken occasion to go to the country in question and speak to the authorities, suggesting that they had better mend their ways in this or that detail, or else the thing would have to be brought before the Council. This was a very useful way of proceeding: it made no open scandal; it did not rouse any great ill feeling on the part of the Government accused; and I think a great deal of good was done. I do not know how far it is still carried on successfully.

Supposing, however, they brought the matter before the Council. Then what was the procedure? Here things became rather difficult. The Council could not take any action without hearing the defence of the Government that was complained against. The Government accused of having treated a minority in some unjust way has the complaint sent to it and is allowed three weeks in which it can say whether it wishes to make any observations or not. It always does. It then is given two months in which to make observations. These observations come in to the Council, but it has always been considered that the petitioners had no right to see them or answer them. This seems a glaring injustice. But it was difficult to say in international law that the minorities had such a right because the international dispute was not between the petitioners and their Government. They both belong to the same nation. The international dispute, as soon as the Council took a question up, was merely between the Council and the Government. The result is in almost every case that the Government makes its answer and things go no further. The Council has called the attention of the Government to the wrong and it considers that

that is enough. There does seem to be a great lack of some method by which the injured minority or the petitioners, or somebody representing them, could appear before the Council and state their case.

Sometimes the wrong done is a question of law, a definite question of a breach of treaty. Sometimes it is something less. One of the resolutions passed in 1922 urged that, whenever there was a question of a definite legal offence, the Council should immediately refer the matter to the International Court. Some such provision seems to me to be obviously right.

v. *Political Difficulties in dealing with these Problems.*

What is the cause of the whole weakness and trouble of the Council in dealing with these questions? It is that the Council is a political body and must inevitably be affected by political considerations. I went twice to speak to an important member of the Council to urge that certain points affecting minorities should be brought up and seriously discussed. On both occasions he said to me the same thing: 'You have no idea what bad blood is produced in the Council as soon as we talk about minorities.' My answer—I was very polite and did not make it—might have been, 'It may make trouble for you in the Council if you do mention a wrong done and try to get it put right; it makes very much worse and wider trouble outside the Council if people learn that the Council's sense of justice cannot be trusted'. Now why is it that sometimes—only sometimes—the Council's sense of justice cannot be trusted? Because it is a political body and is always taking into consideration reasons of a political nature; consequently, I consider that in this, as in so very many of the questions that come before the League, the thing to do as far as possible is to get the problem out of the atmosphere of politics into some other atmosphere. Get the thing settled by law; get the thing settled by the advice of experts, by geographers, by economists; but save the poor people in the Council from this terrible responsibility, from feeling in their hearts: 'If I say what is true, such-and-such a country will be terribly annoyed; if I say what is true, my Government will be imperilled at home; if I say what is true, awful things will happen; therefore, I will say what is diplomatic.' People ought not to be put in that position; one ought to try to save them from it. As a matter of fact, I think I am right in saying that there are only two cases on record where a petition of this sort raising a legal point has actually been referred to the International Court, and perhaps I am not indiscreet in mentioning that those two cases both occurred when Lord Cecil was sitting on the Council.

These are the kind of difficulties that arise. Owing to the machinery being international it is rather heavy and difficult to put in motion; owing to the Council being a political body it is very much hampered in its action; owing to the whole system, the minority or the petitioner has not a fair chance of being heard.

There is another fact in the background which is rather terrible: that this procedure, while it acts on the whole quite reasonably well where there is no great persecution or oppression, where the minority is strong and able to speak for itself and the wrong done is not great, is apt to fail absolutely in the worst cases. The Turks are bound to carry out obligations analogous to the Minority Treaties. Suppose there are Armenians being massacred now in the centre of Turkey (I do not say there are), will this sort of procedure have any effect? In the case of the little boy I mentioned in Macedonia, will this sort of procedure have any effect? It won't.

N

vi. *Some suggestions for improving the Procedure.*

I will now put briefly before you some of the suggestions
that have been made for improving the procedure. There
was first of all one of my own, which was very nearly accepted
in 1922, which deals with this particular point I have last
mentioned. I was enormously struck by two points that
had come into my own experience. One was that in Turkey,
at a time when there was very great friction between Greeks
and Turks, there was a certain district where nothing went
wrong, and that was because there happened to be an English-
man, a commercial man of some description, living in a
particular district, who was a very good sort of man and
who had the confidence of his neighbours. He had no force
behind him, and no official position. But this is what
happened. First of all, nobody liked to commit an atrocity
that Mr. Brown would know about. We all hate committing
anything of that sort when anybody is looking at us. It is
a most profound truth that the way to keep order in a dark
street is not to put six policemen, but to put one street lamp.
This man was a street lamp. In the first place they didn't
like to massacre each other, they didn't like even to quarrel
very badly, when Mr. Brown was there. Secondly, nearly all
bad massacres begin with a lie, the sort of lie of which we had
so may specimens during the war. The first thing is that a
rumour comes to you that the Greeks have horribly maltreated
a Turkish girl in such-and-such a village. You don't go and
look, you only repeat the story, and then the Turks are furious
and they proceed to do the same to two Greek girls, and so
the whole thing starts. What Mr. Brown did was this. Whenever there was a rumour of this sort he said: 'Don't get excited;
I'll go over and see what happened.' He went over, and in nine

cases out of ten would find that nothing at all had happened. I was very much struck by the fact that the mere presence of a civilized and fair-minded man had this wonderful effect. I came afterwards across two other instances, one in the case of a relation of my own who stopped a massacre simply by staying in a village where it was going on. Another was a rather similar case on the Greco-Bulgarian frontier. So I ventured to suggest that there should be 'in places where the conflicts were frequent and serious', resident agents of the League: people who should just live in the neighbourhood and try to keep the two parties in good relations with each other. For various reasons that just failed of acceptance, but I still think that it would be a very useful thing to try— not in ordinary cases, but in cases where there is real danger of violence or massacres.

Then there is a proposal made, about which I have had some difficulty in making up my own mind. That is, that since the trouble about minorities goes on permanently, there should be a Permanent Commission, rather like the Mandates Commission, to consider all minority questions and make quite sure in a positive way, and not merely a negative way, that the full protection of minorities is being carried out. I say a positive and not merely a negative way, because there are two opinions: one is that the Council ought only to interfere when some great wrong occurs; the other, and I think it is in accordance with the language of the Treaties, that it is the Council's business to see that the Treaties are carried out.

The objection to the permanent commission is that it seems to make this protection of minorities a permanency. You accept the position that there always will be in such-and-such a country an alien minority which has to be protected by an external power against its own Government, and people say, with a good deal of force, that surely this protection of a minority against its own Government is a temporary thing; it may be a painful necessity for getting through a particular crisis, but it surely ought not to be made permanent. There are two views taken about that. I quote a passage from Mr. Mello-Franco, who made a Report to the Council on the subject and who took a strong line against anything like a permanent commission. He said:

'We must avoid creating a State within a State. We must prevent the minority from transforming itself into a privileged caste and taking definite form as a foreign group instead of becoming fused in the society in which it lives. If we carry the exaggerated conception of the autonomy of minorities to the last extreme, these minorities will become disruptive elements in the State and a source of national disorganization.'

That is one view. The other view is expressed by Mr. Stresemann:

'The system' (of protection of minorities) 'does not constitute merely a transitional régime, which must ultimately lead to the disappearance of the ethnical and cultural characteristics of the minorities and to their being merged with the majority of the population of the country. On the contrary, the maintenance of this system is the permanent foundation on which the faithful execution by the minorities of all their civic duties towards the State to which they belong must be based.'

So on that point I think there are in theory two views possible; on grounds of practical need, considering the proved inadequacy of the present procedure, I think the constitution of a permanent committee, to advise the Council, has become almost a necessity.

Another suggestion which I think worthy of some attention is to try to get the consideration of the petition taken at once out of the hand of the political Council, for the reasons I have given, and handed over to some sort of legal advisers. The Council already has at its disposition a body of jurists, but I think these advisers ought not perhaps to be pure jurists. They would sometimes have to consider questions not wholly legal, but questions of fact and practice. I think, broadly, something might be done to secure that as soon as the Council was seised of a petition it should hand it over for legal and other advice to some such committee.

Another suggestion—I am not sure whether this has ever been made, but it very well might be—occurred to me from reading an account of the system adopted in England when we still had trouble with Wales, before Wales got into the habit of sending us Prime Ministers. There were constant conflicts between English and Welsh in the fourteenth century, and it was difficult, of course, to get justice done between them, because if you had an English jury it sided with the English and if you had a Welsh jury it sided with the Welsh. The British Government took a very reasonable line, and said that all conflicts between Englishmen and Welshmen should be referred to a mixed jury of six English and six Welsh. The jury was later rather extended, and became in some cases a sort of commission, which made constructive proposals.

I think that some of the countries who have alien minorities, and who resent the interference of foreigners to protect the minorities, might very well consider whether it would not be worth while establishing some sort of informal mixed commission of their own nationals, responsible to their own Government. Such a commission could probably solve a good many difficulties just in an advisory way. There may be objections to that plan, which I have not considered, but I think it is worthy of some attention.

vii. *Removing the Seeds of War.*

Lastly I would just say this. I feel sure that to all reasonably humane people there is ample reason for protecting these minorities in our mere wish not to have human beings oppressed. It is surely an obvious disgrace to our present civilization if you have in so many countries, in the midst of all the culture of Europe, bodies of human beings who are subject to oppression. I should be quite content to base my whole case on that. But, as a matter of fact, there is another reason behind of an even graver character, and which I think one must bear in mind. That is, that every war leaves behind it the seeds of a war of revenge, or at least a war for enabling the beaten party to get back something that it has lost. Let us remember that the end of every war is unjust, and must be unjust, and the end of every war made to correct that injustice will be equally unjust. Mankind can never get justice through war, and so every war leaves behind it the seeds of another.

Of course, by this institution of the League of Nations, we are trying to prevent those seeds from fructifying; but if you have in Europe anything like forty million people seriously discontented and looking beyond the frontier of their own country for the remedy of grievances, not imaginary but real; if you allow anything like that state of things to continue, you give the seeds of war a chance of fructifying, which may well alarm even the calmest among us. This discontent of minorities, though it is often concerned with things which seem to us trivial, is a thing that goes very deep into human nature, and it remains—so long as it is not removed—a serious danger to the peace of the world.

CHAPTER IX

THE ADMINISTRATION OF INTERNATIONAL JUSTICE

MANLEY O. HUDSON:

i. *A Fundamental Conception.*

I PROPOSE to deal with this topic—the Administration of International Justice—as one of the problems of our international society. It seems to me important that each of us should start his consideration of international problems with a conception of the existence of a society of States. That conception is too rare in our writing and thinking about the subject, partly because this society of States is very new in the history of the world. Indeed, it was less than seventy-five years ago, in 1856, that Turkey was admitted by the Powers to participate in the public law and system of Europe. At that time a society of States, so far as it existed at all, was a society of European States. Even later, in the last century, international law was deemed to be a law of the society of Christian nations, or of Christian peoples, and in the middle of the last century Japan and China and other States were not yet deemed to be a part of this society of States. To-day, however, any such distinctions based either on geography or on religion have become entirely obsolete. I think no one would deny to-day that each of the peoples of the world does occupy a place in this society of States. There may be some peoples, like the people of Nepal, for instance, who do not care to assume an active role in that society, but they may be deemed, nevertheless, to be the beneficiaries of the order which has been and is being established by the society itself. Nor must one confuse the society of States which exists in the world with that organization of a large part of the society which we call the League of Nations, or *la Société des Nations*. There are States which do not form part of the *Société des Nations*, but which are members of the society of States; and I think we should discuss the topic which we have this morning as it relates to the whole of that society.

ii. *International Justice and International Law.*

Now the administration of justice is a problem common to all societies. We generally think of it as the administration of justice according to law, but I would suggest to you that there is also a necessity of our thinking of the administration of justice which is not according to law. I know it may run counter to the thinking of some of you if I say that I have never placed much reliance on the formula that law is to be substituted for war. Law covers and can cover but a small part of human endeavour. Most of the activities of most individuals, and most of the activities of States, are not governed by law, and in my judgement cannot be governed by law. I cannot foresee a development of international law which would make it possible for all relations between States to be handled in accordance with law. It is extremely necessary that there should be a conception among us, I think, of justice which is not according to law, of the handling of international affairs by extra-legal methods. It is for that reason that we have created, in the course of these recent years, the Council of the League of Nations and various other organs whose primary duty it is to achieve justice in the relations of States, but which are not bound by the limitations of law in their efforts to that end.

The Council of the League of Nations, for instance, does

not act as the Permanent Court of International Justice acts. It does not act with the same limitations; it does not hold itself in the same *cadre*. It attempts a solution of problems according to the judgement prevailing at the time, frequently without regard to the historical legal tradition, and frequently without consideration of the extent to which its action in a particular case may be taken as a precedent for the future. A tribunal which acts within the limitations of law can never neglect the historical legal tradition that has been handed down to it, and it can never neglect the necessity of taking such action that it may form in the future a precedent for the handling of other cases. I know a great many books have been written in recent years about the Council of the League of Nations and about other organs of the League of Nations, as if they were purporting to act in accordance with the law of a given situation. That is not the case. The Council of the League of Nations is, and it ought to remain, in my judgement, a political instrument; it effects political solutions of different problems; it makes compromises; it is there to adjust differences. It is a conciliating tribunal which does not act within the limitations of law.

If that conception is established, I think one will not fall into the error of supposing that it is ever possible for us to create an international law which is going to cover all of the problems that may come before the States of the world. Some of my friends have talked in recent years as if it were quite adequate for the society of States that we should have a strong international court. Well, I think no one desires a strong international court more than myself, but I think no one appreciates more than I the need for instruments other than a Court, the need for such an instrument as the Council of the League of Nations.

In general, we may say that we have two methods of administering justice not according to law—not in violation of law, but outside the limitations of law. First, of course, is the diplomacy which is conducted by each State with the others, and second is the organized method in such bodies as the Council of the League of Nations. It is not the administration of justice in that sense that I am talking about to-day. It is rather the administration of justice according to law with which I would deal.

Now what are the characteristics of that administration? In the first place, justice administered according to law must be predicable; it must be possible for lawyers to know in advance what it is going to be. The predicability of law is one of its chief characteristics. It is a characteristic that does not apply to the Council of the League of Nations. Lawyers cannot predict what kind of political solution may be reached in any circumstances, but lawyers ought to be able to predict how a court is going to handle any difficulty.

In the second place, the administration of justice according to law ought to be free from the considerations of convenience or the considerations of expediency which may prevail at the time. I do not mean to say that it is ever possible to administer law without regard to the consequences of the results that you may reach. The consequences are as important as anything else for judges to consider; but they consider the consequences in quite a different attitude of mind from that of the Council of the League of Nations. There expediency must rule, convenience must guide; but, in an international court, considerations of expediency, of convenience, have far less weight, and the court must act within the limits of its historical tradition, and it must apply rules which can maintain a future validity.

iii. *The present body of International Law.*

We have to-day, contrary to the popular notion, a very large body of international law, but a relatively small part of it is that part which the popular mind regards as international law. A very large part of our international law to-day is contained in treaties and in written engagements. I have recently made a study of the registration of treaties by the Secretariat of the League of Nations. In the course of the past ten years, almost 2,400 international treaties and engagements have been brought into force and registered with the Secretariat of the League of Nations. It is quite possible that some treaties have been brought into force by the Members of the League of Nations and have not yet been registered, and it is clear also that States not Members of the League of Nations have in this period made some treaties which have not been registered; so I think one may say that, during the course of the last ten years, there have been no less than 2,500 treaties brought into force by the States of the world, the States that are members of the society of States. In other words, we are making treaties at the rate of some 250 a year. The content of these treaties forms a large part of our stock and store of international law when we come to administer justice according to law. Some of them, a very large number of them, are collective, general treaties, multi-party, multilateral, to which various States are parties; perhaps 300 such treaties have been brought into force in the course of the last ten years. These constitute a very large body of international law which we may rely upon in our administration of justice according to law. I stress that point because, in the popular discussions of the Permanent Court of International Justice during these latter years, it has been supposed by many people, not only by people who are not lawyers, but by lawyers themselves, that there is no law for an international court to administer. It is a strange assumption that is being made in many quarters to-day that, without a codification of international law, there is no basis for the action of an international court.

iv. *Justice according to Law.*

May I now ask you to consider for a moment the machinery which exists in the world to-day for the administration of justice according to law. In the first place we have a large number of international tribunals created by groups of States. Two States, States A and B, for instance, may have many legal questions pending between them. It may be necessary for those two States to create some sort of international tribunal which will administer justice according to law for themselves. These we have sometimes called Claims Commissions; at other times we call them Arbitral Tribunals; at other times we apply other names. A considerable number of such tribunals exists in the world to-day. I think perhaps the best instances for me to give are the claims commissions which have been created in recent years by Mexico with various other States: there is a Mexican-French Claims Commission, that deals with justice according to law in a whole series of relations between Mexico and France; there is a Mexican-American Claims Commission, and so on. These claims commissions are extremely busy. They frequently have many cases on their dockets, but their cases usually cover a long period of the past. If one can judge by the history of the last one hundred years, a person who has a claim against a State will be fortunate to have it settled in this manner in the course of the lifetime of his great-great-grandchildren. That is, if you should be injured by State A while you are travelling in State A, and if you should succeed some day in having that case referred by your Government and by the Government of State A to a claims commission, you might hope that your great-great-grandchildren would reap some benefit from the claim and would be able to enjoy what you have lost. It is an excellent way of bequeathing something to your posterity, to be injured in another country.

The results of the work of these claims commissions are on the whole quite satisfactory, if one will forget that they involve delay. They act according to law; the members of the claims commissions are not called judges but they are judges in fact, and it is their judgements and opinions upon which we rely for a great deal of the judge-made part of international law.

Then we have, as distinguished from the claims commissions, various arbitral tribunals set up to handle particular questions which have arisen in the relations of different States. It is a common and popular assumption that arbitration somehow differs very radically from adjudication, and that an arbitral tribunal does not apply law in the sense that a judicial tribunal would apply it. I find nothing, or almost nothing, in the history of arbitral tribunals to justify that assumption. In fact, most arbitral tribunals behave most of the time precisely as they would behave if they were created as judicial tribunals. They attempt to find out what the law is; the members of these arbitral tribunals are usually lawyers, and, whatever clothes you may ask a lawyer to wear, you cannot put him on an arbitral tribunal and ask him to leave at home his legal psychology. He has to bring that along; he must treat precedent as lawyers treat precedent; he must consider the element of predicability as lawyers consider it;

he must consider the possibility of laying down a rule for the future.

In these agencies, then, we have a very extensive machinery for the administration of justice according to law. But we do not stop there. For more than a generation now, we have been engaged in an effort to create some agencies which would serve the whole society of States for the administration of justice according to law. We began that effort at The Hague Peace Conference of 1899, when we established the Permanent Court of International Arbitration, which still exists, and which in the course of thirty years has made a very great contribution. I think that no fewer than nineteen cases have come before the Permanent Court of Arbitration in the course of these last thirty years. The Permanent Court of Arbitration was deemed to be unsatisfactory by many people at the time it was created: it did not go far enough, it was permanent only in the sense that there was an outline of procedure and a permanent panel of possible members of an arbitral tribunal. So that, with the establishment of the League of Nations, we naturally turned our minds to the creation of a really permanent agency to serve the society of States for the administration of justice according to law. For nine years now, we have had experience with the Permanent Court of International Justice, which has handed down sixteen judgements and seventeen advisory opinions.

In nine years we have succeeded in getting for the Permanent Court of International Justice a world-wide support; not the support of all the States of the world, for there are still a few which have delayed giving their support to it, but the support even of certain States which are not Members of the League of Nations. When Brazil withdrew from membership in the League of Nations, for example, she did not think of withdrawing her support from the Permanent Court of International Justice; and Turkey, which is not a Member of the League of Nations, has been before the Permanent Court of International Justice on several occasions. If it is not world-wide in the support which it has, the Court is; nevertheless, world-wide in the service that it is prepared to render to all States.

v. *The Influence of the Court.*

Now what is the influence of this machinery? In the first place the cases that are actually brought before the Court have a great importance. They often do not relate to acute crises; they do not deal with the kind of problem that you have been considering here in this Institute; they frequently do not deal with a situation between States A and B where bad feeling has arisen which needs somehow or other to be dissolved. Its cases relate very often to abstruse problems, problems far removed from the headlines of the newspapers, problems about which States can almost never go to war. Only a few years ago France and Turkey had a very important case before the Permanent Court of International Justice, which lawyers have talked about a great deal since, and which we shall continue to talk about for fifty years to come; but it was not the kind of case about which France and Turkey might ever have gone to war, I think, even under the most embarrassing and exigent circumstances. The actual cases have an importance; but they do not relate very directly to the peace of the world. I think the cases in which the Permanent Court of International Justice has been called upon to give advisory opinions relate much more directly and much more intimately to the peace of the world. When the Court is giving an advisory opinion, it is sometimes trying to find a solution of a legal difficulty which has arisen in the course of the handling of a dispute by the Council of the League of Nations. It serves as a handmaid to the Council of the League of Nations, which must deal with the political phases which often cannot be separated from the legal phases of disputes. So that if the Permanent Court of International Justice has an influence, a direct influence for the maintenance of peace, it is rather through its advisory opinions than through its judgements.

A second influence of this machinery is that it is building an accumulating case law to guide us in future relations of States. We are gradually adding to the stock and store of international law, and in nine years the Permanent Court of International Justice has made a very great contribution.

There is a third influence of this machinery, however, which is far greater than either of those I have mentioned. That is the moral influence of the machinery on the actions of States. You and I are seldom in court. I have been coming to Geneva for ten summers, and I have never been drawn into a court in Geneva. However, the fact that courts exist here has a good deal of influence on me, especially when I am driving my automobile. Such is the moral influence that the courts exert, not merely in the cases which come before them, but in the cases which never come before them. Such is the moral influence of the Permanent Court of International Justice. It is always possible for people to talk about the referring of a dispute between States A and B to the court; if A doesn't want that dispute referred to the court, it usually doesn't even want people to talk about referring the dispute to the Court. Therefore its action will be very much influenced by the mere existence of the machinery that I have described.

vi. *The Enforcement of Judgements.*

I must now deal for a moment with the sanctions of justice according to law. Being a lawyer, I am usually satisfied with saying what the law is, leaving it to other people to choose whether or not they will act according to law. When the Permanent Court of International Justice hands down a judgement, it does not busy itself in any way with the execution of that judgement. It is not there to enforce the judgement and there is no machinery in the world for enforcing the judgements of the Permanent Court of International Justice. We had one very interesting example of that. One of the early cases to come before the Court was the case of the Steamship *Wimbledon*, involving the freedom of the Kiel Canal in time of war. It was finally determined by the Court that a vessel under French charter had been improperly excluded from the Kiel Canal, and the Court adjudged that Germany should pay a certain sum—I think 140,000 French francs—to the French Government as damages, which the French Government might pay over to the French charterers of that vessel. The German Government was quite willing to pay the sum and it actually applied to one of the agencies of the Reparations Commission for permission to pay it; but that agency would not give its permission, so that the judgement has never in fact been carried out. The Court did not busy itself with the question; it was not the province of the Court to see that Germany should pay. We talk a great deal about sanctions, but in the main it seems to me quite satisfactory that we should have an instrument which may give a judgement, leaving it to public opinion and to various other influences to see that the judgement is carried out.

o

vii. *The Optional Clause.*

In the course of these latter years we have had a great movement for extending the province of our justice administered according to law. The feeling has grown that it is not enough to create machinery to which two States may carry their dispute if they desire to do so; there is coming to be a very wide sentiment to the effect that State A ought to be able to hale State B into court, even though State B will not agree to go at the time. For instance, two of us may have a dispute and you may hale me before a court of Switzerland or France or Great Britain or the United States; you don't ask my consent before we go into the court; you simply go into the court and file your proceeding, and then there is a necessity for me to appear to answer that proceeding, or else to have judgement go against me in default. Now that is not the way that our administration of international justice has been developing up to date. We have said in the past that it was quite enough, or as far as we could go, for State A and State B to have available to them, if both of them agree, an agency to which they might carry their difference. When the Statute of the Permanent Court of International Justice was framed, many people thought that the draft actually went further, and when it came before the Assembly of the League of Nations it was modified. An optional clause was added to the Statute which any State might accept or not, as it pleased. Let me read the Optional Clause:

'The Undersigned, being duly authorized thereto, further declare, on behalf of their Government, that, from this date, they accept as compulsory, *ipso facto* and without special Convention, the jurisdiction of the Court in conformity with Article XXXVI, paragraph 2, of the Statute of the Court, under the following conditions . . .'

Article XXXVI had said:

'The Members of the League of Nations and the States mentioned in the Annexe to the Covenant may, either when signing or ratifying the Protocol to which the present Statute is adjoined, or at a later moment, declare that they recognize as compulsory, *ipso facto* and without special agreement, in relation to any other Member or State accepting the same obligation, the jurisdiction of the Court in all or any of the classes of legal disputes concerning . . .'

That Optional Clause has now been signed and ratified by twenty-nine States, and the number has very greatly increased since the last Assembly of the League of Nations. The States which have accepted the Clause up to date have not been disposed to act on it frequently. In fact there has been only one case which has been brought before the Permanent Court of International Justice under this so-called compulsory jurisdiction or Optional Clause. (It is rather paradoxical that a compulsory jurisdiction clause should be called an Optional Clause.) That was a case between Belgium and China, in which the Belgian Government claimed that the Chinese Government had failed to observe a provision in one of their early treaties. The Chinese Government had accepted the Optional Clause, but various delays were requested by the parties, and in the end Belgium and China reached a settlement of their difference without any hearing of the petition of Belgium by the Court itself.

Perhaps we have exaggerated somewhat the importance of this compulsory jurisdiction. In the first place, it has been accepted with certain reservations or certain conditions by various States. The British Empire and various other States, in accepting the clause during the course of last year, have made elaborate statements of conditions upon which they accept it, and those statements of condition usually look to the possibility of settling the case outside and by some other means, perhaps by the Council of the League of Nations. There is a disposition on the part of some of my friends to want to see cases brought into the International Court and settled there. I suggest that sometimes it would be better for us to say that we want to see a settlement of differences, and that any agency available for a settlement will be satisfactory to us if it can actually achieve the settlement. Now the British have said, very wisely I think, that if a difference can be settled by some other means then their undertaking to go to the Court will not apply.

The Optional Clause might have been put into the Statute of the Court at the beginning. Why wasn't it done? If twenty-nine States have now accepted it, why could not the original Statute of the Court have been made to include such a provision without any special necessity of accepting the Optional Clause? I think perhaps it was wise in 1920 and 1921 that we did not attempt to go too far at that time. The Court needed to be created; it needed to be established. People needed some experience of it, and there were such fears about this obligatory jurisdiction at the time that it may have been wise not to put it into the original Statute. But in the course of these later years there has been insistence from time to time in different States that the Governments should accept this obligatory jurisdiction. It is rather interesting for one to turn back a page of British history and read the reasons that have been given in the course of these years why Great Britain could not accept the Optional Clause. Great Britain has now accepted it, but these reasons were given during the course of this period as if they were absolutely insurmountable obstacles to the acceptance of the

Optional Clause. I am rather disposed to believe that the incident shows that if one has a will to do a thing he will find it possible to achieve a method for doing it; when the present Government came into power in Great Britain, they had the will to do this thing and the insuperable obstacles immediately melted like snow.

Does the Optional Clause promise what people are saying that it promises ? Is it going to usher in an era of compulsory international justice ? Well, there are various loopholes, there are various bases for arguments to be made that the Optional Clause does not apply in a particular case. To be sure, the four bases for jurisdiction mentioned in Article XXXVI are very broad indeed, but, if you will study carefully the conditions actually made by the States, I think you will agree that it is quite possible for most States to contend that these conditions are not actually met. And there is one phase of the matter which makes the acceptance of the Optional Clause still experimental. It has been accepted by various States only for a limited period of time. I think one of the States to accept it for the longest period of time was the Irish Free State, which accepted it for a period of twenty years. Great Britain and the Dominions accepted it for a period of ten years only. Other States have accepted it for a period of five years. When that period elapses, as it already has done in the case of some States, it is necessary to renew this acceptance of the Optional Clause.

In other words, we are still in an experimental stage of dealing with the Permanent Court of International Justice as a tribunal having compulsory jurisdiction. No case has been handled by the Court under this Clause. Most States have accepted it only for a limited period of time, and we cannot yet say whether it is possible through this means for us to achieve a very great progress. For my own part, I cannot but think that it is one of the encouraging signs of our times that so many States are now bound by the Optional Clause. A thing of this sort, if it was proposed before the war, would have been laughed out of court by most people; it might not have been laughed out of court in the most advanced nations in the world—in Switzerland, for example, or in the Scandinavian countries—but in the countries which I know better, I am sure it would not have been given a hearing; and yet twenty-nine States have accepted the Clause to-day and we are launched upon a very important experiment in the administration of justice.

viii. *The Functioning of the Court.*

May I now say a word about the functioning of the Permanent Court of International Justice ? One of the important items on the agenda of the Assembly this year is the election of judges of the Permanent Court of International Justice. If one will let his mind wander back to the period of The Hague Peace Conferences, what a tremendous advance we have made in your lifetime and in mine! In that period we were discussing methods of electing the judges and we could not agree upon any method, because every State insisted that it must have a judge on the Court if any other State had a judge on the Court. I think I perhaps know one State in the world to-day where people are still of the opinion that they could not give their support to such an international agency unless they were assured of having a judge on the Court: but perhaps I am wrong about that.

We have passed that period. No State is thinking of modifying the present arrangement for the election of the judges so as to provide for itself a sure place among the judges of the Court. We have now got, and I think it is entirely due to the establishment of the Council and the Assembly of the League of Nations, a thoroughly accepted plan by which the judges are to be selected without any necessity of having every State in the world represented. All the judges are to be elected this year. The term of all of the judges expires at the same time. This provision of the Statute of the Court has often been criticized. People have said that it would be much better if some of the judges could be elected every three years. They say it would assure a greater element of continuity in the work of the Court. I think it is not a weakness of the present system that it lacks this continuity. Some of the judges who have been serving in the Court during the past nine years are certain to be re-elected this year. Those judges will preserve the continuity, and I incline to think there is less log-rolling when all of the judges are elected at the same time. I believe that with the system of election by the Council and the Assembly, it is easier to get agreement if fifteen members are to be elected at once than if we had to elect five every three years.

We have also the problem of how to get the best-qualified men in the world to serve on the Court. The members of the old Permanent Court of Arbitration make nominations of candidates for this election to be held in September, and during the course of next week a list of those candidates will be published by the Secretariat of the League. There have been some abuses of this system of nomination in the course of recent years. In one country, for example, the Government had failed to name more than one member of the Permanent Court of Arbitration, and that member of the Permanent Court of Arbitration nominated himself as a candidate for the Permanent Court of International Justice, and he was elected. That was not a compliance with the purpose of our system of nominating judges. I should add that in that country the panel of the Permanent Court of Arbitration has been filled up since, so that if the same person is a candidate this year it will not be necessary for him to nominate himself.

Is the post of judge of the Permanent Court of International Justice such that it can attract to-day the most qualified men in the world? During the course of the last eight years the Court was in session on an average of 147 days each year. In other words, the Court was in session less than five of the twelve months of each year. Under the amendments to the Court Statute now pending, it is impossible for a judge of the Court to have any other professional occupation. The question I would ask is this. Is it possible for us to get the best-qualified men, the men that we should like to see judges of the Court, if they are prevented from doing anything else of a professional nature, and if the work of the Court is to last for an average of only 147 days a year? I think it is a serious problem. Perhaps the Court is going to have much more to do in years to come; it has already had much more to do than I had anticipated in 1921; perhaps the judges will have to be at The Hague longer. I suppose that for some of the judges 147 days in the year is a large assignment, for some of them are of advanced age; but personally I should like to see among the judges very active men, men who have not yet done their work in the world, men who have not finished the work they are going to do, men who are ready to devote a dynamic energy to the work of the Court. Now are such men likely to accept judgeships on the Court if the Court has an average of 147 days a year in its sessions? That is one of the serious problems which I think all of us ought to think about. I must say I see no solution of it, though in course of time the problem may disappear because the Court may be much busier that it has been during the course of these past nine years.

There has also been a feeling in some quarters that the salaries of the judges were not high enough to attract the most qualified men. The statement is sometimes made that the men we should want to serve on the Court are earning much more money than the salary of a judge, and that they do not want to give up their larger earnings. For my part I should think that we do not lose very much if we lose from the Court men who are not willing to make that kind of sacrifice. If this is not the kind of public service that appeals to a person, if he would rather have a larger income at the Bar, then I think the fact itself bears upon his qualifications to serve as a judge of the Court.

If the amendments to the Statute come into force, the number of the judges of the Court will be increased. During the past nine years we have had eleven judges and four deputy judges, the deputy judges serving only if a judge could not serve. There has been at times a difficulty in getting the quorum of the judges. On one occasion, for instance, when the Court met with a bare quorum, one of the judges fell ill and it was necessary for the case to be adjourned for a whole eight months. The proposal to amend the Statute will do away with that difficulty. We shall have, if the Statute is amended, fifteen judges instead of eleven, but we shall have no deputy judges in the future. It is not a very great change. I personally doubt whether it is very necessary to make the change, and it certainly has one difficulty. The way in which the Court works is a very slow and difficult way; yet it is very thorough, and perhaps it is the best system that could be devised. When a case is heard, each of the judges prepares an opinion concerning that case. All the opinions are circulated among all the judges, and in the end an opinion is drafted which represents a consensus of the views of the judges. That is a very laborious system; I feel free to speak of it now because Judge Hughes, now Chief Justice of the United States, in an address published in the *Journal of the American Bar Association*, has recently told us these intimate details as to how the Court works. With such a method of work, isn't it going to be more difficult to carry on if the number of judges sitting in any case is actually increased? There has been some disposition to say that the Court was very slow and dilatory in dealing with some of the cases that have come before it. I think that disposition only arises among people who are not accustomed to such delays as we have in national courts, at any rate in the case of Anglo-Saxon countries. The Courts of France may be more expeditious than those of English-speaking countries, but in English-speaking countries we are accustomed to delay in handling cases. The Permanent Court of International Justice has not been dilatory; when one considers the nature of the cases before it, I think he can say that its work is expedited very satisfactorily.

The Assembly of the League of Nations this year will consider also one other suggested change in the character of the Court. The Finnish Delegation to the last Assembly proposed that the Court should act as a Court of Appeal from Claims Commissions or Arbitral Tribunals which may have been set up by two States, and a proposal is before the Assembly for enabling two States which set up an Arbitral Tribunal for themselves, to agree at the time that any appeal from the decisions of that Arbitral Tribunal shall go before the Permanent Court of International Justice. I may say that I do not look for a very great development in that direction during the course of the coming years.

ix. *Conclusion.*

May I summarize what I have said? We are dealing with the administration of justice according to law. That is but a small part of the need of a society of States for the administration of justice. It is not enough for us to have Courts acting within the limitations of law; we must have, in addition, other agencies which do not act within those limitations. We have in the world to-day various agencies for the administration of justice according to law. On the whole, we have made very great progress in creating the Permanent Court of International Justice; though it lacks the support of some States, it is, in reality, a world agency for the administration of justice. Its influence extends far beyond the actual cases that come before it. I think the advisory opinions are more important than the cases coming before the Court for judgement; but aside from the cases before it, any such agency as this is bound to have a very great moral influence. We are now in the experimental stage of extending the administration of justice according to law. The acceptance of the Optional Clause by twenty-nine States [1] of the world indicates a very great advance, and I think we can take a great deal of satisfaction in the actual functioning of the Permanent Court of International Justice during these first nine years.

The movement for the establishment of common agencies

[1] Thirty-four by October 1930.

for the administration of justice dates from the latter part of the last century. It is a movement which covers more than a generation of effort. Under our eyes we have seen it make great progress, and I am disposed to say that in the course of the last decade the world has leaped a whole century forward in its organization of the administration of justice according to law.

CHAPTER X

THE LEGISLATIVE FUNCTION IN INTER-
NATIONAL RELATIONS

Professor J. L. BRIERLY:

i. *Methods of Legal Development in general.*

LAW develops and is made responsive to changing social conditions by three instrumentalities — custom, interpretation (particularly by judges in the form of judicial precedent), legislation. The predominance of the first of these, custom, is characteristic of a primitive system of law; its importance tends to diminish, though it does not wholly disappear, as a community becomes legally self-conscious, and reaches a stage of development at which it begins to formulate its rules of law with deliberate purpose, and to construct institutions for their administration and improvement. The international community, tardily but definitely, as it seems to me, has arrived at a stage where the inadequacy of a purely or mainly customary system is manifest, and a purposive, as contrasted with an instinctive, development of its legal system has become a recognized and an urgent need.

The second of these instrumentalities, judicial precedent, has hitherto contributed relatively little to the growth of international law, partly because international adjudications have been few and the records of those that have been held not always conveniently accessible, partly because continental systems of law do not attach to precedents the great importance which they hold in the English and American systems. It is both desirable and probable that the influence of judicial precedent should increase in international law. With a

Permanent Court of already established prestige in existence, international adjudication will certainly become more frequent. Much has been done also in the last few years to collect and make accessible judicial pronouncements on questions of international law both by international and also by national tribunals.[1] I do not suggest that we may expect to see the extreme English view of the decisive value of precedents prevail in the international system. That would be unreasonable. But the influence of precedents in legal development is not wholly a matter of juridical theory or of the deliberate policy of judges. It has its source in the natural desire of any Court to maintain consistency in the application of law, so that the judge inclines to give weight to the solution of a problem which has already commended itself as the reasonable solution to other judicial minds. The mere fact that decisions are recorded in a systematic and convenient form, as has begun to be the case in international law, cannot fail to bring this psychological factor into play and thus to have an effect on the development of the system. None the less, the increased influence of precedent in international law, though it will tend to reduce some of the defects of the existing system, particularly its present poverty in detailed rules authoritatively worked out and applied to practical situations, will not of itself meet the present need.

For the capacity of law to grow under the hands of the judges who apply it to concrete cases, though it is sure, is also, unfortunately, slow. Besides being slow it is also limited in scope. Whether we ought to say that judges make new law or not, depends entirely on the meaning we give to the words 'make' and 'new'. Judges mould to a new shape materials

---

[1] e.g. an *Annual Digest*, edited by Dr. A. D. McNair and Dr. H. Lauterpacht, and published by Longmans, Green & Co., has now been established.

which are given to them; they do so much inevitably, because, however abundant the materials with which they are supplied, they can never be sufficiently diversified for the infinite variety of facts to which they may have to be applied. But judges cannot make the materials with which they work; they cannot introduce a wholly new principle into the law, or abrogate one that is already established. For legal innovation in that sense, we need to resort to the third of the instrumentalities of development to which I have referred, namely, to legislation.

Legislation, that is to say, the process of expressly and authoritatively formulating new rules which are henceforward to have the force of law, has been described by a recent writer as 'the characteristic mark of mature legal systems, the final stage in the development of law-making expedients'.[1] It is so much an ordinary and accepted function in the modern State that, unless we have given some thought to the processes of legal growth, we may find it hard to realize how modern it is. But the study of legal history has shown that primitive communities do not regard themselves as the controllers of their own legal destinies, and that the notion of deliberately changing the law is not one that easily suggests itself to their minds. They look upon existing law rather as one of the facts of their environment, almost as a natural fact, something which must be accepted and made the best of as it is. As we may learn from Sir Henry Maine's classical work on Ancient Law, a primitive community, if it is destined to progress to a higher state of civilization, is likely to resort to legal fictions as a means of changing the spirit without changing the letter of its law; it plays tricks with its law, so to speak, for the reason that the straightforward policy of

[1] Allen, *Law in the Making*, 2nd ed., p. 249.

changing the law, when change is demanded by new social facts, has not occurred to it as possible. Even at a much later stage of history than the primitive stage of which Sir Henry Maine was writing, and for long after men have become intellectually aware that the law is a human institution which it is within their power to change, true legislation remains a comparatively rare event in social history. In English history there were occasional spasms of great legislative activity as, for instance, in the reign of Edward I, under the Tudors, and in the seventeenth century, but most Acts of Parliament, even as late as the eighteenth century, were not true legislative acts in the sense in which we are thinking of legislation; they were more often of the nature of ad-ministrative regulations, or local or personal arrangements, than of changes in the principles of the general law. The deliberate and constant overhauling and development of the law, to which we are accustomed to-day, by an organ of government existing for that purpose, has only been a regular and normal activity in English government since about 1830.

ii. *The Conference and the Treaty as instruments of International Legislation,*

If we turn now to the international sphere with this thought of the modernity even of national legislation in mind, we need feel no surprise at the absence there of any machinery specialized to the legislative function. The nearest international counterpart to a legislative body is a conference of the representatives of States, the nearest counterpart to an act of legislation is a treaty or convention; but both the conference and the treaty are very over-worked institutions in international law, since they have to serve a number of different purposes which a developed system of law fulfils by the use of specialized institutions or procedures.[1] The treaty does the work of a contract, of a conveyance, of a charter of incorporation, of a legislative act, but primarily and essentially a treaty remains, from the juridical point of view, at any rate in most respects, a contract or bargain, and when States use it for the specialized purpose of contracting or bargaining about the rules of law to which they will undertake to conform, that is to say, when they use it legislatively, it still retains the disadvantages of its origin. In particular it retains the characteristic that what is agreed upon in such a case is, as in other cases, only binding upon those who agree, so that, except in the unlikely event of every State having joined in a treaty, treaty-made law is never *universally* binding. A majority of States cannot impose their views on a dissentient minority.

Let us admit at once that the need of securing unanimity in the process of law-making by treaty is a serious inconvenience, but, on the other hand, do not let us assume without inquiry that it is a fatal one, or even quite as formidable as it appears at first sight. *A priori* judgements on political institutions are no substitute for careful observation of the way in which institutions work, and they are, in my experience, nearly always wrong. On this matter of unanimity, for example, the data for a conclusion are not all on the surface. For one thing, it is not absolutely necessary, though it is generally convenient, that legal arrangements should be universally binding; the importance of mere uniformity is easily exaggerated and a certain amount of diversity of legal obligation in the international community does no great harm. We may take heart, too, from the history of national government in this matter. How did the principle that the

[1] Cf. McNair, *British Yearbook of International Law*, 1930, p. 100.

voice of the majority is to be accounted the voice of the whole come to be established there? My historical friends tell me that the answer to that question is extraordinarily obscure. Certainly it is not a primitive or an instinctive principle of government. Maitland, writing of the English Constitution as it was in the twelfth century, says that 'the notion that the majority of an assembly could bind a recalcitrant minority or could bind those who were not present had hardly been formed and would have been as unpopular as the notion that the King himself can extort just what he wants'.[1] By what stages the notion of majority rule did eventually establish itself is a question which the mere lawyer would rather expect the historians to be able to answer for him, but my friend, Professor A. F. Pollard, who would be likely to know the answer if any one does, tells me that they cannot do so. He has reminded me, too, that even modern national government has not, in every case, passed beyond the rule of unanimity; English practice, for example, still requires that the verdict of a jury, or the advice of the Cabinet to the King, should be unanimous. Obviously the formal unanimity of the jury or the Cabinet must often conceal a good deal of real divergence of opinion, which has somehow or other to be reconciled before decisions can be arrived at. The point of interest is to note that the requirement of it does not often produce a deadlock. The jury and the Cabinet are institutions which somehow work, and there is no intrinsic impossibility in making the international conference and the treaty do the same. That they can be made to perform this function of legislation with a fair amount of success is clear from results.[2]

[1] *Constitutional History*, p. 67.
[2] For statistical evidence supporting this statement see, e.g. Manley O. Hudson, *American Journal of International Law*, 1928, pp. 341–6.

If we ask why it is that a rule of unanimity does not necessarily paralyse the working of an institution to which it applies, the explanation is, I think, in the main a psychological one. Sir John Fischer Williams, writing on the rule of unanimity in the League,[1] puts it in these words:

'Nobody', he says, 'likes being in a minority of one. When it is ·clear that in the interests of the whole organization, e.g. on financial matters, some decision must be reached, a small minority does not willingly incur the odium of putting the machine out of gear. Thus when a spirit of loyalty and co-operation prevails, the rule of unanimity tends in practice to mean that decisions, except on certain special occasions where strong political motives are at work, go through.even against the wishes of small minorities. Strong minorities, on the other hand, have the power of maintaining the *status quo*.'

It is, I think, unlikely that in our time we shall see any formal abrogation of the requirement of unanimity in international decisions of first-rate importance. There do already exist numerous exceptions to that requirement, which are important in themselves, as, for instance, under Article V of the Covenant, in the Universal Postal Union, and in other international administrative unions, and the number of these exceptions will probably increase. But I do not think—to take an illustration which students of the League would probably regard as a sort of test case—that it is at all likely that Article XIX, which provides that the Assembly may advise 'the reconsideration of treaties which have become inapplicable and the consideration of international conditions whose continuance might endanger the peace of the world', will be so modified in the near future as to confer legislative powers on a majority of the Assembly in the matters to which

[1] *Chapters on Current International Law*, p. 421.

it relates. It is not merely that international opinion is not ripe for such a change; it is also that the difficulty of devising a satisfactory and practicable scheme is almost insuperable. At any rate I shall assume, in the considerations that I am about to suggest to you, that unanimity, modified on the one hand in matters not of first-rate importance by certain express and perhaps increasingly numerous exceptions, and on the other hand by the psychological factor to which Sir John Fischer Williams refers, will remain the rule in international legislation.[1]

iii. *The Hague Codification Conference*, 1930.

In the spring of this year there was held at The Hague, on the invitation of the League of Nations, a Conference for the 'codification' of international law. Delegations attended from forty-seven States, including both members and non-members of the League. The agenda of the Conference consisted of three questions which had been proposed to the Council as ripe for international regulation by a committee of experts, who had been discussing the matter for some years —viz. nationality, territorial waters, and the responsibility of States for damage done in their territory to the persons or property of foreigners.

On the subject of nationality, the Conference adopted one convention, three protocols, and eight recommendations, but, in the words of the Rapporteur,

'although the Conference has succeeded in drawing up the texts mentioned, it notes with regret that it has been unable to accomplish at present the main object of its work, which was to provide

[1] In a more technical discussion of the problem of international legislation it would be necessary to say something of many other important matters which affect the application of these instruments, the conference

full regulations, by means of a convention, for the problem of nationality. It has encountered almost insurmountable obstacles, due to divergencies in the different laws and also to the more or less marked tendency of each delegation to press the claims of its own country's laws.'

On the subject of territorial waters, the Conference found 'that there exists a divergence of views in respect of certain fundamental points which, for the present, renders the conclusion of a convention impossible', and it had to content itself with drawing up thirteen articles 'with a view to their possible incorporation in a general convention' at some future time, and adopting certain recommendations. On the subject of the responsibility of States the Conference was unable to reach any conclusions at all.

It is not possible here to analyse in detail the nature of the difficulties which this Conference—to the preparation of which an immense amount of time and labour, official and unofficial, had been devoted—discovered in the course of its work. But I think it must be said that the results of the Conference are generally regarded as discouraging. Some of the hopes that have been placed in codification, more particularly in America, could not in any circumstances have been fulfilled; the movement has been hampered throughout by the thoughtless enthusiasm of adherents ignorant alike of the processes of law and of the general conditions of international life. But even its more sober supporters, who have realized the magnitude of the difficulties all along, had probably expected rather more than this first attempt has

and the treaty, to a legislative purpose, such as the means of stimulating ratification by signatory States, the facilitating of accession by non-signatory States, and the revision of concluded conventions. But into problems of technique of this kind it is impossible for this paper to enter.

given us. It is hoped, indeed, that the experience of this Conference may perhaps be used to make a subsequent conference more fruitful of results than this has been, and the Conference itself has made certain suggestions to that end, which will be considered, together with the whole question of the attitude of the League towards the so-called 'codification' of international law at this year's Assembly. But it may not be out of place, while a decision on future policy is still pending, to suggest a doubt whether the method which is being pursued is in itself a sound one.

In the first place, to call what is being attempted 'codification' is a misnomer and a dangerous one. It suggests that the task is much simpler than it really is. 'Codification' proper is the reduction to written form of rules of law already existing in unwritten form and generally accepted as law. It is a technical task which can safely be entrusted to lawyers, for the qualities that are needed are mainly knowledge of the existing law and skill in draftsmanship. But the codification of international law in this sense, and in the present state of the system, is impossible, nor is it being attempted. What is being attempted in fact is to arrive at agreement, not so much on what the law is, but more especially on what it shall be in the future; in short, the attempt is really, in the main, an attempt to legislate, and it cannot at present be anything else. Legislation, however, is not, like codification, a merely technical task for which lawyers are specially qualified, but one that involves at every turn a consideration of national interests and policies; and, of these, statesmen and not lawyers are the special guardians.

In the second place, if this so-called codification turns out to be really legislation, the wisdom of the method that is being followed begins to appear more doubtful. We codify, if we think fit, for the sake of codifying, because a codified form of law, in the opinion of those who believe in it, is preferable to uncodified law. But we do not legislate for the sake of legislating; we legislate because, and only when, we have convinced ourselves that, not law in general, but some particular provision of the law, needs to be reformed. We note something unsatisfactory, something unprovided for, some 'mischief' as English lawyers say, in the existing law, we frame a policy for curing the mischief, and we embody that policy in principles of law: that is legislation. It is not an end in itself, as codification is; it is merely a means to an end, a means to some specific social reform, and it seems to me that at present we are making the mistake of trying to legislate without having a legislative *policy* which we desire to carry into effect, and imagining that we can succeed by miscalling what we are doing codification. Instead of a single legislative policy, or programme, we have a diversity, due, in the significant words of the Rapporteur which I have quoted, 'to the more or less marked tendency of each delegation to press the claims of its own country's laws'. This diversity of policies is not an accident, and it does not even denote any particularly large dose of original sin in the Governments which instructed the various delegations; it is the inevitable result of setting out to legislate, not in order to introduce some reform which we are all more or less agreed in desiring, not to do away with some particular evil which we all feel, but merely under a vague, not very insistent, impulse to do something in a general way to improve the law. I do not believe that such an impulse has ever led to the development of living law. Law grows in response to felt needs, whether the instrument of its growth is the judge or the legislator; it does not grow in response to the demands of a general theory that more law would be a good thing, however sincerely that theory may be held, and however much abstract truth it may contain. It does not grow, either, without interfering with vested interests : every extension of law is necessarily a diminution of the present legal liberty of States to pursue their own immediate interests irrespective of the effect of their policies on the interests of other States. Its development cannot be a painless process, a sort of easy short cut to an international millenium. If we would pay the price there would be no difficulty in drawing up an international legislative programme: in one vitally important field the Economic Conference of 1928 has already provided us with one. The difficulty is rather to focus the vague aspirations which have inspired the enthusiasts of the codification movement on particular mundane problems which need a clear purpose and not merely an idealistic spirit for their solution.

Finally, there seems to me to be a risk of something worse than ineffectiveness if the work of codification is carried on on its present lines. An unsuccessful codification conference does not leave things as they were; it makes them worse. For the whole purpose of formulating general principles of law in a form which is to be finally binding is to introduce a greater measure of certainty and agreement into the law, and there are signs that this movement is likely to produce exactly the opposite effect, that it is exaggerating existing differences, and even creating new ones. It is not difficult to see why this should be so. When we are asked to bind ourselves irrevocably to some particular formulation of a general principle, necessarily a comprehensive formulation, even of a principle with which we more or less agree, we naturally look first at all its possible implications. We look for its disadvantages, however improbable they may seem at the moment, for now or never is the time to secure our national interests, even possible future ones. Interests which no one is threatening now, and which perhaps never will be threatened at all, begin to seem to need protecting; we reflect that it may be safer to qualify the principle, or to withhold our adhesion to it, even though we have hitherto regarded it as more or less established. The whole tendency of the procedure that has been adopted, and, in its main outlines, necessarily adopted, is to throw doubts on hitherto accepted propositions. Differences, again, that are of no great importance in practice, in which we should probably not press our own view very strongly if a concrete case arose, begin to loom large when we argue about them in the form of abstract principles; I have more than once seen heated controversy arise at a codification discussion over a difference of theory which was in the highest degree unlikely ever to lead to an actual dispute in a concrete case. There is an *odium juridicum* as well as an *odium theologicum* of which we shall do well to beware, and the discussion of general principles is the soil in which it flourishes best. It seems to me that the real service that the movement for the codification of international law has rendered is to have directed attention to the great importance of the task of making international law more nearly adequate to the needs of international life than it has been in the past, to have disturbed the complacency of lawyers and statesmen on this point, and even to have aroused a sincere and wide-spread popular interest in a matter hitherto regarded either as a technical mystery or as not in itself very important. It has been less successful in taking the real measure of the problem or in devising methods for its solution; and it has been wholly noxious, when it has been represented, as it has by an influential school of thought

among its supporters, as a sort of substitute for, instead of
an ideal which can only be realized through, the further
institutionalizing of international life, for which the League,
and, in the present state of things, nothing but the League,
offers the necessary means.

iv. *The working of International Legislative Procedure.*

Whatever may be thought of these criticisms of the codification ideal, the movement does not, in the form it has hitherto
taken, even profess to cover the whole field of an international
legislative process. It is concerned at most with the improvement of the law of everyday application, and that only within
the circumscribed field within which States have traditionally
more or less accepted in principle the legal regulation of their
relations, not with any wide extension of the *range* of international law into new fields, such, for example, as the economic, nor with the possibility, in case of need, of changing
anything fundamental in the international order without
resort to the traditional method of change, namely, war.
But the full function of international legislation differs in
no way from that of legislation within the State. It is simply
the redress by peaceful methods of felt grievances, the
introduction into the social order of changes, great or small,
never for the mere sake of change, but on those occasions,
which must necessarily occur in any society, when change is,
on the whole and for practical reasons, necessary or desirable.
How far is our present international organization adequate
to this wider conception of a legislative purpose ?

It is easy to make an unfavourable comparison with the
legislative machinery of the State. The existence of a Parliament or Congress, with specifically legislative functions and
taking its decisions by a majority vote, is quite obviously

superior as a legislative instrument to the undifferentiated international conference acting under the rule of unanimity. On the other hand, if we look behind the external structure at the way in which these contrasted institutions actually work, the difference, though it remains important, is, I think, less important that we might expect. I have already suggested one mistake which the superficial observer is likely to make, that of assuming, contrary to experience, that a unanimity rule must necessarily lead to perpetual deadlocks. In the passage which I quoted above from Sir John Fischer Williams, you may have noticed that his conclusion was that a deadlock tends to occur in such a system in two contingencies, firstly, where a decision is opposed by a small minority acting under some strong political motive, secondly, where the minority is itself a strong one. But the position is really not very different from this in the State, with all its apparent superiority of legislative machinery. The existence of a majority rule is no infallible guarantee against deadlocks in national politics. When we wish to emphasize the shadows in the international picture, it is easy, even for those who are ordinarily quite aware of the imperfections of the State and its institutions, unconsciously to idealize the latter. We do so constantly when we think of the problem of war as if it were a purely international problem, and advocate, as universal panaceas, measures which every State has practised in its domestic affairs for generations—sanctions, arbitration, outlawry—without having yet succeeded in making *civil* war impossible. We make the same mistake if we suppose that social changes are normally introduced into the national order without friction or just as soon as a majority has decided that they have become necessary. The will of the majority in the State is *not* all-powerful, whatever the theory of it may be, and it is fortunate that it is not so; it is, in fact, likely to find its limits very much where Sir John Fischer Williams suggests that deadlocks occur under a rule of unanimity, and we shall not be very far from the truth if we say that in a constitutional State a majority cannot as a rule, in any really important matter, impose its will in permanency upon a strong minority, and that it is difficult, and more often than not inexpedient, to impose it even on a small minority, if that minority is actuated by a sufficiently strong motive for dissent, which is unlikely to be removed by argument, by patience, or even by experience of the change proposed.

This apparent paradox is easily illustrated from the recent history of politics in our two countries. M. Siegfried [1] has pointed out that in the United States the most important measures, such as prohibition or the limitation of immigration, are not carried by one party over the opposition of the other; they become law when, but not before, their advocates have persuaded *both* parties to adopt them. The position in England is much the same. Great changes like the introduction of woman's suffrage, or the granting of self-government to Ireland, were not made by a majority ruthlessly overriding the opposition of a minority, but only when opposition had practically disappeared. In the same way the real danger at the present time—or hope, if you prefer it so—of a system of protectionist duties in England lies not in the Conservative party winning a bare majority at the next election, but in the Labour Party coming to accept, or at least to acquiesce in, the protectionist gospel.

Only last week [2] three events occurred in English politics, each of which illustrates how far we are from a system in

[1] *America Comes of Age*, p. 254.
[2] This lecture was delivered on 29th July 1930. Ed.

which a majority imposes its legislative will on a minority as a matter of course. The first was the appointment by the Government of a Commission to consider the position of the Unemployment Insurance Fund. It consists of two members from each of the three parties, who are to try to arrive at an agreed policy. The second was the breakdown of Lord Ullswater's three-party conference on electoral reform. It broke down because each party in the conference held out for a policy of its own and no agreed policy could be arrived at. Theoretically the Labour Party might now proceed to carry its own policy into law, or at any rate a modified version of it which the Liberal Party might support. I venture to prophesy that that will not happen. The deadlock will remain, just as surely as it would if legally there could be no legislation by a majority vote. The third event was the passage through Parliament of the Bill for regulating the coal-mining industry, and the process leading up to this piece of legislation is instructive in the matter we are discussing. Notoriously the present Labour Government is largely dependent for its existence on the support of the Trade Unions, but it is not on that account using its majority to impose a purely Trade Union policy upon the coal industry; on the contrary, throughout the history of the Bill its constant endeavour has been to devise a policy which both sides of the industry would accept. Whatever the merits or demerits of this particular Bill may be, the method is not only right, but in modern social conditions almost inevitable. Legislation has to work; to do that it has to be accepted, more or less willingly, but anyhow accepted, by those upon whose co-operation its working will depend, and for the working of modern legislation the co-operation of an increasingly large number of people is tending to become necessary[1]. A majority may take risks in this matter; it may use its power to coerce a minority and rely on the minority acquiescing afterwards, either because the minority is small, or because its dissent does not go very deep, or even because of the prestige which law, merely as law, carries in a civilized community. But its possible autocracy is limited, though the limits may be indefinite; somehow or other the acquiescence of the minority has generally to be secured, rather than their obedience enforced. Modern legislation is becoming less and less an authoritarian act, and we need not despair of our international machinery because from its very nature it rules out authoritarian methods either for introducing a change or enforcing it afterwards.

It is instructive to compare the recent history of a national problem like that of the coal-mines in England with that of an international problem like reparations, remembering that for the solution of the former all the facilities of an active and legally omnipotent legislature have been continuously available. There is a striking similarity behind the superficial differences. Both were questions which aroused intense and widespread feeling. Both were debated for years, and there were times when a solution of either seemed practically hopeless. Both have recently been settled, though in neither has it yet been possible to secure a settlement which is likely to be more than provisional. In neither, again, was a settlement which would have given all that it claimed to the party which, for the time being, was the stronger attainable by that party; radical compromises have been necessary in both, and the party political view in the one case, the nationalist view in the other, have had to yield to the realities of the situation as these have been revealed by disinterested expert opinion.

[1] Cf. Delisle Burns, *Democracy*, ch. iii, v. passim.

This latter is a novel factor, to the significance of which, both in national and international affairs, General Smuts[1] has recently called attention.

'The Dawes and Young Commissions', he says, 'were not only valuable because of the great work they did, but even more because they are typical of a new method of dealing with such questions. In the storm and stress of our time a new mechanism is thus being evolved and put into the vast growing machine of human government . . . They applied the forces of science and expert skill and wisdom to a problem which had been hopelessly vitiated by human prejudice, and they succeeded in finding a solution, however temporary in character it may prove to be.'

General Smuts puts the claim of the expert higher than I should be inclined to do, for he looks forward to a time when

'the Permanent Court of International Justice, acting within the purely legal domain, should be paralleled by a system of expert international advisers, who will have no executive power, but whose authority in the domain of applied science, finance, and all the vastly intricate problems which confront the modern world, will be as readily accepted and will be as unquestioned as that of the International Court itself.'

Lord Salisbury, you may remember, had another view of experts, for he wrote that

'no lesson seems to be so deeply inculcated by the experience of life as that you should never trust experts. If you believe the doctors, nothing is wholesome; if you believe the theologians, nothing is innocent; if you believe the soldiers, nothing is safe. They all require to have their strong wine diluted by a large admixture of common sense.'[2]

By all means let us supply the common sense. The expert

[1] *Africa and Some World Problems.* Ch. VI, Democracy.
[2] Quoted by Algernon Cecil, *British Foreign Secretaries*, p. 295.

must be an adviser, not a dictator; we must use him, not he us. But his function in government is an essential one, and happily we are realizing that it is so. The advisory and technical organizations of the League are already among its most valuable contributions, and they seem likely to become increasingly influential. They are more essential to the smooth working of the international legislative process than the creation, even if it were within our power, of a new organ with avowedly legislative functions.

If it is right, as I am suggesting it is, that we should regard the enacting of a new law, whether by the vote of a majority or by unanimity as the case may be, as merely the culmination and not the whole of the legislative process in social life, it will follow that we must not look for quick and sudden results in this field. Friction, verbosity, procrastination, efforts that seem wasted at the time, deadlocks that seem to defy solution, are not accidents but inevitable concomitants of the process whereby we adapt our social arrangements more or less successfully in the end to changes of environment, and the impatience of the reformer convinced that life is a regrettably untidy affair which ought to be set to a pattern —*his* pattern—merely adds one more distraction to the mêlée. A recent instance of international legislation, the settlement of the Optants question between Hungary and Rumania, is an interesting commentary on that text. The Council of the League was severely criticized for its conduct of the earlier stages of this affair. It was accused of weakness, of improper political motives, of betraying the sacred cause of international justice, and so on. In fact what it did was to look, behind the legal façade in which the issue was presented to it, to the political realities of the case, and it wisely refused to arrogate to itself the powers of an international dictator by following the facile advice of critics who would have had no responsiblity for the consequences if their advice had miscarried. The vindication of the Council's method of action has come in the recent settlement at Paris, and a familiar item has disappeared from the Council agenda. But the price of the settlement was the tedium to which members of the Council patiently submitted themselves through years of discussion over this matter.

I have tried to show that, although legislation in the international sphere is at a disadvantage compared with national legislation because of the poverty of its institutional apparatus, the conference and the treaty, yet the disadvantage is less than we might expect on a superficial view. The justification of such a view is that the processes which lie behind the formal culminating act of legislation within the State are, in modern conditions of social life, more important than the act itself, and they have already begun to be organized in international life under the inspiration of the League. But the institutional backwardness of international organization is not the only, nor even the chief, obstacle to necessary legislative changes in the international field. Another lies in a profound difference of our mental attitudes towards change in the national, and change in the international, orders. In any even moderately progressive State we all, even the most conservative of us, regard change as a normal incident of social and political life; every settlement of a problem there is provisional, not final, subject as a matter of course to revision as its defects become obvious. But the mental attitude with which most of us, even the radicals among us, approach international affairs, is quite different. As Mr. Norman Angell[1] has lately written,

[1] *Foreign Affairs*, May 1930.

'One of the great defects in our attitude towards the international problem heretofore has been to regard the management of international affairs as a matter of settling crises as and when they arise, what one might call the "catastrophic method", rather than as a problem of finding means of adjusting ever-changing conditions—the way in which we regard the problem of managing national affairs. In international affairs we are apt always to be looking for some "once for all" settlement, and after that the Millennium. One of the commonest demands as we approached the Versailles peace settlement was that it should be, this time, a "permanent settlement". Of course, there can be no permanent settlement, since human society, being a living and growing, is also a changing, thing. Suppose in respect of national affairs we said: "Now let us get once for all good laws, a permanent settlement of grievances, and then disband Parliament and wind up the Constitution'. We should regard that as implying a gross misunderstanding of the nature of social and political problems. But it is a very usual attitude towards international problems.'

I believe that this mental attitude contributes, more than any defect in our apparatus for international change, to the backwardness of the international social and legal orders. Partly it is a result of apathy, of the lack of any sustained popular interest in international affairs, but that is not the whole explanation. It is partly also the result of a reasoned view of the right international policy to be followed, of a view which looks for security in an immobility to which international relations never can attain. It is a view which of recent years—I speak without offence of a view with which I do not agree, but with which I can sympathize—has been particularly associated with French policy. The strength with which it is held was revealed by an incident at the League Assembly of 1929, when the Chinese delegation attempted to use Article XIX to bring about a revision of the so-called 'unequal' treaties. Such an attempt was foredoomed to failure. But it resulted in a resolution which is on record to remind even those who do not like it that the Article is still in the Covenant. The words of the resolution were studiously vague, but in my view neither its exact wording nor even that of Article XIX matters very much. Both stand for a new mental approach to international problems which needs all the strengthening we can give it. A settled current of opinion —and opinion is what we are concerned with here—does not suddenly leave its accustomed banks and begin to flow in a new channel; the channel has to be prepared. From that point of view, even little incidents like this resolution are not unimportant. Cumulatively they go to prepare the new course into which the stream may eventually be diverted.

v. *The Legislative Process and the Problem of Peace.*

In conclusion, I shall try to express to you, as I see it, the bearing of this problem of international legislation, that is to say of the peaceful introduction of change into the international order, on the general problem of the maintenance of peace. Recent discussions have accustomed us to regard the problem of maintaining peace as if it were merely one of the peaceful settlement of international disputes. We need a far more profound analysis of the problem of peace than that identification implies. The word 'dispute' is quite inadequate to denote the infinitely complicated series of acts, events, and, above all, emotions, out of which wars arise, and the word 'settlement' is equally inadequate to express the process whereby the element of danger can be eliminated from the situations to which these acts, events, and emotions may lead. Both words are too definite, too clear-cut in their implications, to bring before our minds a true picture of the nature of the causes of wars and the means by which we may hope to prevent them. For example, the murder of the Archduke in 1914 may be said to have given rise to a 'dispute' between Austria and Serbia, the issue of which was whether or not Serbia was responsible for that crime. But that dispute was not the cause of the war; if it had stood alone, it could, and probably would, have been 'settled' without any serious difficulty. The causes of the war would have remained, because the process by which they might conceivably have been removed without leading to war is something far more complicated and difficult to define than anything that the word 'settlement' suggests to the ordinary mind.

This is not a matter of mere terminology, for the identification of the problem of peace with the mere settling of disputes is a misleading simplification which distracts attention from the real difficulties. In particular, it leads to an undue concentration on the judicial, or quasi-judicial, in preference to other, sides of international organization. The judicial side is important, but it is also on the whole already good. No drastic reforms are needed in it. Judicial action, too, is essentially conservative, and though the conservative type of mind is needed in the international as it is in other spheres of life, neither there nor elsewhere can the path of safety ever be found in conservatism alone. In any case, it is a work of supererogation at present to work at strengthening the defences of international conservatism.

The real problem of peace is a problem of adjustment or arrangement, of removing or mitigating causes of discontent, of satisfying when that is possible, and of soothing when it is not, national interests or desires. It is the problem with which this lecture has been concerned, which, for want of a better term, we are calling the problem of legislation, because it is the same problem as that which keeps our national legislatures incessantly in activity. Neither courts of law nor a police force, however efficient, are our safeguard against civil war within the State; they can deal with the violent acts of individuals, acting singly or in mobs, but they cannot deal with the acts of men sufficiently numerous and sufficiently moved by dissatisfaction with the existing order to have organized themselves for the co-operative disciplined violence which is war. Against that the only ultimate security, within or without the State, is to deal with the sources of dissatisfaction, and that is exactly what legislation seeks to do.

No one would desire a condition of international life in which the revision of a treaty or the alteration of a frontier or any other important change in the legal order would be a matter lightly effected, but such a state of legal instability is not even a danger on the far horizon. What is dangerous is to cling to the delusion that there can be finality in one particular class of social arrangements, the international. The existing order will not be permanent in that, any more than in other departments of life. It has been changed in the past —in big affairs either as the result of war, or by conferences hastily improvised to avoid war and arrogating to themselves ultra-legal powers which only the extremity of the emergency could justify—in smaller matters, haphazardly, inefficiently, and generally long after changes were due. The League has indirectly provided us with a better way of doing these things—it has made it possible for civilized nations in the future to recognize the forces making for change before the legal order snaps beneath the strain. It stands for them to use in guiding those forces, if they will.

CHAPTER XI

ORDER AND SELF-DEFENCE IN THE WORLD COMMUNITY

W. ARNOLD-FORSTER:

YOU and I are here in Geneva to-day because we are conscious that the mastery of international anarchy, which M. Rappard spoke of in the first lecture, is indeed the supreme political need of our time. Whatever country we come from, we cannot help being oppressed by a sense that, unless the world does evolve some international order, peaceful and subject to reason, man's new powers of destruction are likely to smash civilization. We must all recognize, too, that such conquest of anarchy has its price: it can only be achieved if the nations will renounce those so-called 'rights' of sovereignty which are mutually destructive.

I propose to trace this process of renunciation of the incompatible liberties of States. I shall have to leave aside the economic field, and speak only of the changes directly affecting war and peace. I want to show how each successive renunciation has cleared the way, and shown the need, for a further renunciation; and, in particular, how the renunciations already made involve a revision of the old anarchic ideas about neutrality and self-defence.

i. *International Anarchy.*

We began with chaos. And it is worth remembering, if at times we feel depressed at the slowness of achievement, that the enterprise of building order out of that chaos is still very young—hardly more than thirty years old. Perhaps we may take The Hague Conference of 1889, and the Argentine-Chilian Treaty of 1902 as the first definite contributions. Up till, say, thirty years ago, no legal limitation whatsoever had been imposed in advance (apart from a few special provisions such as those about Swiss neutrality), upon the liberty of every nation to exploit war and the threat of war at any time and for any purpose. Anarchy was absolute.

I believe one of the most important tasks before the peace movement is to spread understanding of what that chaos was really like. Not every one is able or inclined to study the volumes of pre-war documents published by the various Foreign Offices, or even such an admirable and readable book as Lowes Dickinson's *International Anarchy*. But if you want to fortify any one's conviction of the need for international order, give him the facts about the way the threat of war was used on such occasions as the Fashoda incident or the Moroccan crises. Every one ought to know, as part of his historical equipment, how anarchic, how really lunatic, were the assumptions upon which responsible statesmen conducted international relations, at least so lately as twenty and thirty years ago. All the Foreign Offices were engaged in a deadly game of bluff and counter-bluff and genuine menace, with war as their ultimate instrument. The Kaiser described the game with refreshing candour when he wrote in 1899, apropos of The Hague discussions on arbitration, 'In practice I, at any rate, will henceforth rely and call upon God and my bright sword alone; and damn their resolutions.' The Kaiser was not alone: that is what they were all doing in greater or lesser degree—relying upon their own bright swords and their exclusive alliances with God.

Let us now trace the stages by which this anarchy has been curtailed, not chronologically but in logical order. The

first step in logical order, though not in point of time, was
the renunciation of the right of *immediate* war.

ii. *Right of Immediate War.*

Renunciation of that right, which might be called 'the
right to pounce', is obviously the first, least, easiest of the
possible steps. It has the enormous advantage of providing
for a cooling-off period in times of crisis, during which
reason may mobilize its forces in favour of a peaceful settlement. It is represented by the Bryan Conciliation Treaties
of 1913–14 and other conciliation treaties made by the
United States. The Covenant, of course, includes the same
principle, whilst going a good deal farther. Its signatories
agree that in all disputes 'likely to lead to a rupture' they will
'in no case' resort to war until pacific procedure has been
tried; but, besides that, they accept in general the principle
of legal *settlement* in legal disputes: they agree that if the
League Council reaches a unanimous report in a dispute
submitted to it, they will not resort to war against a party
which complies with that unanimous report: and they agree,
furthermore, in principle, that if a State resorts to war in
breach of its Covenant, they will take joint action against
it to put a stop to the breach.

The practical value of these renunciations of the 'right
to pounce' is very great; and the framers of the Covenant
were not mistaken in calculating that, although they did
allow an ultimate right of war to survive, renunciation of the
right of immediate war and the partial renunciation of the
right of ultimate war would make actual war far less probable.
And it may well be that at that juncture, in the Paris of 1919,
they were well advised not to attempt a complete renuncia-

tion of war, even if they had been able to secure its nominal acceptance.

But whether the decision of 1919 was tactically appropriate or not, a time was bound to come when further renunciation would be imperative. The famous 'gap in the Covenant' has become much more than a mere symbol: it has impeded the growth of international order in a hundred ways, morally, technically, and politically. Through that gap the League's moral case against aggressive war has been draining away. Through it the War Departments' technical case for competitive armament has found admission; for the Departments have been able to argue with some show of logic that they must provide not only for genuine self-defence and for collective action against a peace-breaker but also for a possible private war permitted by the Covenant. And whilst the gap exists, we have had no chance of getting rid of all those political and legal embarrassments inseparable from the right of private war, such as the nursing of exclusive alliances against private enemies, or the irreconcilable opposition between neutral and belligerent interests in private war. Arbitration, Security, Disarmament—all three have been compromised by retention of the ultimate right of private war.

Nothing in post-war history has been more promising and significant than the rapid recognition of this fact. Year after year, with astonishing persistence, efforts have been made to close the gap in the Covenant wholly or partly, and to get rid of the ultimate as well as the immediate right of war. Even before the first Assembly had met, the jurists drafting the Statute of the Permanent Court were trying to close the gap, so far as legal disputes were concerned, by providing for definite acceptance in advance of the Court's obligatory jurisdiction. At the first Assembly, the majority shared the jurists' view; and the Optional Clause was the sequel. In 1924 we had the Protocol: in 1925 a series of affirmations of faith in the principle of the rejected Protocol: in 1926 the resolutions recommending the principles of Locarno: in 1927 the Nansen all-in arbitration treaty, and the Polish resolution condemning aggressive war: in 1928 we had the General Act, and outside Geneva we had the Kellogg Pact: in 1929 we had the demand for amendment of the Covenant so as to close the gap: and in 1930 we may hope to see such amendments formally accepted.

Such widespread and unremitting effort in the one direction is a sign that it is time to move on from the first stage of renunciation to the second: to give up the right of immediate war has been recognized as not enough: we have to renounce the right of resort to war even if pacific procedure breaks down.

iii. *The Right of Ultimate War.*

How far has this second renunciation been carried? As regards the Covenant, the position is plain. We have already renounced the right to begin a war against a State which complies with a unanimous report by the Council: and now, if the proposed amendments of the Covenant are accepted, we shall be bound to comply with a unanimous report,[1] and bound never to begin a private war even if the report is not unanimous.

As regards Locarno, also, the position is plain. Germany and France, Germany and Belgium (but not Britain and Italy) are bound not to begin war against each other even if the Council's report is not unanimous: and they are bound in principle to settle all their disputes by peaceful means.

But as regards the Kellogg Pact, the position is still in

[1] See p. 237.

some essential respects uncertain, for the right of self-defence has been reserved but has not been defined. That makes a gap in the Pact of incalculable extent, which I will deal with presently.

But first, before we look this gift-horse in the mouth, let us give thanks for such a magnificent contribution to the conquest of anarchy as the Pact ought to prove. We are only now beginning to work out its implications: but already we can be sure that it will powerfully help to embody in our social ethic the idea that private war is a crime no better than private murder: and we can see that this renunciation should help to clear the way for arbitration, security, and disarmament. But it is clear, too, that the principle of the Pact, the mere renunciation of war, is not enough: it represents a necessary stage in the evolution of international order, but only a stage. I propose to devote the rest of this paper to a consideration of some of the major questions which the renunciation of war raises but does not answer.

(1) First there is the question: If war is ruled out, what is to be the alternative method of settlement of disputes? and

(2) Secondly, What is to be the alternative method of effecting necessary changes?

(3) Thirdly, What is to be done about preventing or in the last resort putting a stop to a breach of the Pact?

(4) Fourthly, What is to be done to prevent the Pact from being stultified by unjustifiable use of the plea of self-defence?

iv. *Peaceful Settlement and the Right of Self-Judgement.*

Take first the question of peaceful settlement. Having renounced the right of immediate war, we had to go on to renounce the right of ultimate war: and having done that, we have again to go on to a further renunciation—renunciation of the right of deadlock, the right of ultimate self-judgement.

The discussions on the Pact and on the amendment of the Covenant have helped to clarify this point.

At first, the effect of the Pact as regards pacific settlement was often misunderstood. Even Lord Cushendun, who signed the Pact·on behalf of Great Britain, and Mr. Baldwin, then Prime Minister, misconstrued its effect: they declared during the last General Election in England that the extension of Britain's arbitration engagements, by such means as the Optional Clause, was no longer of any importance, since the Pact already committed us 'to settle all disputes by peaceful means'.

Actually, however, the Pact does not do this: its obligation is negative, not positive. It binds us never to seek a solution of our disputes 'except by pacific means', but it does not bind us to *settle* our disputes by peaceful means; it leaves us free to refuse a third party's judgement in the last resort, free to maintain a deadlock. And deadlock may prove a very powerful and dangerous 'instrument of national policy'.

Thus, as President Hoover has more than once emphasized, the Pact should compel us to go on to 'perfect the means of peaceful settlement'; instead of making the extension of arbitration less important, the Pact makes it more important than ever. In taking away war as a means of decision, it compels us to put something in its place.

The discussions on the amendment of the Covenant have brought out the same point. The League's Committee last January, which had to draft amendments, intended only to bring the Covenant into line with the Pact: they meant to stop at renunciation of the right of ultimate war. But when they came to grips with their task, they found that they couldn't stop there: they felt bound to go beyond their strict terms of reference and to propose an additional renunciation of the right of deadlock. They had to deal, you remember, with Article XV, paragraph 6, which says that, if the Council's report is unanimous, Members will not go to war with any party which complies with the recommendations of that report. The original British proposals for amendment suggested that this should merely be so changed as to bind members to take no action inconsistent with the Council's unanimous report. But the Committee concluded that the obligation could not be left negative: it must be transformed into a positive obligation to *comply* with a unanimous report. So they proposed a radical amendment, by which Members would 'agree that they will comply with the recommendations of the Report. If the Council's recommendation is not carried out, the Council shall propose suitable measures to give effect to it'. I have referred to this controversial proposal not in order to discuss its merits but only to draw attention to the reasons for which it was made. The Committee explained that in dealing with Article XV they had been guided by 'the general principle—that the elimination of war should have as its consequence the extension of the procedure of pacific settlement. Otherwise, war would only be forbidden by the law and in practice there would be a danger that, in default of any other solution, States would be led to adopt a warlike attitude'.

That particular proposal of the Committee may be open to criticism: but the argument upon which it was based will remain valid, whether the proposal is accepted or not.[1] Sooner

[1] Shortly after this lecture was delivered, the First Commissioner of the Assembly of 1930 advised against acceptance of this proposal. This

or later, having renounced war, we must go on to renounce
the right to be judge in our own cause: we must accept in
advance some means of all-inclusive pacific settlement.

Growth of Arbitration. Needless to say, the nations
did not have to wait for the Pact and the amendment
of the Covenant before trying to do that. Indeed,
the very first definite step in the gradual conquest of
anarchy which I have been describing was an all-inclusive
arbitration treaty between Chile and Argentina in 1902.
I must not weary you by recalling the various types of
arbitration treaty that have been evolved during the thirty-
one years since the discussions at The Hague Conference on
arbitration. Some of them, such as the Anglo-French Treaty
of 1904, were so vague and limited as to be almost valueless:
others, like the Italo-Swiss Treaty of 1924, amounted to
unqualified acceptance of third-party judgement. All these
efforts have prepared the way for the remarkable extension
of the arbitral principle that we have witnessed in the past
year. Great Britain's long delay ended, and at once there was
an advance all along the line. The Optional Clause has been
accepted by so many more States during the year that its
signatories now include the majority, not the minority, of
League Members: and the Clause, being multilateral, covers
a field which hundreds of bilateral treaties would not have
covered so well. We have still to see the signatures of Japan,
and of Poland, Rumania, Persia, and Chile amongst others.
China's acceptance has lapsed, and Italy's ratification has not
been given. The United States have not yet actually adhered
to the Court, and Russia is still far away. But already the

revised amendment, which will be considered in 1931, only says that 'the
Council shall *invite the parties to comply*': and themselves are not to support any party in refusal to comply.

rule of law has been enormously extended: the right of dead-lock has been renounced to an extent which we are only now beginning to appreciate. And that is not all. Within the last two years we have seen the General Act drafted, endorsed by the Assembly, accepted with or without reserve by five States, and now approved by an overwhelming majority in the French Chamber. The British Government is committed to acceptance of it, and we may hope to see many accessions to this Act within the coming year. The Act is, I think, a very imperfect document. But such accession is, I believe, the greatest contribution that an individual State, by itself, can make at this juncture towards the conquest of anarchy.

The General Act. May I, in passing, offer one comment on the General Act, since it will come up for review in a few years' time? The drafters of the Act purposely omitted reference to the League's machinery, in the hope of facili-tating adhesion by States not Members of the League. You will remember that a covering resolution by the Assembly in 1928 was intended to make plain that, despite this omission, the functions of the Council are to be main-tained unimpaired. But, personally, I have always regretted this experiment: I thought it would have been better to specify the League's role quite frankly, as was done in the Nansen Draft Treaty of 1927 and the Draft recommended by the Labour and Socialist International; and it seemed very unlikely that any State not Member of the League would, in fact, accept a system of arbitration so rigid as that offered by the General Act itself. I venture to predict that by the time that the General Act comes up for review two or three years hence, it will have become plain that the omission of reference to the League was unavailing: the price was paid in vain: no outside States will have come in. And in that case there will be some advantages in making plain just what the role of the Council is to be. The Act is, I venture to say, capable of very substantial improvement, as regards both form and substance.

I will refer in a moment to one common criticism of the Act which I believe to be ill-founded. But first let me point out how much still remains to be done, even now, in regard to arbitration.

Arbitration: what remains to be done. First, there are still many signatures missing from the Optional Clause! and, we are only just beginning to secure acceptance of the principle of the General Act. Where the ground is not covered by multilateral treaties like these, bilateral treaties have their uses. For instance, a bilateral all-in arbitration treaty between France and Italy, like the one already existing between Italy and Switzerland, would be a valuable contribution; though it would, of course, be better still if Italy as well as France were to accept the General Act. Another bilateral treaty is needed between Britain and the United States; for the Root Treaty of 1904 lapsed two years ago, and the American alternative draft has not yet been accepted by Great Britain. From the standpoint of the present British Government, it is evident that the American draft, in the form accepted, *faute de mieux*, by France and other countries, so far from going too far, would not go nearly far enough. The present British Government, with the approval of Parliament, have accepted the Optional Clause without any special reservation as to belligerent rights: and, if they accept the General Act without any damaging reservation, as I expect, they will have said, in effect, to the United States, 'Look, we are willing to make as comprehensive a treaty as you will accept; for our part we should like it to be all-inclusive.' I hope it may be possible now to get something better than the original American draft, which included the damaging provision customary in American arbitration treaties that the advice and consent of the Senate must be obtained in each case. But if nothing better can be obtained, half a loaf, even if it is not a very good loaf, may be better than no bread.

Lastly, I venture to refer to the further contribution to arbitration that might be made by the United States. At present that country, the pioneer of the arbitral principle, is still, strangely enough, the most backward as regards obligatory pacific settlement, although it has accepted the Pan-American Conciliation Treaty. But there was one Treaty, the Pan-American Arbitration Treaty of January 1929, signed by the United States, which did for the first time omit the provision about the Senate's consent (that provision which, as President Roosevelt wrote in 1905, would relegate the United States to the position of 'making arbitration treaties on each separate subject that comes up', and would make nonsense of any treaty of general arbitration). This Pan-American Treaty does provide for a *compromis* in each case, but if the disputants fail to agree upon this within three months, the arbiters are empowered to formulate it. This important treaty, which in some respects is a sort of Optional Clause for the Americas, has been signed by the United States but not yet ratified.

Lastly, American adhesion to the Permanent Court has not yet been given.

v. *Peaceful Change and the Rights of the 'Status Quo'*.

So much for peaceful settlement.

Next I must refer, however briefly, to the still more difficult subject of peaceful change. What is to be done when the rights established by treaty cease to be right? When the *status quo* comes to involve 'interactional conditions whose continuance might endanger the peace of the world', how is that to be changed without war?

These are questions which, as Professor Brierly showed in an earlier paper, become more insistent than ever when we renounce war as a means of change, and accept a system of pacific settlement such as that of the General Act. I must not embark now upon a discussion of this enormous subject: but I will mention two points.

First, it would be a mistake to suppose that no important change can be effected peacefully without formal revision of treaties. The *status quo* established by Treaty is continually being readjusted by peaceful means. For instance, the régime contemplated by the Treaty of Versailles has already been radically changed in many respects: and in some cases movements of population have weakened the case for a change of frontier. Article XIX of the Covenant is far from being the only means of peaceful change.

My second point relates to that criticism of the General Act to which I alluded. It is sometimes objected that Chapter III of the Act, which provides for final decision by a body of arbitrators if conciliation fails, is unacceptable, on the ground that it would not settle, and might even aggravate, the problem of peaceful change. Any such provision for 'all-in' arbitration, it is contended, should be avoided unless and until we have perfected means of peaceful change: for the arbitrators must give their finding on the basis of respect for existing law, unless the disputants agree that they should deal with the case *ex aequo et bono*, i.e. on broad grounds of equity and balance of advantage. To refer so-called 'political' disputes to such arbitrators might, it is urged, either 'stereotype the *status quo*' unduly, or else put too severe a strain upon the system of peace-keeping.

This criticism would, I think, be even more formidable than it is, if the League's machinery of conciliation, &c., were not available to temper the rigid system of the General Act. The right way to meet the criticism, I suggest, is not to reject the principle of all-in arbitration, but to lay stress on the League's part in the system, and to grapple courageously, as soon as the League is strong enough, with Article XIX of the Covenant, which becomes a more important element than ever. That article is still almost *terra incognita* on the League's map, though the League of Nations' Union in England has made one gallant reconnaissance: sooner or later we shall have to tackle the exploration of it, as suggested by the Chinese Delegate at the last Assembly.

The mastery of anarchy will be impossible if dissatisfied communities are reckless of the major interests of the commonwealth, and do not try honestly to make the *status quo* work as well as possible. But, equally, anarchy will be invincible if the satisfied powers insist on liberty to veto for ever necessary changes in the status established by treaty. Satisfied and dissatisfied alike will have to recognize the value of the ultimate balancing judgement of such an authority as the League Assembly: they will have to make up their minds to put up with the wisest and most impartial human judgement procurable; for that is the best they will get. Acceptance of such judgement, whether it involves change or maintenance of the *status quo*, is so easy to preach, so infinitely difficult to achieve. But it will be part of the price of international order.

vi. *Sanctions and Rights of Neutrality.*

I have still to deal with two great questions left open by the renunciation of war: one of these is the question of solidarity as regards peace and war. In other words, what is

the effect of the Pact on the old conception of neutrality?
Here again we find that the one renunciation leads inevitably
to another. The old policies of isolation and neutrality were
based upon an amoral and anarchic attitude towards war and
peace: and if now we renounce that attitude—as we do by
the Pact—we cannot well resist the consequential changes
concerning isolation and neutrality.

Those changes are both moral and political. Both Pact
and Covenant condemn certain kinds of war *in advance*: so
that signatories cannot any longer claim that their attitude
towards such a war remains a perfectly open question. Formerly, if you had asked a responsible Minister what attitude
he would wish his country to adopt in the event of a war
elsewhere, he might have replied with perfect justice, 'Wait
and see: it all depends upon whether I think my country's
interest is directly involved'. But now, when his country has
expressed a moral judgement in advance, he could not make so
undiscriminating and amoral an answer: the least he could
well say would be something like what Senator Borah said
of the Pact. 'Of course the Government of the United States
must reserve the right to decide, in the first place, whether or
not the treaty has been violated, and second, what coercive
measures it feels obliged to take. But it is quite unthinkable',
added Senator Borah, 'that this country would stand idly
by in case of a grave breach of a multilateral treaty to which
it is a party.'

Senator Borah here emphasizes one cardinal feature of the
Pact: beside being a moral judgement given *in advance*, it is
a *multilateral* treaty. That is just what makes the Pact so
splendidly damaging to the cause of isolationism. In substance, it is a declaration of international solidarity; for in
pooling the condemnation of war it necessarily pools the

concern for peace. In effect, it extends acceptance of the principle of Article XI of the Covenant: for it makes any war or threat of war by one of its signatories a matter of direct concern to all the others. It is another recognition that peace, in the modern world, is indeed 'the peace of nations', and that in this civilization, which is like a village of inflammable paper houses, no man may dare to say of a conflagration next door, 'Am I my brother's keeper? Let him burn.'

I do not suggest, of course, that the old doctrine of neutrality is dead and buried: far from it. A few States have accepted neither Pact nor Covenant. Even in the signatory States, and even amongst professed supporters of the Pact, there are still some who seek to keep the old neutrality alive; people who can say with no sense of confusion that, if the war we have jointly condemned should happen, there ought to be more neutrality not less. We still hear the misleading slogan 'no entanglements' used, not as a warning against exclusive alliances or against dreams of a benevolent Anglo-American or Pan-European domination, but as a means of shaking our loyalty to the one alliance that is indispensable— the alliance of all people of good-will to respect and preserve the necessary minimum code of international order.

Isolationism is a comfortable doctrine: and I do not suggest that in changing the status of belligerency we have already achieved the necessary change in the status of neutrality. Nor do I suggest, of course, that signature of the Pact imposes the slightest obligation to co-operate in collective sanctions. All that the Pact or its preamble does say is that, if a signatory resorts to war in breach of it, then the others should deny to it 'the benefits furnished by the Treaty'— whatever that may mean. But signatories are legally free, so far as the Pact is concerned, to let their citizens make as

much blood-money as they can out of supplying the Pact-
breaker or his victim: they might even give diplomatic support to those citizens in pressing claims against the League's
war-stopping measures. But although the Pact has not yet
cleared neutrality out of the way, or resolved the uncertainties about sanctions, it has already changed the whole position.
It has cut the roots of the old doctrine of neutrality, so that
that tree must wither in due course. And it has eased the
situation as regards sanctions in many ways.

(1) In the first place, it promotes conference between its
signatories. It does not explicitly commit them to any action,
even for the purpose of preventing a breach of their joint
engagement or for verifying that it has happened: but it does
render such conference so obviously necessary as to be almost
inevitable. This is a clear gain, though League Members will
have to see to it that the advantages are not offset by the
disadvantages that would result if the League's tried and
convenient system of conference were, in effect, superseded
by another system alongside of it. It is to be hoped that,
for reasons of both policy and convenience, the League
Council will act as agent of the League's Members in conferences between signatories of the Pact.

(2) Secondly, the Pact should make the sanctions much less
likely to be required. By removing the ultimate right of
private war, and of private blockade, it should remove a
potent cause of fear and war-preparation, and should clear
the way for agreement about Freedom of the Seas. And it
should reduce the temptation to the would-be peace-breaker
to gamble on the chances of the Council being paralysed by
uncertainty as to an American challenge.

(3) Thirdly, it should clarify the distinction between
private war and public sanctions: between war used as 'an

instrument of national policy, and collective coercion to put a stop to a breach of the common peace. And in so doing, it should compel the critics of the League's sanctions to face up to the real problem which the sanctions were devised to meet.

The nature of this problem, and even the nature of these sanctions, is often misrepresented. May I restate the problem, though I cannot hope to give in a few sentences an adequate justification of the policy of sanctions?

(a) *The sanctions problem.* We are trying to master anarchy, to build up faith in contract, and to get rid of all kinds of coercion, national or international. Which course is the more likely to serve that end ? To say to the members of the society of nations, in a world still equipped for private war, 'You must each fend for yourselves, and the devil take the hindmost'. I am afraid if we say that the devil will take the lot. Or to say, 'We must wait and see what we feel disposed to do when the occasion arises'. Or to say, 'We undertake to co-operate loyally and efficiently, within the limits allowed by our resources and location, in putting a stop to the peace-breaking with as little injury and delay as possible'. That is the real choice before us.

This is not, as some critics imply, only a choice for the individual conscience, between absolute right and wrong: it is a political choice, too, for the community of nations, between a greater and a lesser evil.

And this is not an issue that can be disposed of by saying that those directly involved ought to practice non-resistance on a national scale: even if that were achieved it would not solve the problem for the spectators, who cannot help choosing, in the world of modern commerce, whether to maintain or to change their relations with the peace-breaker. Non-co-operation may be as grim an instrument of coercion as the use of armed force, as we found in the latter part of the great blockade.

Nor does it dispose of the matter to say that collective coercion is an evil, and that it raises grave political and technical difficulties. Of course it is an evil. (That is what makes the sanctions issue the most heart-searching and troubling in the world.) And of course it raises grave difficulties, difficulties which may indeed prove insurmountable if we fail to make the sanctions part of a system in which they are least likely to be required. But without sanctions the evolution of world order out of anarchy seems impossible.

(*b*) *The nature of the sanctions.* Let us then see to it that the problem of sanctions is fairly stated. And let us see to it, also, that the nature of the League's engagement is not misrepresented. It has often been alleged (and has apparently been accepted as a fact by President Hoover) that the sanctions of Article XVI may be used for enforcing somebody's political decisions. Our reply to that charge is unequivocal and conclusive. These sanctions cannot be used to enforce anybody's decisions: the text of the Covenant and the repeated explanations of the Covenant make this perfectly plain: the forcible sanctions of Article XVI can only be invoked against a State which has actually resorted to war in breach of its own pledges. Fighting has begun: the League has to put a stop to the outrage.

But, the critic may reply, that is only part of the story: besides the sanctions of Article XVI, against a peace-breaker, there are the coercive measures permitted by Article XIII, paragraph 4. That, of course, is true: Article XIII, paragraph 4 deals, you remember, with the very unlikely case of a State accepting arbitration and then refusing to comply with the award; and it empowers the Council, in such a case, to propose what steps should be taken 'to give effect' to the award. But that does not mean that the Council can call for acts of war against a State which has not resorted to war: the Council may *propose* measures of pressure, such as the withdrawal of heads of missions or even, it may be, refusal of economic facilities; but (as Mr. Politis explained in 1924) it cannot 'go further and employ force against a state which is not itself resorting to force'.

I venture to mention this point, because it is raised by one of the proposed amendments to the Covenant. The League Committee has proposed to alter the wording of this paragraph 4, Article XIII, so that instead of the Council proposing 'what steps' should be taken, it would propose 'what measures of all kinds' should be taken. Personally I regret the proposal: if it were read carelessly, without the context which governs it, it might be taken to mean that the Council might invoke acts of war against a passive but recalcitrant State. Actually, I take it, this passage will remain governed by the absolute prohibition of resort to war in Article XII. But if misconstruction is possible, it may be well that League spokesmen should clarify the position in the way I have suggested.[1]

Who judges if a case for sanctions has arisen. Before I leave the subject of sanctions, let me refer to one more point. Who is to decide whether the occasion for sanctions has arisen?

The Covenant obliges League Members to sever personal, financial, and commercial relations with the Covenant breaker; but nominally it leaves each member free to determine for himself whether resort to war in breach of the Covenant has been committed. If this were really to be the position in practice, the League's sanctions would be uncertain and ineffective; but in fact the Council would be handling this

[1] This was done by Viscount Cecil in the Assembly, 1930.

matter, and their opinion would be a guide which loyal Members could not well ignore. A modest proposal was brought forward by Great Britain in 1921 and again submitted to the Assembly in 1925, which would, I believe, do something to resolve the uncertainties of the position, and would help to give reality to the sanctions as a war-preventing and war-stopping instrument. The proposal was that two new paragraphs should be included in Article XVI, saying that 'it is for the Council to give an opinion whether or not a breach of the Covenant has taken place', and that 'the Council will notify to all members of the League the date which it recommends for the application of the Economic pressure under this article'. This amendment lacks, I think, only the support of Spain and France before it can become effective. Without discussing other, more controversial, amendments of the Article, I suggest that this one at least might with advantage be made operative. Effective sanctions may be—I think they are—a tragic necessity. But ineffective sanctions, such as the League's would surely be if they were left entirely to the individual judgement of members, would be merely a criminal blunder.

vii. *Rights of Self-Defence.*

I have still to deal with one more question—the most difficult of all—self-defence. How is a national right of self-defence to be made compatible with international order?

Here again, as at every other stage in the process I have been tracing, we find one renunciation making another necessary or possible. This problem of self-defence can only become solvable, I think, when we reach a certain stage in the conquest of anarchy and become ready to accept certain indispensable conditions.

Within the State we have solved the analogous problem; we have succeeded in making the individual's right of self-defence compatible with civil order. And we have managed this because we do accept the necessary conditions; we do accept a tribunal for judgement; we do deny the individual liberty of self-judgement; we do recognize the function of the police; and therefore we can safely allow that, if violence occurs in the absence of the police, the individual may be justified in pleading self-defence even if it should in the rare last resort involve 'justifiable homicide'.

Analogies between national and international affairs, especially in this matter of police, are often misleading; but here, perhaps, the analogy is permissible. In the international sphere we have the same problem. Article XII of the Covenant makes a great contribution, but we have not yet wholly solved it. So far as the Pact is concerned, the position remains chaotic. And that, I suggest, is just because its signatories have not accepted the necessary conditions. They do not universally accept some tribunal capable of judging 'when a nation has violated its agreement not to go to war'; they do not universally recognize the peace-keeping and war-stopping function of the public sanctions; and above all they have not wholly renounced the liberty of the individual State to be judge in its own cause in international disputes. The inevitable result is that they can formulate no sufficiently clear principles on which to base their condemnation of war. What they claim liberty to defend is a private, exclusive interest, not the public interest, shared by the whole commonwealth of nations, in the respect and preservation of the world's peace and justice.

May I briefly remind you of the declarations on this subject of self-defence by Mr. Kellogg and Sir Austen Chamberlain, not, of course, for the revival of old controversy, but because their words indicate exactly the points still at issue?

Mr. Kellogg's formula was that 'every nation is free at all times, regardless of treaty provisions, to defend its territory' (mark the word) 'from attack or invasion. It alone is competent to decide whether circumstances require recourse to war in self-defence'. The French Government likewise reserved self-defence. Sir Austen Chamberlain, in expressing his agreement with Mr. Kellogg's formula, went further still; and he added a 'British Monroe Doctrine', claiming 'freedom of action' in regard to 'certain regions of the world', unspecified, but evidently not British, whose 'welfare and integrity' might be regarded by the British Government as of 'special and vital interest for our peace and safety'. The claim was not confined to home territory, or to the British Commonwealth, or even to specified areas such as the Suez Canal Zone or the Persian Gulf, or even to specified lines of communication: the 'vital interests', and even the 'regions' referred to, were left to the discretion of one Government.

Manifestly, if belligerents were to have such incalculably wide freedom of self-judgement as these claims implied, there would be a hole of incalculable extent clean through the Kellogg-Briand Pact: and through Articles XI and XII of the Covenant as well. Belligerents always do claim to be fighting in self-defence, whether in defence of home territory or of 'vital interests' in 'certain regions of the world'. Mr. Kellogg saw the difficulty: self-judgement must be controlled by some third party's judgement. Obviously what was needed was some world tribunal. But, said Mr. Kellogg, in his Armistice Day speech of 1928, the United States will not yet accept a world tribunal 'to decide when a nation has violated its agreement not to go to war: I do not believe that all the independent nations have yet arrived at the advanced stage of thought which will permit such a tribunal to be established.' And so Mr. Kellogg was reduced to expressing the pious hope that 'the tribunal of public opinion'—whatever that may be—would somehow serve the purpose. 'A nation claiming to act in self-defence must justify itself before the bar of world opinion as well as before the signatories of the Treaty.' That was the best he could do in the way of accepting the principle of conference. And that being so, it is no wonder that he went on to assert that no principles of legitimate self-defence could well be laid down in advance. Granted his premisses, I think he was perfectly right.

Sir Austen Chamberlain agreed with him in rejecting the attempt to lay down principles of self-defence: and he, too, was surely right, granted his assumptions. For the British Government did not formulate their Monroe Doctrine for no reason: they meant it to reserve a liberty which the Pact would otherwise renounce: they meant to ensure freedom to fight in defence not of a common interest, the world's peace and justice, but of a private interest, 'our peace and safety' as judged by Great Britain alone. And they rejected the principle of ultimate pacific settlement by a third party's judgement. That being so, Sir Austen was surely right to discourage the attempt to find a criterion of self-defence compatible with world order.

But that does not mean that the problem is insoluble. Far from it. And I want to end this paper by urging that we should not despair of this enterprise, which is both necessary and feasible if we will pay the price. We can, if we will, accept broad principles defining in advance a self-defence that is compatible with order. And we can provide means by which in time of crisis a reliable distinction between self-defence and aggression can be drawn.

The Covenant marks a revolutionary change in this respect. It makes not one reference to self-defence, but it challenges the entire theory of a self-judged right of self-defence. Its signatories agree 'in no case' to resort to war (in disputes likely to lead to rupture) until peaceful procedure has been tried: and, if they violate that engagement, it is not they themselves, but the community, who will decide whether they are entitled to plead genuine self-defence—justifiable homicide—or whether they have in fact been guilty of a 'resort to war in breach of this covenant'. Now, by our closing of the gap in the Covenant, by our extension of arbitration, by working out the means of peace-keeping under Article XI, and by facilitating the League's use of the imposed armistice, we are steadily clarifying the principles of legitimate self-defence and making the proof of it more sure. We are coming to this position—that a State which refuses peaceful settlement and gets involved in war will raise against itself a presumption that it is a peace-breaker; and that, in any case of doubt, the League will use the most automatic test possible, by enjoining an armistice upon the disputants.

I do not suggest that the matter is simple: it is perhaps more difficult than was generally recognized at the time of the Geneva Protocol. This has been very evident in the discussions on the League's Model Treaty for Strengthening Means of Preventing War. But I must not weary you by further analysis of those difficulties. I will only say that the League is, I believe, steadily proving that it is as idle to pretend that the problem of self-defence is insoluble as to ignore the existence of the problem.

But it is insoluble unless we will pay the price.

We shall all have to accept the principle of conference:

otherwise the anarchic claim to be 'solely competent to decide whether circumstances require recourse to war in self-defence' will make nonsense of our renunciations of war.

We shall have to accept the principle of ultimate third-party judgement in our disputes: otherwise no tribunal, no conference, can employ a workable distinction between aggression and self-defence.

We shall have to trust that tribunal with peace-keeping and war-stopping powers: and we shall have loyally to accept a fair share in the responsibility for making those powers effective: otherwise we shall fail to destroy sufficiently quickly the militarist conception of security as depending on the supremacy of each over the other.

Those who continue to reject these principles of conference, of obligatory settlement, and of solidarity against a peace-breaker will bear a heavy responsibility.

For we have not got unlimited time in which to master our new powers of destruction. It is very easy to draw a tidy little picture of the successive achievements in the conquest of anarchy, as I have done: but, if we want proof that victory is far from won, we have only to recall the menacing fact that the armament expenditure of the world is actually increasing.

And that brings me to the final point, that all these renunciations I have catalogued will be unavailing if we fail to achieve yet one more renunciation—renunciation of those competing armaments by which each State has sought to impose its own will in an anarchic world. The task of Disarmament remains at once the proof and the condition of success in our enterprise of mastering anarchy.

But I have already referred to enough renunciations of sovereignty to keep the world busy for a long time, and more than enough to exhaust your patience.

CHAPTER XII

THE LEAGUE OF NATIONS AND THE ENGLISH-SPEAKING WORLD

Mr. J. L. GARVIN:

i. *After Ten Years: A Strange Situation.*

THE League of Nations has been in action for ten years with results that both on the moral and practical side are admirable in many respects. But results have been less good in one respect. I mean the purpose greater than all the rest, for it is the League's object of being. Abolition of war and assurance of human peace by full civilized co-operation were to be in our time the supreme achievement of the human spirit. We hoped, after the Armistice, to bring about by this present date as between nations, especially in Europe, a fuller extent of understanding, agreement, and confidence, than we have been able to attain. At least, this was the hope of those who, while yet in the midst of terrible events, were early advocates of a new reign of reason and of law. The actual world around us is not the world which we, the unworthy but devoted survivors of so many dead, expected to see by now. The twentieth century moves on: this is the fourth decade. It may well decide this cause one way or the other.

What are the signs? If some aspects are auspicious others are strange and disturbing. The League is still far from being the League of all Nations. Two main societies, the United States of America and the Soviet Republic, are not embraced in its membership. Systems of government are much less uniformly democratic than President Wilson enjoined. Nor, where fully self-governing peoples live side by side, do we find that their common possession of democracy provides an automatic solution of their mutual difficulties and respective claims. There is no consensus of opinion that the present demarcation of territories is exactly right, or that the principle of equal liberty between nations has been sufficiently conceded. Again, when in 1930, from our political hill-top here at Geneva we look out widely upon the landscapes of the earth, what do we see ? We see that the world, instead of waving with olive-branches, bristles with armaments, except in some bald areas and patches forbidden to bristle, because certain Members of the League are prohibited from being armed evenly with their neighbours. There is, I say, no consensus of civilized opinion that this disparity is exemplary in itself or serviceable in itself to the ideals of the Covenant, though we all know that present means of remedy are not easy to recommend.

In a word, between the appeals for general disarmament and the demand for particular securities there is danger of a deadlock of ideas. Ten years after the birth of the League of Nations there is still too large a doubt to-day whether, in spite of all we have hitherto done and endeavoured, the divergent forces amongst a number of nations are not once more becoming stronger than the combining influences of the League by itself. I say 'by itself', because that, let me confess at once, is the key of my argument.

If this is the truth, have we not arrived at a very serious point of thought ? In our repose we may and must be idealists with dreams. In our constructive activity we must be idealists without illusions—above all, in a cause like this necessarily the most difficult just because it is the highest and nearest the divine, to which mortal men have yet set a shaping hand. In this spirit let us ask ourselves why the present peace-

s

system is so much less complete and so much more contradictory at this date in 1930 than was hoped and intended when the League was formed. How has the present situation produced itself and come to possess its singular features, as though in a dual mask showing the eyes and brow of Apollo with the mouth and jaw of Mars? You will wish me to face the realities of the case and not to flinch from any part of it. You will not desire me to slur or blur any hard and stubborn outcrops of truth which in the course of this inquiry we must encounter and surmount before we can begin to see our way beyond.

ii. *The Original Plan of Peace.*

Let me take you back with me just for a moment to the time of death-birth, which seems like yesterday. The War was over and the League began. Rising up out of a sea of sorrows, it shone like light after night—nay, let me dare to say that it shone like light emanating from the face of God after that vast fire-riven night of death and suffering when the kindly earth seemed relinquished to infernal powers. When the silence of the Armistice fell upon the guns, memory was vivid and conscience appalled. Compulsive was the vision of a better future. Both memory and vision worked then on the soul of man with a degree of intensity that the majority everywhere cannot now recall. Empires had fallen, dynasties had vanished, new nations had emerged, all things seemed possible. I want to vindicate that great dream in 1919 of the full World-League. So far from being exalted above all common sense by impulses of enthusiastic delusion when the Covenant was designed and proclaimed, it was based upon grounds of fact which seemed as solid as bed-rock, though soon to prove as fugitive cloud.

Why did the full plan seem so well based and enduring? Because when the League was created its sponsors commanded together the controlling resources of civilization. The explosion of Europe had brought about, amongst other things, the full intervention of the British Empire, and subsequently the deciding intervention of the United States. This paramount co-operation, never before seen, of the whole English-speaking world continued during the earlier phase of peace. And this created the League.

By no possibility could the League of Nations have been created by Europe alone. Britain and Europe together could not have brought it about. Without America it never could have been established. Nor yet again by America without the full conviction of the British Commonwealth in the same sense and its full partnership in the work of architecture. The Covenant bears the stamp impressed upon it by a powerful collaboration of statesmanship representing all the English-speaking peoples. Amongst these statesmen, one figure indeed was uplifted. Woodrow Wilson, President of the United States, will be pre-eminently remembered as the Father of the League. As matters soon turned out across the Atlantic, this became, no doubt, one of the violent paradoxes of history.

This must not make us forget the strength of the original plan. True that from the constitution of the League, war as a final arbiter was not totally excluded. But, apart from that flaw in principle, the Covenant, when drawn with the support of the United States behind it, was a mighty advance in the state of civilization. Both by direct and indirect means, the restrictions on war, or at least on large-scale war, were made so severe as to amount in practice to suppression. Long delay was interposed between litigation and armed hostilities; thorough investigation and weighty judgement on the merits were ordained; resort to every peaceful means of settlement was commanded; upon any country found guilty of breach of Covenant, stern penalties and deprivations were to be inflicted by combined and overwhelming power. Had anything like these conditions been in force in July 1914, the World-War could not have broken out as it did.

In this way, world peace was safeguarded against the three plainest dangers of the future. Those dangers related to France, Russia, and Germany. By supplementary compact the new frontiers of France were to be doubly guaranteed by the American Republic and the British Empire together—by the whole world-wide strength of the English-speaking systems. Whatever else might result within Soviet Russia itself from the volcanic energies then in full eruption, the lava-streams could not overflow its frontiers. Germany was not deprived of every hope regarding the Treaty of Versailles wherewith the Covenant was painfully associated, for the latter instrument by Article XIX enabled the question of Revision to be legally raised in due time; and, as we are all aware, neither President Wilson nor Mr. Lloyd George intended that Article to remain a dead letter, but regarded it as a vital provision.

There was one thing more. Who could think of violating the Covenant while it had the whole English-speaking world behind it? Who dared dream of that? Who, while America and Britain together were capable of operating with irresistible economic pressure without bloodshed? In these circumstances at the beginning, the prospects of general disarmament with the progress of reconciliation seemed better than fair. The new peace-system seemed as sound in its whole fabric as it was majestic in its aspect and splendid in its symbolism. No, we were not dreamers in that marvellous springtime after the war. We had the right to think that the sure promise of peace between nations had entered into the life of man.

iii. *Pact and Parity: The Invisible Revolution.*

But then came the sudden revulsion. The chief single support of the League disappeared in a way that weakened every other upright and girder of the construction. It was a staggering change, as many of us felt, yet it has proved even more far-reaching than we surmised. I want you to let me look its consequences full in the face. They have altered, and they are still altering, every single factor in the problem of world-peace.

America seceded from the League. Wilson fell. With him fell half the mass of the original peace-plan. The fall was not heaviest in the outer edifice, but within the edifice. Externally, the forms remained almost the same at Geneva. One nation amongst so many was missing. But the nation that went out was equal in weight to any twenty or thirty of the smaller nations who form half the League. Internally, half the strength of the construction had dropped out.

In the further sequel America's withdrawal was to involve certain consequences which no man could then foresee. They were not for a moment intended by the United States, and they are not yet adequately understood on either side of the Atlantic. These consequences affect more and more the whole English-speaking world in connexion with the League, and they profoundly influence the working relations of Britain and the British Empire with the League under the present articles of the Covenant. We must just see how this has come about. The process somewhat resembles the manner in which the orbit of one planet may invisibly influence the motions of another.

First, we must look at the United States separately and consider what developments concerning this subject have taken place on American initiative since the withdrawal. Those developments are of two kinds. On the one hand, you have the rise of American sea power which marks a new epoch in oceanic history. On the other hand, you have the evolution of American policy as concerning world peace.

After secession from the League the United States possessed all the financial and technical advantages required for attaining sea supremacy in the English-speaking world and in all the world. No power with the same opportunity of aggrandisement glittering in sight had ever resisted the temptation. But this time American statesmanship and the American people put the temptation away. Instead of seizing superiority in maritime armaments by comparison with the mother-island, at the Washington Conference they proposed equality. This, as a new kind of principle, is an unprecedented thing in history; and, as we shall see, it changes profoundly every former calculation regarding sea power, sea trade and sanctions.

During the half-decade or so following the Washington Conference, the ideals of world-peace, continually advocated by the Churches in the United States, were able to rouse a popular movement, perhaps the widest and most earnest that exists in any country, in support of the same cause. Once more American statesmanship went hand in hand with the American people. The result was another great stride. The Kellogg Pact was signed in August 1928. In principle—I say nothing just yet of practice—it is stronger than the Covenant. So far as solemn engagements of an almost universal scope can secure, it closes that gap in the Covenant which kept open the possibility of war by permission. The Kellogg Pact, including its Second Article, has received the adhesion of nearly sixty nations—a slightly larger number of nations than belong to the League. The date of engagement is more recent. On paper, therefore, the Kellogg Pact, though as short as it is simple, is the paramount instrument of the world's law. Allow me to recite to you the brief terms of the Second Article:

'The High Contracting parties agree that the settlement or solution of all disputes or conflicts of whatever nature, or of whatever origin they may be, which may arise among them, shall never be sought except by pacific means.'

Never, it says. The point to be marked next is one that no stress can over-emphasize. Here is the unconditional renunciation of war and the unqualified acceptance of pacific methods only. It is supported by almost universal pledges. Yet by many members of the League the Pact is regarded as of very doubtful value in emergency. Now, mark. That doubt does not exist with regard to the English-speaking part of the world. For that part the Second Article of the Kellogg Pact is of absolute validity in the practical application as well as in the moral sense. It is the overriding engagement for all the English-speaking peoples. It is the categorical imperative of lasting peace between them all. In that sense it is every day made more secure by circumstance as well as contract. And we shall see also that this big fact is not meant in the least as a separate assertion of Anglo-American egotism, but ought to be welcomed in all quarters by every thoughtful and far-seeing friend of general peace.

And thus we come to the third and most recent development of Anglo-American relations. It was directly and deeply influenced by the Kellogg Pact. Needless to say, I refer to the Naval Conference held in London during the last few months. The Washington Conference settled equality in battleships. Doubts and disputes had arisen about the meaning of equality in the other effective details of fleets, cruisers, and the rest. This controversy came to an unhappy height at Geneva three years ago and led to an angry breakdown of negotiations. For a time there was unfortunate feeling between the two Governments and between the noisier minorities, though not the quiet majorities, of the two peoples. At one moment there was the prospect of a colossal increase in American naval expenditure and construction. But this further cloud was almost instantaneously dispelled. And how? By a spontaneous outburst of that deep peace-feeling of the American people which as a direct practical force is not adequately appreciated anywhere in Europe. Then the whole sky began to clear. Mr. Hoover became President of the United States. Mr. Ramsay MacDonald became Prime Minister of Britain at the head of a Labour Government. Negotiations were resumed with an energetic resolution to settle that part of the world's naval question which involved Anglo-American relations. The need for more clarity about parity was as strongly felt in Downing Street as in Washington. Persuaded against the grain to bring down their requirements in cruisers to an irreducible minimum, our Admirals were full of misgiving. Happily, American Admirals remained equally perturbed. Despite their professional differences with each other, these gallant sailors on both sides could shake hands upon the sentiment that the political land-lubbers everywhere will ruin us all. How on earth—and in the name of Neptune how on sea—can you ever have peace enough if you are lured to suppose that you can ever have guns enough? But this may appear a frivolous digression into a theme for cartoonists. Enough that the statesmen were determined to settle, whatever their fighting experts might say. That is the guiding example. As regards the English-speaking world—leaving aside other aspects so as not to complicate the present theme —the Naval Conference of 1930 in London was a signal success. It eliminated competition in naval armaments between America and Britain. It did this by the sincerity and resourcefulness of political goodwill. And it secured the parity of American sea power in every substantial constituent and in every maritime implication.

When I say 'in every maritime implication', and say it most deliberately, the meaning of the words goes very far. The meaning is that the freedom of the seas for every kind of American traffic, commercial and personal, cannot be peaceably interrupted without America's full consent; that any kind of unpeaceable interruption never will be attempted nor supported by the British democracies; and that as a result of the new practical circumstances in the English-speaking world, war between Britain and America has not only become unthinkable in mind, but impossible in fact.

iv. *Britain, America, and the Unamended Covenant.*

This brings us to the reverse of the medal—to the British side of the English-speaking question in its relation to the League, in view of such an emergency of danger as will bring us all to the real test sooner or later. That matter urgently requires closer attention. What has been the effect upon that vast, strange, British system which is linked with the League? In regard to maritime and economic sanctions, Britain, under the unamended Covenant, is still expected by some people to discharge the whole of that enormous responsibility which, when the Covenant was framed, was to be fully shared by the United States. Had America's withdrawal been foreseen that instrument would have been made subject to modification and those obligations would not have been assumed without precaution. For what now?

Changes by imperceptible degrees have brought about what amounts, by comparison with the conditions of 1919, to an invisible revolution. We must remember what the British system is. Partly an Empire proper, partly a true Commonwealth, it stretches round the globe. It includes a quarter of the earth and nearly a quarter of the human species. In extent and diversity it is unexampled and almost inconceivable. It knows no present nor past analogy. The essential truth, however, is that it is an oceanic system and nothing else. It was created, and maintained, by sole sea supremacy. Now it has to depend only on parity. Where there are two equal halves of a thing, in no case can one half act as though it were the whole. This is to say that the oceanic system of the British Empire cannot be maintained except by a policy which puts Anglo-American concord first and absolutely excludes hostilities with the other English-speaking partner in sea power. In a word, Pact and Parity have had the most penetrating, the most pervading, influence on the life and working of the British Empire, and, above all, on those conditions of maritime and economic action which the Covenant contemplates. This is the invisible revolution.

How difficult and embarrassing are these consequences in relation to the League I must now show. Take Article XVI of the Covenant, which still stands unamended. My conviction is that its amendment is vital to the League and to the full co-operation of the world for peace. What is the essence of that Article ? If any defaulting member shall be declared guilty of war against the League and put to the ban, Article XVI provides that all the other members shall take action in the following ways:

First, they shall *immediately* subject the culprit 'to the severance of all trade or financial relations' and to 'the prohibition of all intercourse between their nationals and the nationals of the Covenant-breaking State'.

Second, 'the prevention of all financial, commercial or personal intercourse between the nationals of the Covenant-breaking State and the nationals of any other State, *whether a member of the League or not.*'

Now, in my judgement, these formulas and injunctions, which might have been sufficiently workable had the power of the United States remained behind them, are totally inoperative, as they stand unamended, amidst the real conditions of 1930. By the logic of these terms the separate and parallel sovereignty of the United States is ignored, as well as the nature of its Constitution. Its right to neutrality is by implication refused, though the refusal is useless in view of the bare fact that no decree or opinion issued by the Council of Geneva can constrain in the least the free judgement of the American people or change the working of American government. America's freedom on the seas is to be intercepted. Its diplomatic connexions as well as its commercial connexions with some foreign country or countries are to be 'immediately' severed. Yet its concurrence on the merits of the case is in no wise strictly required, under the letter of the unamended Covenant.

And by what executive authority are these decrees to be enforced ? Either it is all meaningless, to-day; or else the British fleet is relied upon for summary enforcement.

Britain is to interrupt American commerce. Britain is to suspend America's financial connexions without regard, for instance, to those very large American investments in Germany which have been made in the last few years. Britain is to restrict on the high seas not only the movements of ordinary American citizens, but the normal communication between the Washington State Department and its Ministers and Consuls abroad. And all this, as though American equality in sea-power were a cipher instead of being one of the most redoubtable of all known realities? Need I say that this fantastic nightmare never can enter the realm of day?

But take the theoretical dilemma. Either the United States, in the emergency supposed, must be fully consulted or not. If it *is* consulted, subsequent procedure must be determined by the diplomatic exchanges, not by Article XVI, to which the United States is no party. If Washington is *not* consulted, the immediate actions contemplated against a free non-member of the League would be acts of force and acts of war. They would violate the Kellogg Pact. They would mean the rupture of the English-speaking world. In that case, other consequences, both in Europe and Asia, would destroy the general peace of the world even more widely than before; and the League itself would perish. An Anglo-American conflict, doubly, nay trebly, ruled out in principle by pact, friendship, sanity, is further impossible in fact because none of the Dominions would consent to it, and because for obvious reasons in the circumstances of to-day it would mean swiftly the economic and financial suicide of the British people at home.

Is it supposed by any sane mind that the South American and Central American nations, members of the League, and Canada to boot, shall take action against the 'financial, commercial or personal' connexions of the United States if the United States demurs ?

There is another aspect chiefly concerning Europe. Article XVI seems to contemplate sanctions against some single challenging State. Does it not seem improbable that this simplicity would occur ? Does it not seem more likely and almost certain that there would be several simultaneous challengers, if any; that the Council, so far as it remained intact, would not be unanimous; that the course of several nations assumed to be committed to the sanctions could not then be calculated; and that a general European war might result, to the frustration and dissolution of the League ? In that disastrous predicament the world at large might be deeply divided upon the respective merits of rival causes; and not only American opinion, but the opinion of the English-speaking world as a whole might be very slow to judge between the belligerents.

It would be impossible for the British part of the English-speaking world to move and operate in anything like the same manner as in the last conflict without the full conjunction of American power or the sure benevolence of American neutrality. This means that consultation between London and Washington would be imperative, and would have to be thorough, notwithstanding the provision in Article XVI for 'immediate' action against non-members. To retain that Article as it stands is sad make-believe. The reference to non-members should be cut out. Its retention can only encourage delusions either soporific or dangerous.

v. *What America is asked to do.*

John Stuart Mill says somewhere in effect that any man who means to be an honest thinker must follow the truth of his thought whithersoever it may lead, not jibbing at any hard inference he would have preferred not to meet. This is a law never to be forgotten. In obedience to it I find myself brought to a conclusion which is the core of this address. Deepened by every day of the long consideration I have given to it, the conclusion is this—that whatever we have done or declared hitherto, on either side of the Atlantic, is not yet enough; that we are not yet justified in assuming lightly, or in presuming at all, that we shall succeed by present arrangements in saving world peace.

The reasons for this view cannot be developed here in detail. I need only ask you to look around and consider with a surveyor's eye those national strains and stresses in the fabric of post-war Europe which, if not eased and corrected in good time, will destroy stability. Remember, also, the rift in civilization opened by the system of Soviet Russia, whose future is still incalculable; whose distinctive principles are not in themselves favourable to the present basis of social organization elsewhere; and whose revolutionary statesmen, while possessing their own visions of final peace, do not believe that intermediate peace on existing terms is the highest international ideal.

If, then, as I think, the League as now composed is not and cannot be sufficient for the world's safety without the co-operation of America in emergency, what further steps can the United States be expected to take? And what can the League do in response? This second question is not so frequently raised as the former; but I truly believe that the two questions are vitally interdependent and that their inseparable relationship will have to be realized.

Nothing will convince the English-speaking peoples that the Kellogg Pact, binding for themselves, is, as it stands even now, of no substantial value to other nations. Were we to assume that this universal pledge and unexampled engagement is hardly worth the paper it is written on, then we would have to assume that peace never can be protected by anything but force; and this fatal contradiction would be a warrant for the perpetual maintenance of rival forces and for the eternal recurrence of war. This sinister yet foolish view sometimes claims the name of realism, but it mingles the perversities of cynicism with the morbidities of fear.

The Kellogg Pact as it stands is a solid reinforcement of general peace to this extent, that, though the United States is not positively bound to take any action when the Pact is broken or imminently imperilled, no sane signatory could violate its pledge and resort to hostilities on the bare assumption that America, flouted with facility, would be practically inert and morally impotent. No more unsafe assumption could be supposed. Against those so assuming might be set in motion with decisive effect the whole concerted resources, maritime and economic, of the English-speaking world. In my idea this is a tremendous contingency that no nation or group of nations on earth will wantonly incur. We may be sure that each rival nation or group, were an outbreak of hostilities threatened between them, would seek as soon as possible to predispose the American Government and American public opinion in their favour. This sort of communication would amount to consultation. Nor is it thinkable that Washington would refrain from making early diplomatic inquiry on its own initiative. As Mr. Kellogg himself puts it, 'Consultation is inherent in the Pact.' [1]

---

[1] Cf. also President Hoover's Armistice Day address in 1929: 'What we urgently need in this direction [i.e. assuring a pacific settlement of international differences] is a further development of methods for the

All this in the eyes of the English-speaking peoples, bred in the maxim that 'probability is the guide of life', ought to be regarded as a real guarantee of increased world security.

Ought to be? But the general mind of Continental Europe does not take the same view. We must recognize, unfortunately, that the Kellogg Pact has had no effect whatever in one great and critical quarter. It has had no effect on the dissensions, the inequalities, the anxieties, or the armaments of Europe. Accordingly, America is urged to enter into closer contract. She is asked to pledge herself— more or less in the spirit of Article XVI of the Covenant— to fortify the defence of Peace in one or all of several ways.

First, America is asked to declare that consultation shall be compulsory.

Second, with reference to the declaration of the Kellogg Pact that settlement of any international dispute whatever 'shall never be sought except by pacific means,' America is asked to take the lead in defining what is meant by 'pacific means'; and in arranging the methods of adjudication or adjustment which are to replace the excluded resorts of ordeal by bloodshed and decision by force.

Third, America is asked to join in naming the 'aggressor' or 'aggressors'; and then either to proceed with full force against the nation or group of nations so named; or else, and at least, to abstain from nourishing both sides of the war indifferently—without regard to respective merits under the Kellogg Pact, or to the present ideals of the peace movement on either side of the Atlantic, or to morals of any kind. (Let me say that the latter fear expresses a gross notion of American

reference of unsettled controversies to joint inquiry by the parties, assisted by friendly nations, in order that action may be stayed and that the aggressor may be subjected to the searchlight of public opinion.' Ed.

materialism which I do not share, but must mention, though with some contempt, because it is far too prevalent.)

What are the prospects for these three further steps proposed to America by most of the adherents of the League? I believe that, as between the signatories to the Kellogg Pact, the principle of consultation prior to hostilities—already in my judgement virtually secured—will become an established rule in consequence of the natural developments of American statesmanship and opinion in the next few years. Equally do I believe that, as a result of consultation, the general imperative of the Pact—where it says that solution of disputes shall 'never be sought except by pacific means'—will be implemented by definite terms of appeal to some mediating tribunal, not necessarily the same in each case, whose investigations would compel a prolonged and perhaps saving postponement of war; while its delivered opinion, even though not obligatory in the letter, would have in most cases a full pacific effect. I hold that it is our duty, and with the utmost of our earnestness, to plead with the American people —plead with them to go thus far in the next stage by instituting as between the signatories to the universal anti-war pact, including all the Members of the League, regular processes of consultation, mediation, investigation, and recommendation.

But as conditions stand, these processes, though of inestimable usefulness, can only be adopted on the clear understanding that Americans are left free at every stage to act in the sense of enforcement or not. Their temperament and institutions being what we know, that people will, in fact, be more likely to act, and to act in the right way, if it feels itself in no danger of being dragged into war against its real mind. To strive with all our hearts and with frank appeal to American sympathies for a further extent of regular but free co-

T

operation by the United States with a view to the postponement and restraint of war—and to the sure avoidance of
some wars that might otherwise occur—this, I feel certain,
is the wisest and most promising work to which we can bend
ourselves in the immediate future.

vi. *What Europe must do for itself.*

But what after? You may tell me, and rightly, that after
this suggested stride in progress, the great question will
remain—how to secure the full and lasting peace of civilization by restoring in new ways that predominance of authority
which was presumptively inherent in the plan of the Covenant when originally framed in conjunction with a President
of the United States. America is urged to complete the
broken circle by binding itself in advance to join in declaration and action against the 'aggressor' or 'aggressors' found
guilty of defying the absolute prohibition of international
war by the Kellogg Pact. To secure so much seems at present
impossible; and likely to remain impossible unless and until
further steps are taken by the League itself and by its Members. It is of crucial importance to examine the chief reasons
for this difficult position, whether we agree with the reasons
or not.

The American people feel—and the English-speaking
world as a whole feels—that as matters stand in Europe, or
must come to stand unless Europe does something for itself,
the alleged 'aggressors' might not be the principal offenders
against wisdom and justice. To maintain regional ascendancies by superior force of arms in peace-time—is this
non-aggression? To resist such ascendancies—is this
aggression? Neither side in such a case is likely to agree that
right is on the side of the other. Here we must think of

Hegel's warning word: 'Tragedy is not the conflict of right and wrong, but of right and right.' Or at least of equal and opposite convictions at the time concerning right and right. Still to-day, as always before, that is the deepest psychological danger. Take the deadlock on disarmament and the vicious circle in which security revolves. America believes that, without progressive disarmament under the Covenant and the Pact, there can be no security for international peace itself, whatever security there may, or may not be, in the end for the special interests which armaments in action are intended to protect. The whole English-speaking world believes that disarmament for its own sake is good and necessary; that it makes alike for relief and reconciliation, for peace and security; and that risks in this direction are the lesser risk. Rival preparations for war are amongst the surest causes of it. Again, the whole English-speaking world shrinks with horror from the thought of helping the armaments of any part of Europe against any other part of Europe in any business of killing, mutilation, and heart-break called sanctioned war. Sanctioned war, like any other sort of war, means the same massacre of the innocent on both sides; and the same fearful divorce between personal fate and political responsibility. Twelve years after the Armistice, and after those first ardent visions of the League, you have certain members of it free to arm themselves to the eyes while other members are forcibly deprived of the same privilege; and amongst those so subordinate is one of the greatest nations of all.

This in its kind is a spectacle of unparalleled inequality, and though we must believe our eyes when we behold it in 1930, history knows not the like. So long as this or anything like it continues, you will not induce America to define the 'aggressor' or 'aggressors' in accordance with formal arguments or immediate appearances, apart from more general considerations touching their own kind of feeling and conviction regarding equity and the rights of man.

And I doubt, to say the least, whether any Parliament in the British part of the English-speaking world would take a different view. Remember that Britain has gone very far in setting an example. While her world-wide responsibilities remain, and while the island is in some ways more peculiarly vulnerable than any other country of the same rank and fame, she has relinquished her centuried sea supremacy; she is at a disadvantage in air power; and her army in these circumstances is less than ever capable of aggressive action.

The chief point here is that there will have to be large measures of disarmament in Europe before the American people can be induced to fetter their free judgement in emergency or to tie their hands in any way. I think they might begin to change their minds if the magnitude of present armaments in this continent were conspicuously diminished and compulsory inequalities removed.

But for any complete change of mind regarding entry into any joint system of concrete guarantees, even of an economic nature, prior steps by the League itself would be required in yet another sense. This question, though of profound significance, is so delicate and controversial that I shall touch it gently and pass on. The close association of the Paris Treaties with the Covenant has been from the first a serious moral difficulty in various quarters, but most of all in the United States, where respect and admiration for at least one of the ex-enemies stand very high. 'Strict maintenance' of the Treaty of Versailles by armaments and alliances, and in all its territorial details, and for ever—that is not a view which can be actively supported by the English-speaking world in general or by the United States in particular. They regard it as a view bound to perpetuate the war-mind and to become in the end perilously inconsistent with the spirit of peace, perhaps mortally inimical to it.

Treaties of peace throughout history nearly always contained the seeds of coming war when war was the only means of revision available, before the foundation of the League. But is the League to be a real means of revision? Wilson said, Yes. A number of its Members say No. In the spring of 1919 many thinkers in the English-speaking world were utterly convinced, and they as strongly insisted, that to provide some peaceable means for the reconsideration of treaties within some given period after their conclusion is a general principle that belongs to the very essence of any good peace system. Article XIX of the Covenant, though far too casual and vague, was fully understood by the English-speaking world to recognize that principle of reconsideration. This question, as we are all aware, and there is no use in shutting our eyes to it, is quite certain to be raised in earnest in the Assembly during the next few years; and is quite likely to become a dispute which, according to the Kellogg Pact, must be settled or solved by 'pacific means'. It seems to me that, as long as the rigid theory of 'strict 'maintenance' enforced by arms and alliances makes a dead letter of Article XIX of the Covenant, the United States will decline to enter into any system of joint action such as is contemplated by Article XVI of the Covenant; that America will exercise a free judgement if an emergency arises on this issue; that in these circumstances, if it comes to wide hostilities in Europe, procedure by Britain against American 'financial, commercial, and personal' connexions, in the manner nominally ordered by the clause as it stands, will be out of the question, as we have already seen; and that, in short, the consequences of Pact and parity make Article XVI, in its bearing on non-members of the League, totally unworkable so far as the English-speaking world is concerned.

vii. *A New Awakening.*

This involves for many European minds a distress of thought. But is it really an evil, and even a presage of disaster, as at first sight they may be disposed to assume? Or is it a blessing and a saving principle that has entered unawares into our work? I believe with my whole soul that the latter is true.

Rupture between America and Britain for any reason would not only be in itself the most unnatural and disastrous violation of peace that can be imagined. It would destroy universally and for generations all human faith in the idea of peace. It would mean the wreck of the League and of every purpose of the League. The means would destroy the object. Every original hope for the ideals of the Covenant, as now reinforced by the Pact, remains possible, with inviolable peace between the English-speaking peoples. Without that there would be no hope. Darkness would cover the waters and wrap the earth.

Nothing, then, to come back to it, is more necessary than to amend Article XVI as soon as may be, by excluding the present instruction that, in the full exercise of sanctions, Members of the League shall *immediately* interrupt the freedom—commercial, financial, and personal—of non-members of the League, like the United States on one hand and Russia on the other. Had America's withdrawal been conjectured, the clause never could have been inserted as it stands. It cannot remain as it stands. Were it literally interpreted in emer-

gency, no surer receipt for universal war could be concocted.[1]
For in the case supposed, and in the actual situation we have

---

[1] The Members of the League have already gone a long way to meeting
the difficulties contemplated by Mr. Garvin through a common-sense
interpretation of Article XVI and its relation to the rest of the Covenant
system for preserving peace. This is made clear by the following quota-
tions from C.A.S. 10, the Report of the Arbitration and Security Committee adopted by the Assembly and Council in 1928, and, therefore, the
latest authoritative exposition of the obligations of Article XVI as understood by the Members of the League. The views expressed in these quota-
tions are based on a series of discussions in the Assembly and various League
committees and conferences, stretching back as far as 1921, and are, therefore, doubly authoritative:

'It is worth recalling here the words of the [Assembly's] fourth resolution of 1921:

' "It is the duty of each Member of the League to decide for itself
whether a breach of the Covenant has been committed. The fulfilment
of their duties under Article XVI is required from Members of the
League by the express terms of the Covenant, and they cannot neglect
them without breach of their treaty obligations." '

'This doctrine is generally accepted to-day, and even if it were not
the Council could not invoke a text or apply a sanction to oblige a Member to obey a decision of the Council in virtue of Article XVI which
that Member did not consider to be well founded. It is the Members
themselves who must decide on the performance of their obligations
under Article XVI. It must therefore be realized that when they are
called upon to take this extremely grave decision they will be guided
by their own conception of their obligations under Article XVI.

'We may go even further than this. If ever the question of the application of Article XVI arose, the decision of the different countries would
not depend on interpretations, however authoritative, or on the deductions of lawyers; the great question would be whether the principle of
Article XVI was or was not a living reality. To carry out the grave
obligations contained in Article XVI, States would have to be inspired
by the spirit of responsibility and solidarity which is at the root of
Article XVI and of the whole League of Nations. . . .

'The application of the measures provided for by Article XVI does to deal with after ten years, the resisting neutrals, if any, would be many.

not take place at the beginning of a dispute but only when it is proved that a serious crisis is no longer capable of a peaceful solution. The question of the application of Article XVI will therefore not come before the Council and the Members without the Council having first to deal with the conflict in virtue of Article XI and similar articles.' (p. 33.)

'The task of the League of Nations is to maintain peace; to fulfil this task it must, above all, *prevent* war. The application of repressive measures, which cannot but have serious consequences, will only take place in extreme cases in which the preventive measures have unfortunately failed in their object. . . .

'In order to facilitate the application of Article XVI in case of need, it is necessary to make a full and conscientious use of the other articles of the Covenant and especially of Article XI. This article enables the Council to keep in touch with developments in a conflict and so to construct a basis for the decisions which it may be called upon to take under Article XVI.' (pp. 39 and 40.)

In other words, the leading Members of the League, including Great Britain, and the other permanent Members of the Council whose action is decisive in applying sanctions, must first deal with a threat to peace through the Council under Article XI, when they are committed to nothing except to regarding any war or threat of war as a matter of concern to the whole League, and to taking 'any action that may be deemed wise and effectual to safeguard the peace of nations'. Such action, as is made clear by League practice and by various reports and interpretations, extends to attempts to restore peace upon the outbreak of hostilities, and may in the last resort include proposing an armistice to the parties. So long as the leading Members of the League are still trying to restore peace under Article XI they will not, of course, turn to Article XVI. And so long as the Council is still acting under Article XI, the remaining Members of the League are not only entitled but morally bound to support the peace-keeping efforts of the Council by refraining from any action under Article XVI. In practice, therefore, the Members of the League would not consider that a State had 'resorted to war' in the sense contemplated by Article XVI unless and until the Council had announced that it despaired of restoring peace and getting the authority of the League

The sane course is clear. We must cut our coat according to our cloth. The Covenant must be rationally amended in its bearing on non-members. Next, we must recognize that in no country whatever belonging to the League does there exist a peace movement so powerful and wide as in the United States, where it is vehemently inspired by religious earnestness, as it should be everywhere. The Kellogg Pact is its consequence and expression. In that movement lies one of our strong hopes: I think our strongest in the world. Show that we value it. Put quite away the habit of reproaches and sermonizing, of nagging and prodding towards America. In the spirit of appreciation and confidence, and in no other spirit, let us appeal without ceasing frankly and boldly to the peace idealism of the American people. If we do, as they have gone far in many ways making for peaceable settlement, they will go farther. We shall see established some practical definition and application of that reference to 'pacific means', as the only permissible mode of settlement, which is the real core of the Pact. In connexion with it, provisions for consultation, investigation, and recommendation will follow. But, if the Members of the League ask America to consult, let them see well to it that they for their part consult America.

We can only abolish war by extracting the venom of enmity; and that in good time, while opportunity is towards us. No enforced peace can endure. Nothing can endure but the voluntary peace between nations associated on equal

respected by one of the parties. And the first care of the Council when dealing with a situation that threatened peace would, of course, be to secure the widest possible co-operation with the United States, or at least to avoid measures that might bring about a conflict with that country. Ed.

[I had considered carefully the general views so fairly restated in the note above before coming to the conclusion that it is disserviceable to retain Art. XVI as it stands. J.L.G.]

conditions of self-respect and fair dealing. When you have the advantage of power, do unto others as you would have them do to you if the same power were not on your side but on theirs.

Thoughts like these upon the future of the League and the Pact are working throughout the English-speaking world; and it becomes essential that they shall be deeply considered by the rest of the world. Though to some they may seem more mystical than practical, it must be remembered that the mingling of the mystical and the practical is a marked trait amongst the English-speaking communities. This has led, as between them, to results not yet reached elsewhere. War between them, despite the far spaces over which they extend, has been in truth abolished. They have achieved amongst themselves the purpose of the Covenant and the Pact. Yet how has this great thing been done? It has been done by methods the very opposite of those still predominating in Europe. Canada has no visible security against the United States, yet for over a century peace has reigned upon the undefended frontier from ocean to ocean. Naval parity, instead of sea supremacy, does not give substantial security against the United States to Britain or to any part of the British Empire. Yet friendship and accord are the more ensured. No doubt these results have been brought about under exceptionally favourable circumstances—as of kinship, a common tongue, intercourse, and geographical situation.

But the chief part has been played by their mutual reliance on goodwill and good faith. They are convinced that, as their exertions have established their own peace, their example can do much to spread the will to peace. Their view is that if war were made equally 'unthinkable and impossible' between France and Germany—to take one instance—the gain to the whole cause would be equally great and even decisive. For them, the Kellogg Pact against war is not only a declaration but a power. They believe that the rising forces of world opinion will make it so. They do not wish the League in its next decade to become an organization fixing its mind upon expectations of war, and upon steps to be taken in the event of war, instead of upon further measures to remove war's causes by the bold statesmanship of conciliation. If Europe can do this for itself there will be no doubt about the response of the English-speaking world or about its full action against wanton war-makers. Henceforth, like Wordsworth's cloud, 'it moves together if it move at all'. For there will be no doubt about America. The moral forces at our call are omnipotent in the age of women. Let us strengthen the appeal to those forces. Let us set ourselves to put them in full motion. Of late, sullen waves of pessimism have surged against the cause of world peace. We shall save it yet, if we believe. If we believe that our aim is the more sacred the less it is yet assured; that a new awakening of the spirit is demanded from us; that further steps as well by the Members of the League as by America are required for the avoidance and prevention of war; and that peace cannot be preserved in the end, and will not reign as a result of our present movement, unless the policy of the United States in the next phase ensures a community of action in crisis by the English-speaking world as a whole; and unless America and the League, formally separate though for long they may remain, are to become indissoluble associates in the common cause of an amended Covenant and an operative Pact.

CHAPTER XIII

THE DIFFICULTY OF DISARMING

Professor S. DE MADARIAGA:

MR. CHAIRMAN, Ladies and Gentlemen, there is a story about a French wit of the eighteenth century who lived mostly by being invited to the tables of the rich and being amusing at table, and who used to say that his hostesses provided the bread and he provided the salt. As my Chairman has invited you to provide the salt for this meal, I will take upon myself to provide a little bread, but, unfortunately, the price of flour in this particular branch of business has gone up, and when your Committee asked me for the fifth or sixth time (I do not remember exactly) to speak to you on the matter of disarmament, a story came to my mind of the first days of Bernard Shaw's career, when William Archer, who knew all about the theatre—except how to make plays—advised Mr. Bernard Shaw about one particular play and gave him an excellent plot. Mr. Bernard Shaw took the plot to the country, started the play, and a few days later sent him a telegram: 'I am in the middle of the second act: I have finished your plot; please send me more plot.' I was asked to come to Geneva to speak to you about disarmament. I finished my plot three years ago and put it in a book, to which the Chairman has been good enough to refer, and now I have no more plot and I turn to the League and say: 'Please give me more plot.'

i. *The London Conference.*

I know you will tell me there has been a mighty conference on naval disarmament in London. I am not altogether so gloomy a man as the Chairman diagnoses me, and the London Conference in many ways has, far from making me gloomy, rather made me rejoice. I might almost say it has amused me, but I cannot say that it has in any way contradicted, or incited me to alter, my position as regards the main value of disarmament conferences in the absence of a well-organized world community. My view is that, until and unless we have organized the world community in a thorough-going and efficient fashion, without any absentees—Americans please note—it will be impossible to avoid the conclusion that every disarmament conference must automatically become an armament conference: and I should be very pleased to be able to say that the London Conference convicted me of being mistaken; but I am afraid the London Conference has confirmed me in my opinion.

One thing it has produced: it has stimulated the capacity for presenting a bad case in a very eloquent and good way, and I would in particular congratulate the talent of the American Secretary of State, and of the President of the American Republic, Mr. Hoover, in explaining that—considering that, if the London Conference had not succeeded, America might have accepted the scheme put forward in Geneva by Great Britain during the Coolidge Conference, and considering that the difference between the building plan implied by the reduction proposed by the Coolidge Conference and the building plan proposed as a result of the London Conference would be something like a wondrous number of million dollars which I do not care to remember— the London Conference has resulted in a considerable reduction of contemplated expenditure by the American Republic. This argument is somewhat involved, but you might put it perhaps a little more easily in the form of a parable. A sinner arrives in heaven and asks St. Peter for admittance there, and St. Peter says: 'What have you to say on your behalf?' The sinner says: 'I am sixty. I might have sinned, let us say, at the rate of three sins a day—that would have been about 60,000 sins. I only sinned 30,000 times; that means I am 30,000 to the good, and I deserve to come in.' I do not know what the answer would have been to this argument. I know my answer. If I had been in the place of St. Peter, I would have said: 'Your argument is excellent; you are absolutely right. Considering you are a human being, you might have sinned far more than you have sinned. You do deserve theoretically to enter heaven, but, considering you are not in the least humble about it, but are very proud of it, down you go.'

ii. *The Expenditure on Armaments.*

Meanwhile, what is happening? What is happening is that when I wrote my book on disarmament the world was spending roughly at the rate of about 3,800 million dollars a year in armaments. It is now calculated by people who can count up to these astronomical figures—I cannot—that the world is spending in armaments at the rate of 4,300–4,400 million dollars a year. The United States is spending now at the rate of 773 million dollars a year, which is 24 per cent. more than three years ago; Great Britain is in a very good way, it is spending 550 millions, which is 8 per cent. less than three years ago; France is spending 357 millions, or about 50 per cent. more than three years ago; Italy is spending 321 millions, which is 27 per cent. more; and Japan 215 millions, or 1 per cent. more. Finally, there are our friends the Russians, who are spending at the rate of 481 million dollars, which is 84 per cent. more than three years ago. We are getting on nicely!

Let us now imagine that the League of Nations comes along and says to all the nations of the world: 'We have the deepest respect for your sense of security and we do not in the least want you to stop spending all these sums now, but we would ask you for a tiny bit of generosity towards our budget. Would you mind giving us 3 per cent., not more than 3 per cent., of your military, naval, and air expenditure of only one year and only once in the history of the world— we shall never come back again—we only ask that in this year 1930 you give us 3 per cent. of your armament budgets.' Very well, we take that money and we put it into the League bank. What is the result? The result is that the League will not have to bother any more about a budget for the rest of history. It will be able to carry on on the 5 per cent. dividend on that sum very comfortably, without ever having to have a budget voted by the Assembly, or to have the budget ratified by any commission, any Parliament, any authority. Three per cent. of the yearly expenditure on armaments of the present-day world is enough to constitute a capital fund, the 5 per cent. interest on which is more than 6 million dollars a year, which is rather more than what the League is spending at present.

That is the appalling relation between what the world is doing to defend itself against its own absurd idea of its own insecurity and what the world is doing to organize the peace of the future and the community according to which human beings ought to live.

iii. *The Pacifists.*

But why this barrenness in results? Why, in the presence of this extraordinary contrast between the monies spent in preparing for war and the monies spent in preparing for peace, this barrenness, these years without any progress, without any tangible success? That is the point which I should like to discuss to-day before you.

To begin with, I want to be quite frank about it. I believe that one of the heaviest responsibilities lies with the Pacifists. They have got the wrong end of the stick. It is no use putting before people that war is horrible; that war is bloody; that war is criminal; that war evokes in men the wrong feelings of animal fury and of primeval forces of nature. It is no good, because men, all men, love these things. Men love fight, they love struggle, they love courage, they love risking their lives, they love self-sacrifice; they love the glory of war, and, if you want a proof of it, look at the extraordinary success of war books and the war plays. Oh, I know that war books and war plays pretend or claim, most of them at any rate, to present war under a disagreeable aspect; but have you noticed how every one looks at the ugliest face in a drawing-room? No one looks at the most beautiful: every one looks at the ugliest face; the gaze seems glued to it. There is a fascination in unpleasantness and horror. Similarly with war books. All this popularity of war books—Do you mean to say that it is because people say: 'Look at the horrible thing—I hate it: I am going to buy another war book to show myself how much I hate war'? No, it is because people like it: they like the excitement of it; they like the excitement and the horror of it. War is an evil that fascinates human beings, and it isn't by condemning it as an evil that you are going to abolish it. The true policy of the anti-war campaign must be a constructive policy which will appeal not to the emotions but to the reason of people, which will make them realize that the struggle for peace is an even more difficult struggle than the struggle for war; that it requires much heavier and far more difficult sacrifices than the struggle for war, and that, after all, it is a far more noble and difficult thing to consecrate one's life to an exacting task than to give it up in one minute of excitement. That is, I think, one of the reasons why we are not getting on, because the atmosphere, the wide atmosphere of public opinion, is not prepared for what our efforts mean. The public do not really understand, are not really and profoundly interested in, our anti-war efforts. Why should there be any war? They don't realize the importance of this fact. They are far too much interested in the side issues, the side-shows of war, even in the interesting spectacle and sight of big fleets and big armies. Even at this late hour they are very much impressed by a direct and friendly attack on the evils of war, yet they are not sufficiently interested in public affairs, and do not sufficiently understand the technicalities of public affairs, to realize what an extraordinarily difficult thing it is that the organization of the world should be set on its feet in order to stop all drifting towards war. And here is the fundamental opposition. We drift into war, but we must build up peace by conscious and continuous and methodical effort. There is nothing wanted to go to war except to let oneself go; but, if you want to get peace in the world against all the forces of nature that tend naturally to produce war, you are going to work for it with all your brain, and with all your heart, and with all your effort. And it is because it is far more difficult to have peace than to have war that, human beings being lazy, we go down more easily into war than we ascend to peace. In point of fact, we have never had real peace in the whole history of the Western world.

iv. *General Principles of Disarmament.*

Let me now, before I come more directly into my subject, recall what I consider to be the general principles without which I do not believe that this problem of disarmament can be understood, nor any of the incidents and episodes of it be accurately estimated. The first of them is that disarmament is not a problem in itself, but only one of the aspects of the fundamental problem of international life. There is no problem of armaments. It is one of the forms, one of the aspects of the problem of international life; but it is only one.

I should like to be sure that we are agreed on this point. I should like to be sure because there are some people who do not agree with me about it. For instance, such an eminent, well-meaning, and active propagandist of peace as Mr. Clayton C. Morrison of Chicago, believes, if I have understood him on these matters, that the problem of armaments or its cause, the problem of war, can be isolated, and not mixed at all with the other political and economic questions that complicate it. I think that that is wrong, and in these times of compromise and of confused ideas, and of give and take, I think it is good that, when we are sure that an idea is right and an idea is wrong, we should say so quite clearly. I think it is wrong to imagine that the problem of war is isolated. In my opinion it is one of the aspects of international life and it cannot be separated from the other aspects thereof without wasting our time in academic discussions. That is my first point.

My second point, which in reality develops the first and emphasizes it, is that the problem of armaments is not a fundamental problem of international life. It is only a symptomatic problem; it is a symptom, not a disease.

It is true that there are certain symptoms which, if sufficiently strong, may determine the death of the patient. We all know the symptom of temperature. Temperature in a patient is a symptom, but in some diseases it may go so high that it may itself, though a symptom of disease, actually kill the patient off. Therefore, I do not deny that the problem may acquire in certain circumstances—I believe it is now beginning to acquire—a fundamental importance, though a symptom. Nevertheless, if we want to approach it with intelligence, we must realize that it is not an essential problem of the body politic of international life, of international society, but a symptomatic problem.

And now my third point, which again flows from the second and the first and explains them both. What is the disease then, if disarmament, or rather armament, is only a symptom? What is the disease? The disease is that war between nations is not merely the military war with which our imagination is accustomed to connect the idea of this word 'war'. Military wars, which I call hostilities, are only acute fits in a permanent endemic disease of the world, which is war, and it is because war is permanently with us that we are all the time on the verge of hostilities. It may occur at any time, it may occur this very minute, because we suffer from chronic war.

I believe that now the background of our general ideas is complete, at least sufficiently so to approach the problem I want to put before you this afternoon, with some chance of solving it.

v. *Two Methods.*

I should like to draw your attention to a most peculiar set of circumstances. What is the way in which the problem of disarmament has been approached? It has been approached by a mixture of two different methods, inspired in their turn by two different schools of thought. The people who emphasize the question of armaments in themselves, and who say: 'Let us at once deal with the reduction of armaments', insisted on having disarmament commissions, technical experts, disarmament conferences. That explains the Preparatory Commission for Disarmament; that explains the Coolidge Conference, the Washington Conference, and the London Conference. But at the same time other people say: 'No, armaments are only there because there is insecurity in the world. We must organize the civilian side of the world so that there is no chance of attack to the world community. Therefore we must have something else.' And that explains in general the work of the League in relation to security and arbitration; the development of The Hague Court; and finally, as an offshoot of this idea in the American continent, the Kellogg Pact.

Here are two sets of facts. Every one knows that the first set of facts, that which has tried to reduce or limit armaments in themselves, has not made anything like such headway as the second. But in this contrast there lies the source of a very melancholy meditation. Let us look at the progress of arbitration and the progress of friendly treaties and intercourse between nations in the last ten years. It is impressive. There is no question about it. No one could dream in 1914 of anything approaching the magnificent economy of the Covenant of the League of Nations from the point of view of self-denial and of belief and trust in an international judiciary, and in arbitration and conciliation methods. No one could have dreamt of it. And there is the Covenant, signed and ratified by practically every nation in the world,

except three or four; two of which I must confess are very
important.

And then there comes the Treaty of Locarno. One year
before Locarno, no one would have dreamt that nations which
had been through all the terrible tragedy of 1914–18, such
as France and Germany, would sign such an extraordinarily
statesmanlike and advanced document as the Locarno Treaty;
and there is the Treaty, signed and ratified by those very
nations.

Then there is the perfect maze of treaties on conciliation
and arbitration passed in Europe and America, not forgetting
those prepared by the Pan-American Washington Conference,
led by Mr. Hughes, one of which, at any rate, if I am not
mistaken, is already ratified by the Senate, and another will, I
hope, be soon discussed by that august, if slow, body.

And that is not all. Then comes the Kellogg Pact, and
the Kellogg Pact say: 'No more war'. No one would have
believed, say three years previously, that a treaty proscribing
war from the world would be signed by responsible Governments: such an uncompromising treaty, too, without the
slightest reservation in the actual body of it. But there it is,
every nation that matters having signed and ratified it. And,
finally, the optional clause of compulsory jurisdiction, so
awe-inspiring but a few years ago, is now signed and ratified
by many great Powers, while America itself draws nearer
to The Hague Court by a few inches a year. So here we go
year after year depositing solemn oaths on the altar of international peace; and year after year with the other hand
depositing millions on the altar of war. What does that
mean? Does it mean that we are following the precept in
the Gospel, which I thought applied only to pianists: 'Let
not thy right hand know what thy left hand doeth'? Does

it also apply to Governments? Are they signing treaties of
no-war with the right hand and signing contracts of armaments with the left as hard as they can do it? The figures
I gave you at the beginning of my address show you that the
hands of naval war secretaries in the signing of war contracts
have been no less busy than those of peace-loving foreign
secretaries signing contracts of peace.

But isn't this a very serious state of affairs? Doesn't this
look as if the more oaths there are about the less they are
worth? Is it that the law of supply and demand applies to
national oaths of peace? I do not want to be gloomy. I was
forewarned by our Chairman. I don't want to be gloomy;
I am constitutionally an optimist, but surely I want to be a
realist as well. An idealist need not be a fool, and, if there
was any dilemma between dropping idealism or dropping
wisdom, I would drop idealism right enough.

The problem before us is that we have all signed and
ratified that we are not going to have any war, and at the
same time we are all arming to the teeth, and the only conclusion to be drawn from this is that there are far too many
oaths about, and that it is high time we stopped both swearing
that we are going to keep peace and trying to reduce armaments, because we cannot do it. We must try something else.

Now I put this before you. If swearing that we are going
to keep the peace is not enough to stop armaments—if having
direct conferences to stop armaments is not enough to stop
armaments—is there a method which is going to succeed
where these two methods have failed?

Let me, before I answer that question—of course in the
affirmative—let me give you my reason why, or at least one
of the reasons why, this gradual cheapening of the value of
oaths is going on in the world. I believe it is due to the fact

that the nations that sign these papers are in a period of transition, and that they have not succeeded in creating, either in their national public opinions or in international opinion, sufficient harmony between the conflicting ideas which hold the field. There is a Spanish proverb which says that it is good to go on hammering and at the same time praying to God. Nations go on praying to God but, at the same time, 'in case', they go on hammering. Here is the dualism in human nature manifested in our everyday national politics. Now it is no good condemning statesmen in general, much as I would like to attempt to condemn one or two, because there it is. They are held by these tendencies, which go in different directions; and, as men in Government cannot govern in the void, as they must govern with the materials they have in their hands, it is evident that the finished product of statesmanship must reflect the rather motley colour of the human clay that the artist is handling. Therefore I do not propose to take an extremist view of the situation and to condemn wholesale this kind of muddle-headed statesmanship. Nevertheless, I should like to point out a kind of very brief course of evolution which explains the plight in which we are to-day. I may be mistaken, and, if I am, I hope you will point it out to me in the hour of retaliation that generally follows this speech.

I have a feeling that the whole trouble comes from the morning of headachy moodiness that followed the night of orgy after the Peace Conference. There was such an orgy of generosity and idealism in that conference that on the next-day several people felt headachy about it. I am very sorry that I unwittingly landed myself in this metaphor, because a night of orgy is not the kind of thing that goes with the Puritan memories of Woodrow Wilson, but I should say that the fact that the American nation awoke to a perhaps exaggerated sense of realities after the exhilarating effects produced by the Covenant, was the origin of the wave of reaction from which we are now suffering. I do not want to give the impression that I entertain censorious views about the backing out of the Covenant of America. I believe, and I ask that I may be corrected if I am mistaken, that the only reason why America did not ratify the Covenant is because of the slow movements of the Senate. If every other nation had had such a slow body for ratifying treaties, very few of them would have ratified the thing. If any one had noticed what was inside, few would have ratified it. If the Covenant were put to-day as a fresh proposition to any nation in the world, it would not have a chance anywhere. That is my honest opinion.

vi. *The Responsibilities of America.*

I want to say that because, nevertheless, I take a very serious view of the responsibilities of the American nation in this business. I think they can be easily explained in a way which does not in the least reflect upon the American nation, but the responsibilities remain. In my opinion, the original responsibility for the wave of reaction which we are at present passing through must be traced back to this unfortunate fact that the American nation did not see its way to ratify the Covenant.

Why? First, because of the moral effect of it. America backed out of the international community. We need not discuss the reasons. They may have been the best reasons possible. That is irrelevant. It is the effect that matters. America claimed back her liberty from this constitution, from this pact. And, therefore, that example, which is

infinitely more important than any argument, as you all
know who have read the Gospels, that example went right
through every other national character and psychology, and
in every nation in the world there was this feeling, unex-
pressed, perhaps—perhaps subconscious—that, after all, we
wish we were as free as the Americans are. They took the
right course. They are independent; we wish we were as
independent. And that creates inside the Covenant an
antagonistic tendency to get away from it. That moral
effect added itself to the natural effect which, in every nation,
was produced by the cooling off from enthusiasm ; and, when
people began to realize the very important inferences of that
wonderful document and, when encouraged by the American
example, began to find ways, to imagine arguments, to consider possibilities, there began a period of whittling down of
the meaning of the Covenant. The Covenant began to lose
in meaning—began to be impoverished from the inside. Add
to it that, with the disappearance of America, England became
the main prop of the Covenant. Now England, for reasons
that must be respected because they are very grave, cannot
consider the practical possibility of coming to a break with the
nation outside the League framework with which it is linked
with the closest ties of civilization and language. And then all
the clauses of the Covenant in which there was the possibility
of such a breach—or, even without arriving at the idea of
breach, of friction—were immediately considered by England
as impracticable, outside the pale of practical politics; and,
therefore, all those clauses became inoperative in the imagination of statesmen, which amounts to saying that they disappeared from the Covenant, in so far as the Covenant is a
living thing in international politics and not merely a dead
letter contract.

vi. *The Present Condition of Europe.*

And then there came the reaction from the war—the dis-
illusionment about the distribution of dividends; the quarrels,
the territorial difficulties, the jealousies about mandates;
natural reactions which tended to develop national fears for
the nations that had swallowed, perhaps, more than they
could digest, lest they should be deprived of their gains; a
state of unpleasantness on the part of nations that had been
deprived of more than they ought to have been deprived,
according to their way of looking at it. It was quite natural.
And, in the end, there tends to develop in the world a position
of international politics which differs practically in nothing
from the position which obtained in 1914. There is no need
of suspecting the good faith of any one of the nations that
signed the Covenant. They signed the Covenant in good
faith. I think they meant to apply it in good faith in so far
as they could and in so far as it isn't contrary to one of their
direct aims. But what will you have?

I should like to draw your attention to one of the most
peculiar positions that is now developing in Europe, and
which suggests one of pre-war days, and, therefore, which
suggests a coming war. Every nation is now flirting with the
neighbour but one, which is the favourite position recommended by classical strategy. France—I am now going to
quote some names—France has discovered an old historical
friendship with Poland, the next but one. Germany, in spite
of profound differences in the political economy of the two
nations, has discovered an extraordinary interest in Russia,
the next but one. Also, it doesn't dislike the looks of Spain,
the next but one in the other direction. Italy is extremely
interested in the welfare of Hungary, the next but one.

Serbia is interested in France, and France in Serbia, the next but one. And lastly, but not least, even the Labour Government of England is not altogether on as inimical terms as one might think with Italy, the next but one.

I think this is a very serious position. We really are forgetting all about the Covenant. We really are forgetting all about the Kellogg Pact. We have got into a position of familiarity with all those oaths we have delivered and deposited on the altar of peace, and the position is becoming one as dangerous as the tendency to belittle the oaths of fidelity in marriage.

viii. *Enlightened Public Opinion must act.*

What is, then, the outlook? In my opinion—and it is here that I want to justify what I said at first, that I am an optimist, on condition that enlightened public opinion makes itself felt—in my opinion the position need not be allowed to drift if the million or two million people who matter in the world make up their minds that this is going to change; only they must not be allowed to take at its face value whatever stuff they read in their national press. I don't want to remind anybody of unpleasant memories, but I would remind my American friends present that the American Senate was never more courageous than when it started an inquiry into the origin of certain information given to the American press by a famous—shall I call him?—war correspondent in Geneva during the Coolidge Conference. I was myself, at any rate, very sorry that the overwork which afflicts the American Senate prevented them from continuing that inquiry to the present day. I believe that was the right line to take—was at least one of the right lines to take in order to clear the ground for constructive purposes. But that is by the way.

Enlightened public opinion could do much if it had courage; and I say that because I do not believe that all these little efforts at reducing armaments by such tiny fractions that people can argue for years and years as to whether the particular convention in question actually reduced or increased the armaments of the nation concerned—which is what is happening now as a result of the Naval Conference of London—I do not believe that that method amounts to anything. Far from it: I believe that it is positively a danger. We have a Spanish proverb which says: 'As if we were not enough in the family, my grandmother had a baby.' Now, as if we hadn't enough causes of war in the world, we are bringing a new cause of war into the world, which is disarmament conferences. I have never seen more unpleasantness about England in American papers, or more unpleasantness about America in English papers, than during the Washington and Coolidge Conferences, and any one who is honest about it will agree with me. It is a very dangerous position, and I will give you a complete example of it.

Soon after the English had been reduced to a state of hopeless parity by their American cousins, 100 odd American clergymen thought fit to explain to Mr. MacDonald, in a letter full of advice, what he ought to do with Mr. Gandhi. You know advice is the easiest thing to be given and most difficult to be taken, and the London *Times* had a long series of letters about it. Those letters were particularly bitter about America—exceptionally bitter. It wasn't because of Gandhi; it was because of parity, though parity wasn't mentioned in the letters. There is nothing that poisons international relations more than all these ticklish matters of prestige and power that are raised at the moment of disarmament conferences, and you may think what you like about the unthinkability of the unthinkable war, but, if you believe that the unthinkable war is really unthinkable, then I cannot understand a word about the debates of the London Conference, because they have no meaning whatsoever. The only way in which you can put a meaning to the debates of the London Conference is if you assume that there is going to be war between America and England soon, and the two nations want to be sure that neither of them is going to be beaten by the other at sea, at least on technical grounds. If you don't admit that, the debates of the Conference have no meaning at all—I grant that there have been many conferences without any meaning at all, but I should not like to be so rude about the London Conference.

What, then, is to be done to have a positive policy and not a negative one? We do not want to disarm; disarming is a negative affair. We do not want to destroy armaments. We do not want to scrap ships, battleships; a battleship is a beautiful engine; why scrap her? Leave her to live as long as she likes. This insistence that battleships and cruisers must have a short life was once defended by referring to the fact that they are supposed to be feminine and must be very costly; but surely it is carrying it too far when you say that cruisers, according to the new system, and particularly destroyers, are going to be scrapped at thirteen. Too old at thirteen! It really isn't very generous for craft which are supposed to be feminine!

ix. *Some Proposals.*

What we want is something more positive, and I am going to give concrete proposals. The real, or at least one of the most important causes of the trouble between big nations to-day, and the small ones do not matter for these purposes, is the economic rivalry and fight for markets, and particularly for raw materials.

Let us start at once an international organization for the handling of a few very simple economic matters. This is one point. Secondly, let us start at once the international organization of the most dangerous of military arms—I refer to aviation. Now my argument is this. Instead of these piecemeal methods of disarmament which are going to lead us nowhere except to quarrels, let us consider one concrete question like the question of aviation. It is composed of two parts: military aviation, civil aviation. It is composed of two parts for the lay and innocent man; for the man who knows, it is composed of one part—military aviation under military guise and military aviation under civilian disguise. Let us be quite clear; let us take the matter in hand and consider that, in so far as commercial aims are concerned, it is no earthly use, at any rate in Europe, to have aviation at all, unless you are going to cross at least one frontier, and in some cases at least two. Therefore civil aviation is in its essence an international affair. If it is an international affair in its essence let us make it so in law, for the progress of international life consists in turning international in law all that is international in fact. Aviation is international in fact; let us make it so in law. Let us have an international company, if you like— official or private, I do not mind. I am neutral as to socialism or capitalism. You may choose; but let us make an international enterprise of aviation, and let us make it so that its internationalism is going to run from top to bottom of its hierarchy, so that the body of its organization is going to be international, and, therefore, is going to see to it that no civil aviation is prepared with an eye to war, as happens to-day everywhere; that there are men of all nationalities in all the aerodromes, but particularly the nationalities that matter, so that aerodromes in France are run with a strong proportion of Germans, Italians, and so on all round, so that there is no possibility of using these establishments for war. And, once you have settled all these matters, let us have a Convention prohibiting the construction and use of aeroplanes in war.

Here is a proposal that needs no limitation. We are not going to ask any nation how many aeroplanes it has; how many guns, and how big they are, on its aeroplanes. It is a constructive and positive proposal; and, by forcing the nations of the world to work it out in actual practice, it will generate the habit of working together in one particular and important aspect of life, which will ultimately lead to the general education of the world, which will make disarmament a natural course. This is, to my mind, the spirit of the work that ought to be taken in hand at once; and, instead of that, we have oaths on the one hand, armies on the other. That policy must go. I honestly believe that for the last ten years the policy of disarmament has been all wrong. It was a very good thing it was all wrong, because we do not need to do it again now. We know it is wrong, but it is a good thing we realize it was wrong, because we have been ten years at it, and I think ten years in the life of a man—who, after all, doesn't live very much more than a battleship—is quite enough, and henceforth we may begin to look at disarmament with grown-up eyes.

CHAPTER XIV

EDUCATION FOR WORLD CITIZENSHIP

Professor A. E. ZIMMERN:

THE problem with which I have been asked to deal under the title of 'Education for World Citizenship' falls naturally within a series of lectures devoted to the work of the League of Nations. But its place there calls for a few words of explanation. A certain amount of confusion has been caused by the fact that, when the League took this matter up at the Assembly of 1925, it passed a double-barrelled Resolution in which two quite different, though related, ideas were expressed. On the one hand it was recommended that the Member States should see that the younger generation understood the achievements and aims of the League of Nations—a relatively small matter—and, on the other hand, that they should be trained to regard inter-national co-operation as the normal mode of carrying on human affairs. That is a very much larger aim, and that is the real educational problem which is presented to us.

Now, what is education? There have been many defini-tions, and I will give you one just in order to provoke dis-cussion. Education is the harmonization of the inner with the outer, the harmonization of the individual human personality with the society in which we are compelled to live. It follows from this that political education (such education as we are concerned with to-day) involves an understanding of the forces of the contemporary world and the training of character and intelligence so that the individual can control those forces. It involves a training in responsibility, and not simply a training in ideas.

i. *The Society in which we Live.*

Let us look for a few moments at the outer environment. I see three outstanding features in the present-day world for which our future citizens must be prepared. Firstly, international interdependence. The industrial revolution has made the modern world a unity in a sense which was absolutely inconceivable 150 years ago. Not only is there a greater difference between the world of George Washington and of the French Revolution and the world of to-day than there was between the world of 1776 and the world of Julius Caesar, Alexander the Great, the Pharaohs, or King Minos of Crete, but the economic forces set loose by the industrial revolution have given us an interdependent economic system which, on its material side, has created a world community where we are all clothed, fed, and transported as a result of world forces which have come to be indispensable to us. And this world economic community is not national, regional, or continental, but it covers the whole world, and it is totally impossible for any State or any political grouping to separate us, for instance, from that African continent upon which, whatever the culture of its peoples, we are dependent for so much of our indispensable industrial raw material and food-stuffs.

The first big fact, then, is interdependence. The second, also dating back about 150 years, is the spread of democracy. President Wilson rather inclined us to think of Democracy as a force making for internationalism, for a better understanding between nations, for a more united world. The real facts, both historical and psychological, indicate the contrary. Democracy is not a force making—at least, in its first impact —for world unity. It is a force making for disintegration, or at least for decentralization. Democracy has divided the world into far more local units of power, of sentiment, of interest, of opinion, than existed 100 years ago. Democracy means that throughout the world there is a large and increasing number of living and active centres of interest which have a natural human way of asserting themselves and wishing to impose their own will. The extended electorate means more power to local units, more stress laid on local interests, and a greater difficulty in promoting international co-operation. It means that the world is being run to-day increasingly by small-scale minds—that is to say by men and women who find a difficulty in looking beyond the barriers of their own parish, province, or nation. You have only to open your newspaper and see what is happening in all parts of the world. We are constantly exposed to this sudden intrusion of local passions into a world which, on its material side, is endeavouring to become interdependent.

The third big fact is the weakening of the authority of government throughout the world, the decline of politics. The large-scale forces that have been set in motion since the end of the eighteenth century are, on their economic side, making for efficiency, for improved methods of production, and improved methods of administration. On their political side they are making for smaller units, for disturbance and for disintegration. Compare, for instance, the twenty-seven sovereign States in Europe and the large and increasing units of big business. The natural effect of this is to undermine the authority which the science and art of government have exercised over men's minds since the beginning of organized civilization. The economic power of the world is that exercised through new and extremely well adapted agencies. Take such an instrument as the joint-stock company, which

only dates back about eighty years. The political work of the
world, on the other hand, is carried on by old-fashioned
instruments operating within old-fashioned limits, and is,
therefore, giving less and less satisfaction. The work done
in the City of London is in many respects more important
than that done in Whitehall, and that done in Wall Street
of more importance than that done in Washington. How
much more is that the case in those smaller political units
which comprise the greater part of the world's Governments,
and how much more attractive is it for young men to take up
a career in the wide-ranging sphere of business rather than
in the more or less parochial and confined atmosphere of
government and bureaucracy! That creates an immense
problem for all of us who are interested in training for
political and civic responsibility, because the day may come
when private forces may usurp the seat of power hitherto
occupied by what we may call Government or the constitutional authority.

It is clear, in the face of the democratic movement, that
we shall not see a world State. We are not ready yet even for
international co-operative institutions. We are operating with a
public opinion which is, so to speak, in blinkers—these millions
and millions of men and women electors who have been brought
up to see nothing beyond the limits of their own country,
who mostly are unaware of a foreign language, have met very
few people from outside their own borders, and whose minds
and horizon are limited by their own local interests. In those
circumstances, it is a farce even to dream of a world Government based on world public opinion, and such international
institutions as have been painfully brought into existence,
such as the League of Nations, are really suspended in mid-
air, without any adequate foundation. Therefore there is, at

present, practically no public opinion on international affairs. There is a British opinion on foreign affairs, a German opinion, a French opinion, but there is no organic body of public opinion supporting the League of Nations and understanding the problems with which it is confronted. Scattered about the world, in London, Paris, Berlin, New York, and elsewhere, you may find individuals or groups of individuals (of whom I will speak later) who are following this question, but there is no organized democratic public opinion. There is nothing, for instance, corresponding to what we call in England His Majesty's Opposition, to follow critically and to interpret the work done by international bodies.

ii. *The Objective.*

That, then, is our problem. It puts before us two lines of action, a short-distance line and a long-distance line. The short-distance line of action involves attempting to bring into existence an adequate body of public opinion on particular issues, and attempting to make a success of such projects as the League of Nations is engaged on at the present time, namely the prevention of war, the observance of the Covenant and the Kellogg Pact. We are more concerned here with the long-distance line of action—that is, with the development of an adequate education which will bring into existence, by degrees, a public opinion capable of understanding and controlling the conditions of our time. We find ourselves confronted with two sharply contrasted schools of thought—the cosmopolitans and the internationalists.

The cosmopolitan looks at the world as from a distant planet, and he sees terrible confusion. He not only sees that there has been a world war and that millions of people have been killed; he sees also an immense amount of untidiness, innumerable frontiers and languages, far too many religions, far too many varieties of humankind; and his ideal is the establishment of peace by what might be called Roman means, peace involving the breaking down by superior authority of all these barriers, and the establishment of a world civilization, a world uniformity, based on a common scientific education. Cosmopolitans of this type look at the world with the eyes of the natural scientist, and see no reason why citizens of the world should not all be trained on the same lines, in the same schools, and even with the same textbooks.

If you follow that up with the mind of the bureaucrat or the administrator, it leads you to a League of Nations Education Department supervising, and perhaps managing, the schools of all the Member States of the League, and perhaps, if we let our imagination roam, we may be able to conceive Mr. Dufour-Feronce or his successor taking out his watch at 10 o'clock in the morning and saying that many hundred million children throughout the world are at that moment engaged in learning about the Council or the Assembly according to the programme laid down by the world authorities on education. It means a common inspectorate, a common system of finance, a common teacher's certificate, common examinations, and, to manage it all, a vast bureaucracy. Along that line of thinking, I think you see we get nowhere. We get right away from those forces of democracy which are, at bottom, also forces of personality. If you are out to produce a dead world, a mechanical world, that system may work very well, but if you are out to produce a world which has more life in it, more personality, more happiness, you have to set to work in a different direction. After all, democracy and the League of Nations itself, and all our political and social agencies, are only means to an end, and the end is human, human beings living better and freer and happier lives, and, if we hold that view—which is the basis of my whole political creed—then I care not a scrap for institutions apart from the individuals for whom they are devised. The League of Nations was made for man, and not man for the League of Nations.

We must, then, recognize that this democratic movement springs from the deepest roots of human personality, and if the Chinese, the Indian, the Argentine, the Lithuanian, and Canadian, and other groups in this very multiform world want to assert themselves, that is a sign of life which should cause us satisfaction and not a sign of untidiness which should be swept away. In our discussions, then, on international education, let us steer clean away from the ideal of uniformity and adopt the second and opposite ideal of co-operation between all these living forces which will develop increasingly as the world grows older. Perhaps I may say as the world grows younger, because the world releases the forces of youth it has too long controlled, which will develop in Asia and Africa as they have developed in Europe, America, and Australia in the last 100 years. We need co-operation in an increasingly democratic and an increasingly decentralized world. There will never be a World Education Department, but there will be an increasing network of contacts between people engaged in this great task under all sorts of different conditions throughout the civilized world, with a central clearing-house—no doubt here at Geneva—just as there is a clearing-house for colonial government in the Mandates Section, and so on in other departments.

The general effect, then, will be a League of Nations not to run schools but to stimulate national and local effort to

level the backward people up to foremost, to pool and trans-
mit from country to country suggestions and experiences and
stimulation of all kinds, so that each may learn from the other
and adapt its newer ideas to the special local circumstances.

iii. *School Text-books.*

Let us try to come down to earth and apply the principle
of co-operation to some of the problems of school life. A great
deal of discussion has been going on about text-books. Some
people have even desired that the League of Nations should
exercise a censorship over books that make for war and bad
feeling between nations. Something has been attempted
officially in that respect, but it has led to very little result.
Some years ago the International Committee on Intellectual Co-operation, after carefully considering this matter,
adopted a rather elaborate resolution in which they said that,
if it was found that there was an error of fact in a text-book,
it should be pointed out to the National Committee on
Intellectual Co-operation in the country offended against,
and that it might call the matter to the attention of the
National Committee for Intellectual Co-operation in the
country where the book was produced. Note that the
resolution only dealt with errors of fact. If you say that
Germany was responsible for the war, that is not a simple
matter of fact. That is a far-reaching historical judgement
based on the appraisal of a large number of facts, so that the
real matters which cause bad blood between nations cannot
easily be brought within the Committee's formula. One
case has occurred under this procedure. A French school-
book was discovered which stated that the rivers of Spain
ran dry in the summer. This was a statement of fact which
was demonstrably untrue, and the machinery was set in

motion, presumably with the required results. That instance shows you how very difficult it is to use anything like methods of censorship. The better principle, I think, is to encourage good work rather than to attempt to discover, and sometimes to advertise, bad work. You can do that in two ways. You can make white-lists of good books, new books that treat history and other subjects in a more modern way, but, above all, you can instruct the people whose business it is that there should be good books—in other words, the teachers and the historians. Action is being taken in that sense on lines of co-operation. The International Federation of Primary Teachers, which was formed in the first instance by collaboration between French and German primary teachers, has done much work on those lines, and the historians who formed an International Committee in 1926, and later held an International Congress at Oslo, have formed a special sub-committee for dealing with the question of text-books, and are really trying to arouse the professional pride of historians, irrespective of national frontiers, in the production of better historical manuals. After all, the chauvinistic history text-book is, first and foremost, a disgrace to the teaching profession and to the historians of the country where it is produced, and it is they who ought to take action against it.

iv. *The School Time-table.*

Let us now turn to the question of the time-table. It is highly desirable that the League of Nations and such international institutions as we have in the modern world should be introduced to the notice of children in schools. But how and where? The League action in this respect, and the recommendations of the sub-committee of experts, have led to an unexpected result. They have led to a re-consideration of methods of history teaching. You are faced with the fact that the League of Nations exists, that it began to exist in 1920, and has existed for the last ten years. If you are going to teach it, then you should teach it in the history lesson. At any rate, that is one place where it should be taught. But in some countries it has been discovered that the history programmes are apt to stop short, if not at the battle of Waterloo, at any rate somewhere about the death of Queen Victoria, and therefore the putting into effect of the League of Nations sub-committee's recommendations has involved overhauling history programmes, and has compelled teachers to face the task of teaching the history and conditions of the contemporary world. It used to be thought, when I was a boy, that you learned about the present-day world from the newspapers—the newspapers were perhaps a little more responsible in those days than now—whereas you learned about the past in-books. To-day that is impossible. A world fed upon newspapers, which relies entirely upon newspapers for knowledge of contemporary events, would never be a truly democratic world. It is absolutely essential that the historical outlook should be applied to contemporary problems, and one very happy result of this movement for the teaching of the League of Nations in schools has been to lead to a reconsideration not only of the history programmes, but of the principles on which they are based.

In that connexion I would draw attention to a very interesting movement that has taken place in the United States. Although the United States is not a Member of the League of Nations, American educators have really done perhaps more for the teaching of the League of Nations and international co-operation than the educators of any other country. The Americans are very obstinate people, and it is perhaps because their Government refused to take action that they set to work on voluntary lines to do what they can in the face of Government. There has recently developed an extremely interesting movement which has been based on the idea of breaking down in the school time-table the dividing lines between the different studies concerned with the modern world. When I was at school we learned history for certain hours, geography for certain other hours; then we had certain hours for 'divinity'. In certain countries they do not have 'divinity' except in the Sunday Schools, but they have what is called civics, or social ethics. In America there is a movement to associate together in a common programme these studies, to fuse them into a unity under the title of Social Science. I have a programme here of the City of Denver, which is a long way from the Atlantic and a very long way from Geneva, but which has introduced a contin-uous course in social studies covering the whole twelve years from 6 to 18, in which geography, history, and civics have been combined. In this programme there is a whole course of world history, in which the objective is stated to be 'to create a background in the mind of the pupil adequate to explain the life of to-day', and in which, finally, there is con-tinued reference to the League of Nations and its institu-tions. The people of Denver do not take the view that, because the United States is not a Member of the League of Nations, the League of Nations should be banished from the class-room as non-existent. In Germany there have been formed groups of teachers for discussing these problems and attempting to adapt the curriculum to the new needs, and in trying to revolutionize the teaching of history. There are endless possibilities for the development of agencies of discussion among teachers for applying these new ideas, and one of the reasons why I am so happy that there is no chance of centralized League of Nations control is because the personal method, the method of co-operation, will tend to encourage action by teachers and by those who are interested in the problem in different countries, and different local areas will report all sorts of new ideas springing up, and leading, of course, to an equal need for a clearing-house in which those new ideas shall be recorded and discussed.

I have been talking mainly of the curriculum in primary and secondary schools. I turn for a moment to technical schools. The sub-committee of experts' recommendations make special reference to the teaching of the League of Nations in naval and military academies. As a matter of fact, international relations are already studied in several of these institutions. It is just as necessary for naval and military officers as any one else to know the history of the world. It is quite a mistake to think that League of Nations teaching is a kind of Sunday School affair, relegated only to those who are specially impressed with the ideal of peace. A knowledge of the League of Nations is needed by everybody in every profession. It concerns working men, who need to know about the International Labour Organization; it concerns doctors, who need to know about the Health Organization; it concerns people in almost every walk of life.

v. *The Universities.*

I pass to the Universities. What is being done in the Universities to teach international relations? Well, I think in the first place it should be said that international relations is not a subject; international relations is a group of subjects.

To introduce international relations into a University simply means trying to induce the authorities of that University and the students to look at a group of existing subjects from a new angle. Is not history an international subject? Are not geography, political science, and political economy international subjects? Has not law its international side, and is not economics pre-eminently an international subject? Any courses in international relations that are devised must necessarily be based upon a collaboration between existing chairs and existing studies. Any attempt to organize international relations apart from these other studies is bound to fail, and may become supremely ridiculous. A few weeks ago I was talking to a teacher from—I will not say where, but a somewhat modest institution. She told me that she was a professor of international relations, and I asked her what she taught. She said: 'It is extremely difficult, because I am not allowed to teach anything which trespasses on the field of my colleagues on history, economics, or political science.' All that was left to her was the field of what is called 'current events'. That is not international relations, but something very different. That is the very level of journalism from which we are trying to get away.

vi. *Intellectual Co-operation.*

This movement for the study of international relations has had the very happy effect of bringing together those who are teaching the related subjects, the subjects I have mentioned, and teaching them from a new angle. One of the results which has been achieved through the work of the Committee on Intellectual Co-operation has been the establishment of an annual Conference of Institutions, now representing twelve countries, concerned with the study of international relations. This Conference has become a very living thing. There is an enormous field here for the removal of misunderstanding. The technique of this method of co-operation as against the method of uniformity is the weaving of a network of contacts and the promotion of conferences between interested groups in the various technical fields. I have not time to develop this subject any further here, but in a certain number of educational fields regular conferences have either been established or are being projected, and the mere mention of them will be sufficient to show the great possibilities of co-operation along these lines.

The primary and secondary teachers are now internationally organized. Their congresses are becoming increasingly important international events, and very interesting problems are put on the agenda for discussion.

There is now, under the League, an annual Conference of International Students' Organizations.

There is a regular conference of the officials in various countries concerned with students from abroad. They have met and discussed various technical problems. This is the natural body to discuss the problem of the equivalence of degrees, &c.

A conference is projected of the officials in University departments and ministries of public instruction. Then there is a proposal for a regular conference of local administrators, of what are called in the United States superintendents of education.

There is the conference of institutions concerned with the study of international affairs, which may easily develop into a discussion not simply of method but of ideas, because I think, as time goes on, there may be common programmes of research in these institutions, so that these problems which the States are now unable to solve may ultimately be solved through the contributions of experts.

Then, finally, there is the General Educational Conference put forward by the Annual Conference of League of Nations Associations, with rather a wider object, more like a parliament than a technical conference, but which would be extremely valuable in focussing public opinion upon the main lines of advance in this whole field. I think myself that such a conference, or really congress, would need to be very carefully prepared in order to make it effective, but I see no reason why that preparation should not take place, and why such a congress should not become a regular institution.

vii. *Two Vital Principles.*

In this work, it seems to me, there are two very vital educational principles involved, and with those I conclude.

There is, firstly, the unity of the teaching profession. The attempt to enlarge the outlook of the ordinary citizen is not simply a matter for universities or for high schools, but a matter which extends to the primary school, and perhaps even to the nursery school. To-day we should apply the sound democratic principle that all who are engaged in the work of teaching the younger generation form a single profession and should, as far as possible, act together. The second principle I would lay down is the close contact and association between those who are teaching and those who are engaged in research, those who are communicating knowledge and those who are adding to knowledge. It is quite as necessary that those who teach history in the class-room should be up to date in their facts and use modern books as it is for those who are teaching chemistry or physics, or any of the subjects in which there has been so rapid an advance in recent generations. That is why it is so important that investigators should be in closest touch with the work done in school, and that is another reason for insisting on unity in the teaching profession.

I conclude by repeating what I said at the beginning. In a democratic world we are up against enormous difficulties. The natural trend of the human mind is against international relations. The old proverb says: 'Birds of a feather flock together.' Englishmen flock with Englishmen, Germans with Germans, Frenchmen with Frenchmen. If we are going to overcome this natural inhibition in the mind of the growing citizens, we need to evolve a new technique and to keep in the closest touch with one another in different countries. We need to cherish the old educational virtues of intellectual integrity and conscientiousness, and we need, above all, to cultivate among ourselves that larger outlook which we in our daily work are apt to forget among the rubs and difficulties to which we are exposed, and to maintain our own personal ideal for the development of the world and a better life for humanity.